# Modern Business Report Writing

# Modern Business Report Writing

**Salvatore J. Iacone, Ph.D.**

Macmillan Publishing Company
New York

Collier Macmillan Publishers
London

Macmillan Publishing Company
866 Third Avenue, New York, New York 10022

Collier Macmillan Canada, Inc.

**Library of Congress Cataloging in Publication Data**

Iacone, Salvatore J.
    Modern business report writing.

    Bibliography: p.
    Includes index.
    1. Business report writing.   I. Title.
HF5719.I23   1985          808'.066651          84-7865
ISBN 0-02-359410-1


Printing: 1 2 3 4 5 6 7 8     Year: 5 6 7 8 9 0 1 2 3

ISBN 0-02-359410-1

*To Renee, Alexis, and Hadley*

# Preface

*Modern Business Report Writing* is designed as a practical guide to preparing well-written business reports in the 1980s. My goal was to devise a format that not only combined theory and practice but offered actual step-by-step procedures for writing a report. As a result, the text proceeds from a discussion of the nature of reports to techniques for gathering, evaluating, and organizing information, writing the rough draft, including illustrations, revising the report, constructing an abstract, and if needed, transforming a written report into an oral one.

In an effort to reflect truly modern considerations when writing a business report, discussions of computerized information retrieval systems, word processors, computer graphics, and teletext have been included. Because writing mirrors thinking, special attention has been given to overcoming writer's block and getting started, critical thinking skills and problem-solving techniques. Throughout the text, there are samples of actual business reports and questionnaires, and realistic report writing assignments. My goal was to create a text that would leave the reader an experienced and confident report writer by the last chapter. My hope is that both instructors and students will find that the techniques for writing effective business reports have been presented in an informative and enjoyable manner. A teacher's manual is available as an added resource for instructors who use the textbook.

I want to thank the following people for providing material and granting permission to reprint: Michael Blake, J. Garrett Blowers, Mary Bois, Laura White Dillon, Richard W. Everett, Guy Henle, James F. Henry, Renee Peterkin Iacone, Ronald L. Koprowski, Daniel Langdon, John Morris, Thomas Nugent, M. Susan Ueber Raymond, Werner Renberg, Leonard Schwartz, James G. Stier, Ronald and Jill Wulkan.

To my editors at Macmillan: D. Anthony English, for his initial support of this project; to William Oldsey, for his uncanny advice, unwavering support and encouragement; to Wendy Polhemus, for her diligent efforts and expertise in transforming the manuscript into a finished text, my grateful appreciation. I would also like to thank Dubose McLane, production manager and Holly Reid McLaughlin, book designer.

To my colleagues, friends, and family for their helpful comments and kind support, my deepest gratitude.

S. J. I.

## ABOUT THE AUTHOR

**Salvatore J. Iacone, Ph.D.,** is a specialist in effective writing skills programs for universities, private corporations, and federal government agencies. As a consultant, Dr. Iacone conducts business and technical writing skills seminars for such organizations as AT&T, Hoffman-La Roche, the Federal Aviation Administration, the United States Departments of Defense and Commerce, and Army research and development units.

In addition to his consulting activities, Dr. Iacone is an adjunct professor of writing skills at Adelphi University and has taught at the City University of New York. He received his Ph.D. from St. John's University.

# Contents

## **5** Organizing and Outlining the Information    **75**

## **6** Report Formats and Elements    **95**

## **7** Writing the Report: The First Draft    **113**

**APPENDICES**

# Modern Business Report Writing

# CHAPTER 1

# The Nature of Reports

**THE COMMUNICATION PROCESS**

The communication process involves the transference of information from one mind to another. Often that information consists of knowledge of people, places, objects, events, ideas, and relationships. Whether expressed orally, in writing, or through bodily gestures, successful communication depends upon clear expression. Business reports provide essential aspects of the communication process. They transmit facts, opinions, and numerical data crucial to the effective operation within and among many kinds of organizations—large or small, public or private.

In general, breakdowns in the communication process result in frustration, confusion, and, at times, violence. In the business world, the failure to communicate information clearly impedes productivity, disrupts the flow of ideas, and invariably results in the loss of millions, perhaps billions, of dollars. In recent years, the introduction of and increasing reliance on computers, word processors, satellites, audio-visual equipment, and other highly technological inventions have resulted in the more rapid exchange of information and the availability and processing of data. Although much of this wizardry has led to greater convenience and efficiency in the office or home, these innovations have neither lessened nor replaced the need for well-written business reports.

A well-written report minimizes the possibility of someone misinterpretting, not fully understanding, or subjectively distorting the information being conveyed. Although even the clearest and most direct of reports can be misconstrued, the likelihood of this occurring diminishes if the ideas are communicated simply, clearly, accurately, logically, and concisely.

Good writing reflects a person's ability to think critically, to analyze problems and situations logically, and perhaps most of all, to employ common sense in reaching solutions to the myriad of problems and issues addressed in reports. Business reports require planning, time, discipline, good organization skills, and a sound grasp of the basic principles essential to expressing ideas on paper clearly. Nowhere in the communication process is directness, clarity, and accuracy more valued than in a report. For an organization, a report that truly communicates information is efficient in terms of time and money. For the writer, a well-written business report has its own rewards, because it can prove the best and most reliable source of recommendation for increased respect, responsibility, and perhaps promotion.

## THE NEED FOR REPORTS

Just as necessity is the acknowledged mother of invention, the need to convey information for a specific purpose is the basis for preparing and writing reports. Effective communication is essential to the daily operation of any organization, public or private. Due to the variety of purposes they can serve, written reports are crucial to the successful exchange of information in nearly every profession. In fact, few fields exist in which the need to prepare a report, whether written or oral, is not required either on a routine basis or when a special need arises.

Corporate managers, stockbrokers, doctors, bankers, engineers, scientists, government and military leaders, educators, and international secret agents all use reports to transmit or receive information. Even the local auto mechanic may be obliged to prepare a written diagnostic report before repairing a customer's car. In some instances, reports are prepared on a regular basis, as in the case of salesmen and women who must file daily or weekly sales and field trip reports, accountants who compile yearly audit reports, and large corporations that issue annual reports to their stockholders.

Sometimes reports are prepared on an as-needed basis or when they can prove crucial to the decision-making process within an organization. For example, a senior executive may require extensive background information before expanding plant operations in a particular area. Or perhaps a national sales manager is considering opening new markets for company products. Both may decide they need a great many questions answered about the feasibility of these ideas, and they might possibly commission reports on the subjects. So too would an investment banker want accurate data about a specific municipal bond offering before committing large sums of customers' money to it. Similarly, a food company president would want information about changing patterns in consumer nutritional awareness before introducing a new product.

In each of these cases, the need for a written report would arise if essential information could not adequately be transmitted either orally or through simple memos and letters. Although memos and letters can and do often incorporate reports, they can prove to be of limited use when the subject of the report is highly complex or if it demands extensive analysis. For example, a report that describes the need for new office furniture for a five-person office may be incorporated in a memo, but one that attempts to analyze the means of improving mass transporation in a large city may run three hundred pages, and need to be presented in a formal format.

All reports, then, serve specific needs by conveying particular information to people who require it. Yet in terms of their nature and function, reports can be as diversified as some of the world's most renowned conglomerates. Written reports are needed to do the following:

- *Analyze facts* and other relevant data to provide a basis for a decision.
- *Present the results* of an experiment or findings of an investigation.
- *Measure the progress* or development of a project or task.
- *Describe a process* or method.
- *Provide the history* or background of an issue, project, procedure, or task.

- *Initiate* an investigation.
- *Suggest a solution* for a new or ongoing problem.
- *Recommend* changes or measures for improvement of existing systems, materials, or procedures.
- *Recommend* action.
- *Transmit* creative ideas.
- *Evaluate* a proposal or idea.
- *Record* information for future use.

A report can serve one or all of these needs, depending upon the nature and complexity of the topic and the amount of detail required. For example, a report concerning the improvement of mass transportation in a large city would *provide history or background data* on existing systems, *describe* present conditions, *analyze* problems, *suggest* solutions, and *recommend* feasible means of improving the present system. By contrast, a report on the progress of the construction of a new dormitory would *describe* the various tasks accomplished, *measure progress* in terms of time and activities completed, *discuss* existing or unexpected problems that might hinder construction, *suggest* a solution, and *outline* future tasks. A report's purpose, therefore, largely determines its contents and format.

## CLASSIFICATION OF REPORTS

As a result of the diverse needs they can serve, it would appear that written reports defy either formal definition or a classification system. Nevertheless, general common factors and characteristics apply to all reports. For one, reports tend to present *factual data* in an *objective fashion* for a *specific purpose* to a *particular audience* or reader. Unlike memos and letters, reports offer little opportunity for cordiality and the expression of personal feelings. While reports can be written in either a formal or informal manner, the very objectivity often associated with the serious treatment of a subject insists upon greater distance between writer and topic and writer and reader. While reports can contain opinions, their conclusions and recommendations are based more often on facts than on personal feelings. The report writer's observations should be rendered *objectively*, *accurately*, *thoroughly*, *logically*, and *clearly*.

Yet before writers relate their perceptions and comments, they should anticipate the *length*, *function*, *subject area* and *tone* of the report. Classifying a report according to these factors will enable the writer to focus precisely on the information and ideas to be expressed and the best format in which to present them.

**Length**    The scope and complexity of a topic often distinguish its length. In some cases there is little information to report, as when a project or problem is initially studied. Perhaps with further study, the information will increase either in quantity or in complexity, and longer reports will be required. In other instances, a great amount of information may be available to the writer, who must then select which data will best satisfy the needs of the reader.

One mistake to avoid is to confuse quantity with quality. Despite the unfortunate fact that quite a number of people can be more readily impressed with physical magnitude rather than with intrinsic merit, the report writer who confuses quantity with quality will likely produce overly long reports that go partially or completely unread. No one wants to read five hundred pages when fifty will suffice. Also, length is a relative consideration. A long report in one organization may number ten pages; one hundred in another.

**Function**    Another helpful approach to preparing a report is to classify it according to need and function. The following are reports classified according to functions most commonly addressed by the report writer. (Examples of most of these types of business reports can be found in Appendix B.)

*Fact-Finding or Informational Report.*    In a fact-finding report the writer gathers and presents background, historical, or factual data without providing analytical comment, conclusions, and recommendations. The purpose of this report is to inform the reader of details relevant to an issue, problem, procedure, or topic. For instance, suppose that someone employed by a large department store chain is asked to report on the various fringe benefits available to all employees. The writer would be responsible for listing and describing the benefits, which might include medical and dental insurance, pension plan, paid number of sick days, personal days, and a 60 percent discount on all store purchases. Any opinions, judgments, and conclusions the reader might reach would result from his or her personal interpretation of the facts.

***Analytical Report.*** The writer of an analytical report studies, interprets, and comments upon information. He or she may offer conclusions and recommendations. With respect to the department store report on fringe benefits, the writer could additionally suggest changes for improving the benefits. He or she could recommend raising the amount of available medical coverage after taking into account inflation and rising medical costs, or decreasing the number of allowable paid personal days in an effort to trim overhead. In brief, factual information would be enhanced by the writer's viewpoints and judgments.

***Performance Report.*** A performance report evaluates either an individual, product, or activity. The writer summarizes and highlights behavior or trends on a weekly, monthly, or otherwise regular basis. This type of report would be used by one of the department store supervisors to evaluate buyers and salespeople recently hired. The writer would take into account such factors as the success of particular merchandise introduced by the buyers for various seasons, and the employees' rapport with past clients and skills in handling problems concerning production, shipping delays and defective products. The writer's role is that of observer and evaluator.

***Progress or Status Report.*** A progress or status report states developments concerning work on a specific project, problem, or activity. Consider the example of an account executive developing a new advertising campaign for a client. He or she is expected to prepare a detailed description of progress or obstacles encountered either weekly, monthly, or periodically. The report would outline the various tasks undertaken in developing the new advertising campaign. It would also note future steps and efforts the project would entail.

***Feasibility Report.*** The writer of a feasibility report gathers data and offers conclusions and opinions concerning the probable chances for success or failure. The report also evaluates the advantages and disadvantages of pursuing a particular project, goal, or activity. If a beverage manufacturer wants to know the potential for successfully marketing beer in bottles rather than cans, or the president of a hamburger franchise chain is debating whether or not to introduce additional kinds of food, such as pizza and hot sandwiches, both executives might commission an expert to write a feasibility report before making their decisions.

**Process Report.**   A process report conveys how-to information, instructions, or methods for implementing a project, procedure, or activity. The subject might concern assembling a sales staff or transforming an office that uses traditional office equipment into an electronic one fully reflecting modern technology. In each case, the writer must carefully outline the various tasks essential to each activity.

**Problem-Solution Report.**   A problem-solution report calls for the writer to identify the nature and causes of a specific problem and to offer possible solutions. A company chairperson seeking to improve the oral and written communication skills of middle managers might ask someone to prepare a report that studies the extent of the problem. After careful analysis, the report writer might conclude that improving such skills would save the company a considerable amount of money. One solution might be to hire a communications consultant to teach weekly in-house seminars. The chairperson could then accept, reject, or modify the writer's conclusions and recommendations.

**Field Trip Report.**   Field trip reports are useful in recording activities at branch offices, project locations, sales meetings, out-of-town conferences, and on-site inspection visits. The writer usually outlines activities chronologically or in order of importance. For instance, an architect might visit a construction site to check on the progress of an office building. The field trip report could include information concerning the day and time spent at the site, discussions with individuals in charge of the construction, a notation of an unexpected obstacle (such as delayed delivery of plumbing materials), and any other relevant information.

**Sales Report.**   A sales report conveys weekly, monthly, or annual sales figures and may include an analysis of present market conditions.

***Marketing Report.***   A marketing study can be prepared by an individual or group. It presents analysis and discussion of potential markets for goods and services. Well-researched facts are studied and judged for effective marketing strategies.

***Audit Report.***   Economic efficiency, as well as gross and net income, profit and loss, expenditures, and taxes, is recorded in an audit report, which is usually prepared by an accountant. While the emphasis is on numbers, the writer often summarizes useful information in an introduction or running commentary.

***Annual Report.***   Often presented in an attractive format, accompanied by photographs, charts, and diagrams, an annual report presents an overall perspective of an organization's administrative structure and personnel, a description of its products or services, an analysis of recent operating procedures and future goals, specific accomplishments, and financial data. This report can be prepared by one person or a group of writers, whose task is to present factual information in an interesting manner as well as to project a particular public image.

**Subject Area**   Classifying a report according to its subject matter enables the writer to focus more clearly on content and on the specific issues to be addressed. Limiting the scope of a report according to its topic helps the writer to more readily concentrate on the report's central concerns. For instance, if someone employed by a large fast food chain plans to study the sales potential of foods foreign to American tastes, the writer's first step is to classify a report according to a general subject heading, such as "Foreign Foods." After sorting out the specifics of what to discuss about this topic, the writer might decide to concentrate on foods characteristic of three countries—India, Japan, and Mexico—and their chances for acceptance by the public. Subsequently, the writer not only alters the title of the report to "The Sales Potential of Indian, Japanese, and Mexican Food in the Fast Food Market," but also has a clearer idea of what the report should or should not include.

***Tone and Format***   Reports are often classified according to tone and format. Generally, reports divide into two types, *informal* and *formal*.

> ***Informal.***   Informal reports are characterized by a personal tone and a conversational writing style. Pronouns such as *I, you,* and *we* are often used to communicate ideas. Informal reports might concern routine matters or initial inquiries. Such reports assume either a familiarity between writer and reader or a mutual understanding of the topic. For example, two people working for the same organization might prefer using informal reports to share their ideas, findings, or other observations concerning a particular subject. They may pass information along on printed memo sheets or company stationery. The information is either handwritten or typed, and may average one or several pages. Many of the components of formal reports, such as fancy covers, letters of transmittal, prefaces, introductions, and appendices are optional.

> ***Formal.***   Heightened objectivity, accompanied by an impersonal tone of voice, elaborate layouts, and attractive bindings, often distinguish formal from informal reports. Often the very length and complexity of the subject lead the writer to incorporate his or her observations in a clearly structured format to enhance the reader's understanding. Some topics require many details that must be carefully organized and presented in a framework that does not suggest familiarity either between writer and reader, or reader and subject. Formality is dictated by the content, the relationship of the writer to the potential reader, or by the occasion. For instance, an advertising executive who believes that a firm should explore the marketing potential of cable television may report this idea informally to colleagues. Yet that same executive might prefer a formal approach when the same information and observations are presented to a national conference of advertising executives. To appear more professional, the style would perhaps be more reserved, and the ideas might be arranged in an attractive binder that included a table of contents and visual aids such as charts and graphs. Yet, whether reported informally or formally, the information expressed should be clear, accurate and thorough.
>
> Annual, financial, market-research, and feasibility reports are usually formal in tone and format. Reports that indicate a title or professional standing of the writer, or a particular relationship to an orga-

nization requesting a report, are usually formal. Such reports are labeled *professional*, *public*, *private*, *independent*, *internal*, *external*, *government*, *executive*, and *administrative* studies.

## MODERN TECHNOLOGY AND BUSINESS REPORT WRITING

Modern technology, particularly in the forms of *computers* and *word processors*, will have a substantial impact on the way business reports are prepared and written. While computers have been in use for a number of years, they are becoming increasingly helpful in providing access to and retrieving information, as well as in analyzing raw data, disseminating statistics, and organizing information quickly and efficiently. At the same time, word processors are increasingly becoming standard office equipment in large and small companies, where they serve a variety of time- and labor-saving functions, including the editing and correcting of letters and reports, program planning and forecasting, information storage and retrieval, graphics design, and printing. Because report writing involves gathering and presenting information, computers and word processors will be of immeasurable value in terms of time and money.

Yet some aspects of report writing will not change. The writer will always need the ability to think critically and to write clearly and effectively. While modern wizardry can be of assistance, there can be no substitute for the human ability to exercise sound judgment based on experience and observation in understanding the nuances and subtleties of complex problems and issues. Nor can any machine generate writing that is as lively as it is informative and thorough. Computers can help a writer gather information, but they cannot offer conclusions and recommendations based upon careful human thought and analysis. Word processors facilitate the writing process, but no machine can generate ideas in the same manner as the human mind. Nor can a machine enhance the writing with any degree of style, wit, and intelligence.

At best, automation and technology should free the report writer from time-consuming and tedious tasks. As long as reports are written for people, they will be written by people. No amount of technology can ever change that fact. Thus the need to plan and prepare business reports that are helpful to decision making and problem-solving in any field will not be diminished by the introduction of modern technological equipment. Rather, the writer will all the more require an understanding of the planning procedures and writing skills essential to the success of every kind of business report.

***Word Processor***     *Word processing* is a fast and accurate means of transferring ideas and information into typewritten form. The equipment varies according to different needs, but a basic word processor consists of a keyboard, a screen to display the text, and information-storage and retrieval components. In brief, a word processor looks like a typewriter that has a television screen attached. Its advantages are formidable: increased productivity and cost-effectiveness in typing, editing, and correcting textual errors. The features include textual display, the ability to store and retrieve, to rearrange sentences, words, and paragraphs, to consolidate several pages into one, to number the pages automatically, to correct spelling errors, and to design graphics and charts. A word processor is especially useful in preparing the following:

- Letters.
- Mailing lists.
- Proposals.
- Financial information reports.
- Sales reports.
- Annual reports.
- Audit reports.
- Inventory reports.
- Marketing reports and letters.
- Letters of transmittal.
- Administrative reports.
- Status reports.
- Insurance reports.

***Videotex***     *Videotex* combines television, print, and data processing technologies to transmit information to home or office by telephone, cable, or over the air. Information flows from a computer to a television screen. The operator uses a small keyboard to select "pages" containing such information as stocks and bonds prices, or articles in magazines, journals, and books.

Though still in the development phase in the United States, videotex systems offer business news, weather, home banking and shopping services, electronic mail, and stock quotations to subscribers. In

Great Britain, France, Japan, and Canada, videotex systems have been operating for some time and continue to attract new users as new services are developed. For the modern business report writer, videotex may prove a revolutionary means of obtaining and transmitting information either during the preparation phase or in the presentation of reports.

## CHAPTER REVIEW

### Questions

1. What, in your own words, is a business report?

2. What is the relationship between reports and the communication process?

3. List ten functions reports can serve.

4. Identify the qualities of an effective report.

5. How might reports be classified?

6. Define five types of reports.

7. Distinguish between informal and formal reports.

8. How will modern technology affect the writing of business reports?

### Exercises

1. Describe three situations or problems at your college or job that would warrant reports.

2. Classify each of the following requests for reports according to one or more of the categories discussed in this chapter.
   a. "I must know if it is worthwhile to hire a marketing firm to test our new cereal."
   b. "What have our research teams been doing lately on the X-20 project? When will I receive the results of their investigation?"
   c. "How can we improve our latest video cassette recorder?"
   d. "Why did our Phoenix store sell more shirts than those in New York, Dallas, and San Francisco?"
   e. "The committee needs some idea of the history of that company before considering a merger."

  f. "Why have we sold every condominium in Miami and only a handful in Key West?"

  g. "What caused the slowdown in our production lines last month?"

3. Begin thinking about preparing an informal report on one of the following topics:
  a. Your academic standing this semester.
  b. The quality of food and services in the college cafeteria or local restaurant.
  c. Getting in shape for a marathon race.
  d. Hiking in the woods.
  e. Tuning a car engine.
  f. Setting up a tent.
  g. Building a model.
  h. Selecting video games and equipment.
  i. A persistent campus problem.
  j. Ways of improving registration procedures.
  k. Your side of an insurance claim account of an auto accident.
  l. The best car for your money.
  m. How a local movie house can increase business.
  n. Ten best stocks and bonds.
  o. What makes a successful television commercial?
  p. The need for a new gymnasium on campus.

Be sure to pick a topic you feel can be adequately discussed. Then, to ensure completeness, consider its possible length and amount of required details before writing. It might be helpful to determine the nature of the report (status, process, feasibility, progress, problem-solution, etc.) at the outset.

## Report Project

To provide actual practice for each phase of preparing and writing a business report, each chapter includes supplementary questions designed to reinforce the major ideas and procedures. Topics should be selected from the report writing assignments listed in Appendix A. For Chapter 1, select and classify a topic according to the criteria discussed. Determine the amount of detail required, and decide if the tone will be informal or formal.

# CHAPTER 2

# Planning the Report

**PLAN THE REPORT**  Despite the maxim lamenting the uncertain course of the best-laid plans of mice and men, a successful report requires careful planning. However, the amount of planning will vary among assignments.

In one situation, the writer may be thoroughly familiar with the subject matter and demands of the report, and may know precisely, or at least with a modest amount of confidence, the format and scope of the assignment. At another time, the writer may not fully understand the topic and may be unable to predict the amount of work the project requires.

As the writer's name often appears on the title page or front cover, he or she will be praised or condemned by the reader. All reports reflect the writer's ability to think, to compile and organize information, and to analyze problems and offer observations, solutions, conclusions, and recommendations essential to everyday business operations. One certain way to convey a positive impression of these skills is first to analyze the assignment and clarify its purpose. Next, the writer's aim is to limit the topic and to identify potential readers. Finally, he or she should devise a work schedule that will reflect the demands of the report.

**ANALYZE THE REPORT ASSIGNMENT: CLARIFY ITS PURPOSE**

Before preparing a report, the writer should analyze the assignment to clarify the aim and to focus precisely on its purpose. One way to gain a clear understanding of a report's purpose is to consider how it will be used by those who requested it or by those who will read it. Two questions to ask are (1) Will the report provide background information so that management can obtain a thorough perspective of an issue or problem? (2) Is the report's purpose to analyze and solve a problem, to outline the progress of a specific project, to study the feasibility of certain actions or policies, or to supply data essential to an important decision?

Often it is useful to ask the following question: "Why am I writing this report?" The answer will help the writer understand the demands, scope, and objectives of the report. For example, a company's senior vice-president for sales might request a report on recent sales trends and figures for several newly introduced products. The writer, after asking this question—in addition to "What does this person really want to know?"—may conclude that the report should focus on two aspects: sales regions where the new products have been marketed, and the corresponding sales figures for each area. He or she soon realizes that this report involves gathering and organizing sales data for each new product according to regional distribution. The report will also demand analysis and comments on strong or weak sales performances. Also, it may become clear that apparent trends, such as preference for a product in one area and not in another, should be noted. After analyzing the purpose of this report, the writer would *not* feel obliged to provide a detailed history of the development and marketing of each new product. Unless the writer were requested to include this information, such data would be outside the primary needs of the vice-president who asked for the report.

Establishing the *purpose* results in greater focus on those aspects of the subject area that are truly relevant. If the purpose appears vague or confusing, the writer should discuss the aims of the report with the person who has assigned it. Pondering a report's relationship to an organization's goals, priorities, daily operating procedures, or specific areas of interest will help the writer gain a perspective of its importance. Clarifying a report's purpose prevents the waste of time, effort, and, invariably, a great deal of an organization's money.

## LIMIT THE TOPIC

Limiting the topic demands an awareness of the need to proceed from a general to a specific understanding of the report's concerns. One helpful technique is to construct a *purpose statement* that may be broad in scope, and then to refine it by eliminating words or expressions that do not precisely characterize the report's purpose. For example, suppose the writer must compile a report on recent changes in consumers' spending attitudes and expectations toward buying new cars. At first, the writer may jot down this purpose statement:

A report about people's buying habits towards new cars.

After further consideration, the writer concludes that the report must outline buying trends and patterns in recent years. Yet how does one define recent years? Two? Three? Five? Another question to consider is whether the report should concern specific regions or represent a national perspective. Additional thought might be given to the role of advertising and peer pressure, as well as political, social, and economic factors. Quite a number of possibilities emerge about scope and content. Quite possibly, the more the writer thinks about the report's purpose, the more apparent the need becomes to highlight those factors directly related to the initial purpose of the report—to evaluate what changes have occurred in terms of what the public wants and will spend for a new car. If the writer decides to highlight consumer trends in new car purchases in the last three years, the revised purpose statement will read as follows:

This report will analyze and discuss changing consumer attitudes and trends towards purchasing new cars in the United States between 1983 and 1985.

Now the writer has a clear idea of the precise goal he or she must work toward in preparing the report. Other ways to formulate the purpose statement include posing a question:

What trends are apparent concerning consumer attitudes toward purchasing new cars between 1983 and 1985?

or

Did consumer purchases of new cars from 1983 to 1985 form a pattern or indicate a trend?

The writer may also postulate an hypothesis or statement that will be proven either true or false after careful research or analysis of available facts and figures:

The trend among consumers in buying new cars from 1983 to 1985 indicates a significant shift away from large cars to smaller ones.

**CONSIDER OTHER FACTORS**

Once the writer formulates a purpose statement, he or she can grasp a clearer understanding of the report's scope by considering other important factors. One approach is to jot down any relevant factors that will pertain to the report's goals and function. For instance, perhaps the board of trustees of a college needs an information report concerning the nature of present parking facilities. After noting the purpose statement, which might read

Present Parking Facilities at Adelphi University

the writer can consider these factors:

1. The physical availability of parking space.
2. The number of faculty, staff, and students who drive to the college.
3. Peak hours when the parking lots are used.

However, if the writer is asked to analyze the *adequacy* of these parking lots, the factors have to be expanded to include such information as the following:

1. Adequacy for present number of people who drive to the college.
2. Adequacy for potential future students, staff, and faculty.
3. The ratio between those who commute by bus and rail and those who drive.

The writer might also be expected to offer conclusions about adequate present and future parking, as well as several recommendations for improving or modernizing the existing facilities. If the writer concludes that additional parking facilities are necessary, he or she may pose this question:

Where is the best location for additional parking?

and then list factors essential to arriving at an answer. Factual data must then be analyzed before the writer can offer explanations and reasons for judging one location preferable to another. It may prove necessary to consult several other people for advice. All of the following factors must be considered if the report is to be thorough:

- Cost.
- Convenience.
- Aesthetics.
- Professional planners' opinions.
- Possibilities for future expansion.

Comparative criteria against which several hypotheses can be tested might also include the following:

1. The old baseball field is the best location.
2. Uncleared land owned by the college would be best for constructing parking lots.
3. The most feasible approach to building additional parking lots is to demolish several old laboratory buildings.

Whatever the conclusion, the writer's perspective will benefit from having reviewed the important factors that will prove crucial to producing a reliable, incisive report.

## IDENTIFY THE READER

To know who will be reading the report is just as vital as to be aware of its purpose and to limit its topic. Therefore, the writer must have a considerable understanding of the reader's background, interests, and needs. The reader could become frustrated and confused if the content required specialized knowledge and insulted if the approach is overly simplistic or incomplete. Ideally, the report should appear custom-tailored to fit the reader's needs and concerns.

One way to accomplish this is to try to understand the preferences and needs of the individual who assigns or commissions the report. Does he or she enjoy a wealth of detail or prefer a study that focuses on central issues concisely? Does the individual appreciate abundant visual aids, such as graphs and drawings? Do other responsibilities take up so much of this person's time that the report should consist either of a summary of key points and observations or conclusions and recommendations that appear at the beginning rather than at the end? A wise writer will ask many questions.

At the same time, the writer should try to identify readers other than the individual who assigns the report. Are they familiar with the subject? Are they experts in the area the report addresses? Are they members of the board of directors, company managers, stockholders, technicians, supervisors, plant foremen, government officials, or the general public? Their needs and backgrounds must be kept in mind if the writer is to avoid writing over the readers' heads or underestimating their ability to comprehend the report's findings. Experts will naturally expect an in-depth and perhaps highly detailed approach, but the general reader will appreciate a simple and concise overview of the subject.

Although tastes may vary, one standard that does not is the need for clarity and precision of expression. Unless the writer knows the names and specific job functions of the readers, he or she can never assume that the audience will easily follow the discussion and instinctively understand each point. The communication process breaks down the moment someone fails to understand another's meaning, no matter how simple the concept may appear to the writer.

In Figure 2–1, the writer has failed to consider the readers' needs in lieu of personal preferences for exhaustive and wordy sentences and description. The reader is more than likely to experience frustration and confusion in trying to understand exactly what this writer is attempting to say. It is hard to imagine a reader's interest being aroused and maintained over several pages of this kind of writing. Whenever a writer is unfamiliar with the readers' expectations and needs, it is best to use plain language instead of jargon (specialized or technical words and phrases) to express ideas. In Figure 2–2, however, the writer conveys the information in a manner that employees at all levels can understand.

## ADAPT TO THE READER'S NEEDS

When two people interpret a poem or novel, each is entitled to his or her own views and feelings. Reports, however, should not lend themselves to a variety of interpretations by the reader. Instead, the ideas should be explicitly expressed. One fatal assumption a writer can make is to assume that what appears clear to him or her will be clear to everyone else. Two key elements to consider when adapting style and content to the readers' needs are *time* and *personal interest*.

Personality, job title, and familiarity with the report's subject all play a part in the reader's response to a report. Subsequently, no report will appeal to or please everyone. Yet whether the report is intended for senior level executives, middle managers, or plant super-

# Memorandum

Subject:  Reports/Forms                              March 25, 1984

To: Manager, Facilities Division

It seems that we are constantly feeding a gigantic multi-headed, nice to have, information monster.  Every head wants the information in a little different format or the same information with one or two different quirks of equivocal information requested.  If there is not a genuine requirement for information, and some function is going to be performed with the information; other than to feed one of the monster's heads, or nice to have so I will know if he asks, whoever he may be; we can save a lot of manpower if we eliminate this practice or consolidate reports.

Specifically, we question the tangible benefits that will be derived from the most recent form requesting data on SMP/S&G projects.  We are presently feeding SMP/S&G data in an ADP Run, when we receive it; on Procurement Requests (PR's), by SF-19's, EA Form 6030-13, EA Form 6030-12, and Purchase Orders (SF-44's).  The one or two quirks this request has that can not be obtained from all these other reports/forms (hopefully someone is looking at them), is that this one asks for projects "out on the street," "projects actively being prepared but not ready for advertisement," and something I'm not sure of.  (Form is enclosed.)

The questions that we should be asking are:

1.  Do we really need this information?  If so, what are we going to do with it?
2.  Is this the most efficient method to use in obtaining it?
3.  Is this information somewhere else?
4.  Can we consolidate reports to include necessary information thereby eliminating waste and saving manpower?

We realize that certain information is necessary and some is just desired.  We should be sure it is required before we ask for it since we must utilize our work force to gather the information and prepare the reports/forms.  Our people are our most valuable resource, and as our staffing dwindles, we need to insure that we are utilizing them in the most efficient manner to realize maximum productivity.

Enclosure

FIGURE 2–1.    *Poorly constructed memo characterized by rambling phrases, wordiness, and repetition.*

**MEMORANDUM**

*To:*       All Associates, Secretaries and Staff Personnel

*From:*     Accounting Department

*Subject:*  Personal Charges

*Date:*     May 28, 1984


As of June 1, please present all reimbursable
personal charges on the last day of each month
on one Personal Expenditures form.  Personal
charges include taxis, automobile rentals, air
travel, overnight lodging, meals, and telephone
credit calls related to company business.

If you have questions regarding this new
procedure, please call Aldo Vannucci (X1225).

*FIGURE 2–2.   A model memo characterized by clarity and precision of expression.*

visors and technicians, its readability depends on the clarity of the writing and the fact that the writer has truly identified probable readers. Having even a general understanding of the reader's needs and background can prove invaluable while planning a business report. Perhaps the most helpful question for the writer to ask at this stage is "Would I want to read my own report?"

**DEVISE A WORK SCHEDULE**

Once the writer has defined the report's purpose, limited its topic, and analyzed potential readers, a tentative work schedule should be devised to provide a general idea of the tasks involved in preparing the report. In determining the schedule, the following questions might be considered:

***1. Do I Know Enough About My Topic?*** While most people will readily agree that no one can be knowledgeable about everything, few people care to admit to deficiency in any area of knowledge. For this reason, a report writer's success often depends upon the willingness to admit to not knowing enough about the subject, and to recognize the need for further research and investigation. Additional knowledge can be pursued easily enough if the writer consults informally with people who may be able to offer valuable insight to the topic or its particular problems. The people consulted might be either inside or outside the organization, and they may express opinions privately or in a professional capacity. At other times, the writer will be familiar with the issues or problems the report must address but still feel the need to learn more about the topic. Therefore, the extent of further research will range from personal observations and informal discussions with others, to consulting books, magazines, journals, encyclopedias, pamphlets, and brochures. Specific information-gathering methods are discussed in Chapter 3.

***2. Is the Subject Matter Simple or Complex? Will the Report Require a Great Amount of Details?*** The simplicity or complexity of a report is determined by the nature of the subject and needs of the reader. At times relatively complex material, such as an analysis of the latest computer technology or stock market trends, must be simplified for an audience lacking expertise in either field. On other occasions, apparently simple or easy-to-understand topics call for lengthy analysis or careful explanation of the smallest details. Such is the case when a doctor writes an article on the need for a balanced diet. A mass market publication, such as *Readers Digest*, requires more elaboration than does a professional medical journal, for whose readership there is not so great a need to explain every detail. On occasion, the subject of a report may be complex due to the specialized jargon and terminology needed to explain its nature and function. This would occur with a report explaining how a word processor operates. Sometimes a report's complexity rests in the need to discuss multifaceted concepts in-depth. One sure way to simplify any report is for the writer to determine what does *not* have to be stated after considering the readers' backgrounds and needs.

**3. Will the Report Be Long or Short?**   Although the question of length is a relative one among business report writers, determining the simplicity or complexity of the subject matter will provide some idea of a report's length. One ironic factor to bear in mind, however, is that the simplest topics do not necessarily result in the briefest reports. A great deal of the writer's time can be absorbed searching for unavailable data or from unexpected delays in obtaining information.

**4. Will the Report Provide Information, Analysis, or Both?**   Although reports can serve many functions, generally they are divided into two groups: those that provide information, and those that examine and analyze it as well. In practice, many reports combine both facets, yet during the planning stage, the writer should determine whether the report will be fundamentally informative, analytical, or perhaps a combination of both. For example, a report on the number of students enrolled in college business programs across the country will essentially be informational, because the writer is merely compiling facts and numbers. By contrast, if the report examines the various reasons students choose to concentrate on one area rather than another—investment banking instead of marketing research—then the writer might include opinions, conclusions, and other forms of analytical observation. Understanding the premise of the report enables the writer to plan adequately.

**5. Should the Report Include Illustrations?**   Illustrations should be used to clarify, not merely to beautify, the content of the report.

Complex ideas, statistics, and numerical computations will often be clearer to the reader if they are expressed visually through drawings, charts, graphs and other devices. Taking into consideration the possible need for illustrations is one facet of report planning the writer should not ignore. Illustrations are discussed fully in Chapter 8.

**6. *When is the Report Due?*** Getting a tentative idea of a due date is indispensable to devising a work schedule. Depending upon an organization's needs, routine reports can be due at the end of each week, month, quarter, or every third Friday of each month. For specially assigned reports, the writer should always reach a general understanding or set an approximate deadline with whoever requests the report. If a report is initiated by the writer, then it is clearly his or her responsibility to set a completion date. To avoid undue pressure and anxiety, it is best to allow some extra time for unexpected delays or problems.

**7. *Can Some of the Report's Workload Be Delegated to Others?*** Once the writer has determined the scope of the report and how much time is needed for preparation and writing, he or she should consider delegating some of the workload or tasks to other people. If a committee has been assembled to write the report, various people can share in gathering information, conducting research, organizing the details, and perhaps in actually writing parts of it. For the solitary report writer, knowledge of the resources available within an organization can save time and effort. For example, does the organization maintain its own library, research staff, graphic arts department, computer terminals that can obtain information from outside sources, typing pool, or editorial services? The ability to gain access to any one of these services can and should be taken into account when the writer formulates a work plan.

Answering these preliminary questions can help the writer devise a realistic work schedule that allows time for other daily business or job-related responsibilities. Whether the writer devotes some or all of his or her time to working on the report, having a work schedule helps one to concentrate efforts and avoid the danger of procrastination. Procrastination is especially disastrous to report writing due to the often rigorous demands of research and information gathering, organizing, writing, revising, and proofreading. Unexpected setbacks, for any number of reasons, allow little time for putting off the report for tomorrow.

Good writing takes time and discipline. For these reasons alone, the writer must consider the amount of time needed for the report from inception to completion. To be sure, the following points should be kept in mind:

- Devise a work plan even if it appears that there will always be some free time each day to work on the report.
- Begin the report as soon as possible to avoid the anxiety of feeling rushed.
- Allow breathing space by setting a deadline even if there is none.
- Determine the best time to work on the report, and stick to it.

**PREPARE A WRITTEN PLAN**    Even if the topic of a report seems routine or familiar, the writer can more easily clarify his or her thoughts by preparing a written plan. The plan should not be overly rigid but should allow room for changes. This way, it will provide the writer with a visible but not restricted sense of direction regarding the report's overall nature, objectives, and tasks.

The written plan might include the following:

1. Title.
2. Purpose statement.
3. Reader/audience analysis.
4. Information gathering sources (company files, records, field trips, library research, interviews, questionnaires, etc.).
5. Possible limitations (time, money, availability of information, etc.).
6. List or outline of topics.
7. Report format (memo, letter, formal, printed).
8. Work schedule.
9. Available company resources (library, computers, typing pool, etc.).
10. Tentative completion date.

Although the writer is free to formulate his or her own approach to planning a report, following the various steps discussed in this chapter will more than likely result in reports that are well-organized, comprehensive, logically developed, and direct.

The following is a preview of additional tasks essential to preparing and writing successful reports:

1. Prepare an outline.
2. Gather necessary information.
3. Evaluate the information.
4. Organize the information.
5. Select an appropriate format.
6. Write the first draft.
7. Prepare a table of contents, additional material (longer reports).
8. Select illustrations.
9. Review and revise the first draft.
10. Proofread for content and structure.
11. Compose an abstract or summary (longer reports).
12. Review and submit the final draft.

Each of these steps will be discussed fully in Chapters 5–10.

**CHAPTER REVIEW**

*Questions*

1. List five steps for planning a report.

2. What factors should be considered when analyzing a report assignment?

3. Why is it important to identify a report's readers? What can the writer assume about the reader?

4. How would a report written for a construction company's executives differ from one written for its engineers?

5. What are the advantages of limiting the topic of a report?

6. In devising a work schedule, what questions should be posed by the writer?

7. List the components of a written plan.

8. List the various steps, from idea to completion, that a writer should follow in preparing a report.

*Exercises*

1. Write a purpose statement that limits the problem to be addressed in each of these report-writing situations:

   a. Our sedans and station wagons are among the best our engineers and designers ever produced. They are comfortable, fuel efficient, and reasonably priced. They come in a variety of new colors and styles that should appeal to car buyers everywhere. Yet recent sales figures show that these cars are selling well in New York and California only. Why?

   b. For eighty years, Good Tasting Ice Cream has outsold all other brands. This can be attributed to the use of the finest ingredients and a superb sales staff. Although the brand is a household name for many people, there are still some places where this ice cream cannot be obtained.

   c. Central Savings Bank was the first one built in Main City, Iowa. Its depositors include leading business executives, the mayor and members of the city council, prominent local doctors and lawyers, and other professional people. In recent years a number of these depositors have withdrawn their money and placed it elsewhere. For Central Savings to survive into the 1980's, new depositors must be attracted.

   d. Time Honored Foods has long been associated with quality food products. Some administrators have noted increasing consumer interest in imported gourmet food items. Moreover, a major competitor has begun selling imported gourmet food and has been doing very well with the new line. Is this a sign of possible threat to Time Honored Foods' ability to remain competitive?

   e. An electronics manufacturer predicts that by 1999 every home in America will have some kind of computer equipment. Yet the demands of the public are fickle and varied. Which need should the company's research and development department concentrate on?

   f. The food in the cafeteria of a famous university used to be excellent. It was once rumored that students studied there because of the food more than because of any other factor. Yet nowadays the hamburgers are dry and over-cooked, the salads are paltry, the fish like rubber, the desserts tasteless. However, the hot sandwiches are tops and the Italian and Chinese dishes way above average. Sales vary, according to the manager, depending on what kind of food is served each day. Yet there must be greater consistency in sales if the cafeteria can show a profit and remain in business.

g. At another college, some students in the psychology program are wondering why certain seminars have seventy-five students enrolled when the maximum number listed in the course catalogue is ten. This is occurring more and more often lately, and many people are beginning to feel that the quality of their education may be at stake. Some students are drafting a letter to the department chairman and president of the college. There is, however, some doubt about how to phrase the problem.

2. Devise a business day schedule that allows time for preparing and writing a report on one of the above topics.

3. For three of the problems listed above, construct a written plan according to the one described on pp. 26–27.

4. Select any product or service and write an information report for both the company president and the sales staff. How might the reports differ in scope, tone, and content? Why?

5. For a report designed to evaluate two competitive products, what factors should be considered in the planning stage? Should the emphasis be on providing background information or critical observations?

## *Report Project*

1. Devise a report writing plan for your formal report, taking into account all factors considered in this chapter. Be certain to note the title, scope, purpose, due date, and probable reader(s).

2. Analyze the audience in terms of education, experience, relationship to or knowledge of the subject, interest and need to read the entire report or selected portions. Decide if the report is intended to provide information, offer conclusions, or urge the reader to act.

# CHAPTER 3

# Gathering the Information

**KNOW THE SUBJECT**

Once the writer has determined the purpose and scope of a report, and has identified and analyzed the readers' needs, it is essential to ask this question before proceding further: "Do I know enough about my subject?"

This question must be answered honestly if the report is to reflect the writer's best work. No one, however expert in any field, can know everything about a given topic. There will always be information to acquire about increasing technological innovations, the expanding proliferation of available information, and the complexity of many issues and subjects. While personal expertise and understanding will often suffice when preparing a report, there will be many occasions when a report will require extensive research.

Generally, there are two kinds of research—primary and secondary. In *primary research*, information is obtained first-hand or directly through personal observations, company files, experiments, field trips, interviews, and the use of questionnaires. *Secondary research* involves the gathering of information from published sources such as books, professional journals, popular magazines, trade newsletters, past reports on a related or similar subject, and newspapers.

Once the need for research has been established, the writer may feel confused about where to begin. Secondary research can often provide a convenient overview of what others have observed about a particular topic. More importantly, a review of relevant published material can save the writer a great deal of time. A drawback, however, is that only a portion of the available information may be relevant to the particular focus of the report. It is thus essential to conduct primary research as well.

## PRIMARY RESEARCH

Primary research originates with the writer's personal knowledge, observations, and expertise. In many instances, experience is a source of needed information. Daily familiarity with the workings of a specific project, product, or service often translates into firsthand knowledge that can prove useful in preparing a report. As an example, suppose an aeronautical engineer is asked to report on the possibility of developing an improved jet airplane engine that will offer added fuel-efficiency. If the engineer has a great deal of experience in designing jet engines, that knowledge can be drawn upon to provide background information concerning the limitations and possibilities for developing a new engine. Moreover, if the engineer has been following recent aeronautical trends and advances, the need for secondary research may be less than for someone unfamiliar with the field or who has less experience. Hence, the approach to research is relative to the writer's expertise and experience with the subject. While the point of departure for conducting research will vary among writers, most reports will reflect a combination of primary and secondary research methods.

Another source of primary information can be the writer's own office or department, where memos, letters, previous reports, and any other company files may provide necessary or helpful data. Very often such correspondence can offer information not otherwise obtainable. The only obstacles the writer might encounter in consulting company records are obsolescence or inaccessibility due to classified status. However, this is not often the case, and in many instances such correspondence will prove both useful and available.

When conducting primary research, it is a good idea to solicit suggestions and advice about gathering necessary information either from the person who requests the report or from anyone else familiar with its topic. As time is money, the wise writer saves both by accepting all the help he or she can get from any reliable source.

**INTERVIEWS**    Personal interviews are an excellent means of obtaining firsthand facts and opinions. The benefits of conducting interviews while searching for information include avoiding misunderstanding and misinterpretating data, achieving greater accuracy in the findings, and possibly reducing the amount of time expended in secondary research.

*Before the*    The writer can save a great deal of time by carefully narrowing the
*Interview*    list of interviewees to those who can significantly contribute to the investigation. It is important to consider the individual's background, expertise in relation to the report's purpose, and job function or status. If the people to be interviewed are co-workers, it is easier to arrange an interview on short notice. For those outside the company, it is best to arrange interviews well ahead of time. Express the reason for wanting to interview them, and assure them that their assistance is needed.

*Prepare the*    Whether conducted in-person or by telephone, a successful inter-
*Questions*    view depends on carefully prepared questions. These should be as follows:

*1. Relevant to the Subject.*    An interview requires the interviewee's time, as well as that of the report writer. Thus, every question should relate directly to the report's main concerns. Always avoid or curtail lengthy digressions. If the person chooses not to answer a controversial question, proceed directly to the next question.

*2. Objective.*    Obtaining accurate responses from an interviewee depends in large part on the writer's ability to construct questions that limit or discourage subjective or overly opinionated answers. Even when the writer seeks a valid opinion of particular interest to the investigation, he or she should construct questions that focus on the specific issue or topic. This limits the tendency to offer general opinions that might not be helpful in the long run. Objective questions force the interviewee to give specific answers. For example, the following question will most likely evoke a subjective response:

What do you think about our new word processors?

By contrast, the question that follows will evoke a specific response:

What experience has your staff had with our new *X* and *Y* word processors? Have there been any problems?

The wording of the second question helps the interviewee recall specific experiences that staff had with the company's word processors.

**3. *Clear and Straightforward.*** Unclear questions generate confusion and invite inaccurate and vague responses. The writer should know exactly what must be learned before formulating the questions, and should take time to rewrite or rephrase any question that appears vague or imprecise. Note these two examples:

Unclear
I was wondering if you had any ideas about this?

Clear
How can our organization improve its public image?

**4. *Significant.*** Avoid conducting an interview if the information can easily be found in printed material or if it is a matter of public record. The writer can enhance the value of the interview by asking important questions, not by exchanging small talk. After all, if someone takes up valuable time to answer questions, the least the writer can do is to ask relevant and significant ones.

**5. *Comprehensive.*** Comprehensive, in-depth questions will evoke detailed rather than superficial answers. The writer therefore can avoid the anxiety that results from forgetting to ask a key question or phrase an important one correctly. In practical terms, the writer may be unable to contact the interviewee again before the due date of the report. That person may be ill, on vacation, or working for another company. In short, construct complete questions to ensure complete answers.

**6. *Free of Bias.*** Expressions of personal bias either in the questions or in the responses are detrimental to the integrity of the report's findings. For this reason, the writer should be cautious about composing questions that reflect a biased attitude or that seek to evoke one. Sometimes, for any number of reasons, an interviewee may feel that certain questions must be answered in such a way as to reinforce or justify a particular bias toward an issue or project. The writer should formulate questions so that the responses will not reflect prejudiced feelings and beliefs. Bias would undermine the purpose of all reports—to discover the truth.

Biased
Are you as upset and angry as our firm is over the nerve of those people at XYZ to build a plant in the middle of town?

Do you enjoy preparing sales reports?

Unbiased
What is your firm's reaction to the XYZ Company's plans to build a new plant in our area?

How often do you prepare sales reports?

**7. *Interesting.*** Asking interesting questions often sustains the interviewee's attention and possibly generates better responses. This is not an easy task, because no one can truly foresee what will interest one person and not another. One helpful technique is to make the questions relate to the individual's interests, concerns and area of expertise. Getting someone involved in the interviewing process is half the battle; asking interesting questions that invite free-flowing comments can only insure the interview's chances for success.

For those individuals who are reluctant to comment on certain issues, the interviewer should rephrase and repeat the question toward the end of the interview. Perhaps by then the interviewee will feel more comfortable and will speak more freely. It is not unusual for people to need time to warm up to someone they have never met. At first, the biggest obstacle may be to overcome or penetrate someone's official pose.

Another technique involves appearing enthusiastic about the report's subject. This will often have a positive effect on those interviewed. Boredom or indifference to the subject can result in dull questions; energy and enthusiasm can encourage active participation.

**CONDUCTING THE INTERVIEW**

If possible, send the list of questions to the interviewee a few days ahead of time. Submitting questions before an interviewee allows the respondent more time and thought, and perhaps greater accuracy in response. Avoid sending questions too far in advance or just before the interview. In the former instance, the interviewee may misplace them or forget to look them over; in the latter case, he or she may feel overwhelmed or ill-prepared, and may cancel or postpone the interview.

During the interview, try to appear relaxed and not overly aggressive. Do not interrogate, intimidate, or otherwise cause someone to feel ill at ease. At the same time, convey the impression that the interview will be conducted as quickly as possible. After exchanging the usual pleasantries, get right to the questions. Preface them with brief restatement of the purpose for asking them.

Information can be recorded on notecards, in a journal, or on a tape recorder. If taking notes makes the person being interviewed uncomfortable, put down the pen and either try to remember key points or, if one is available, switch on a tape recorder. Be certain always to ask permission before using a tape recorder.

Jot down responses in outline form or short phrases. Remember to note fully the interviewee's *name*, *title*, and *organization*. Record the time, day, and date of the interview. At the end of the interview, review responses to major questions with the interviewee. This will substantiate accuracy and will diminish the possibility of future refutation of any comments. In some instances, the interviewee might initial his or her remarks. Always express appreciation for the interview, and offer to send along a copy of the report upon its completion.

## QUESTIONNAIRES

Questionnaires that are sent through the mails are helpful in gathering information from large numbers of people or from those who are too busy to sit through an interview. Two advantages of a mail questionnaire are its relatively economical cost (compared with long distance telephone rates) and the leisure afforded each respondent in answering the questions. Some difficulties include procrastination, indifference, or lack of knowledge on the part of the respondent. Also, anyone who designs a questionnaire to determine a trend or general pattern must have the ability to reach a general conclusion based upon individual responses. For these reasons, the writer who uses questionnaires to compile information should have some familiarity with various sampling methods and procedures for designing surveys. This knowledge enables the researcher to minimize inaccuracies and discrepancies among respondents and to maximize valid perceptions.

**Sampling Methods**  The report writer who distributes questionnaires relies on sample returns to determine tastes, preferences, opinions, attitudes, and viewpoints about a product, service, issue, or problem.

In an effort to obtain as truly representative a view as possible, the writer should employ as many samples as possible. Ordinarily, the greater the number of respondents, the greater the possibility that the group will truly reflect the whole. Some basic methods of sampling include the following:

1. *Random sampling* involves the spontaneous and unfocused selection of respondents. Choosing names from a telephone directory is one example of this approach.
2. *Cluster sampling* selects respondents from subdivisions or categories of a larger population or group. An example would be an interoffice survey of employees according to age, sex, job function, or seniority.
3. *Systematic sampling* involves selecting respondents at various numerical intervals from larger lists. Thus, every fifth or tenth respondent's replies may be studied from a group of one hundred questionnaires.
4. *Quota sampling* allows the writer to control samplings by setting quotas. For instance, the conductor of a survey may limit the study to fifteen engineers, ten scientists, twenty executives, and so on, to measure specific data.

In many instances, the report writer will want to scrutinize carefully and weigh the responses of all those surveyed. In the case of some respondents, the writer may value one opinion above another, depending on his or her familiarity with the various individuals' backgrounds and expertise. Yet before information from a sampling can be evaluated, it must first be obtained through a well-designed questionnaire.

**DESIGNING THE QUESTIONNAIRE**  All questionnaires consist of a *series of questions* and either a *quantitative* (i.e., 1–10 rating) or *qualitative* (good, necessary, excellent) means of measurement and response. Instructions and an explana-

---

### *COLLEGE COURSE AND TEACHER SURVEY QUESTIONNAIRE*

The purpose of this questionnaire is to obtain student opinions about courses and teachers. It is important that you answer these questions carefully since information from the survey is used in decisions for reappointment, tenure and promotion at the college. However, the project is voluntary, and you are not required to answer the survey items. To maintain anonymity, please do not record your name on the IBM response card.

**Instructions**

Print the name of the instructor, the course number and the section designation on the left side of the IBM card.

Read each of the items below, rating the statements in terms of the five (5) response categories listed. For each statement, indicate the response closest to your own opinion by blackening IN PENCIL the appropriate space on the IBM card.

Response columns are numbered 1, 2, 3, and so on. Please be sure to use the column that corresponds to the number of the statement on which you are giving your opinion. For example, if you <u>disagree</u> with statement 1, you will blacken in number "2" in the column above response number 1; if you <u>agree</u> with statement 1, you will blacken in number "3" in the column above response number 1.

*(continued)*

---

FIGURE 3–1.   *A model questionnaire characterized by a qualitative means of measurement. Note how carefully the instructions and the questions have been prepared.*

tion of the reason for the survey are standard components as well. While formats may vary, all effective questionnaires are characterized by carefully prepared questions. Effective questions contain the following characteristics:

1. *They are directly related to the report's purpose and subject.* Answering a questionnaire requires time and concentration by the respondent. Therefore, questions should be directly related to the report's scope and purpose. Otherise, both the wirter and respondent will waste a great deal of time with unnecessary data. Thus, the need to develop pertinent questions is of primary concern.

WHAT IS YOUR OPINION ON EACH OF THE FOLLOWING ITEMS AS IT APPLIES TO THIS COURSE OR INSTRUCTOR?

1. The course is well organized.

   0 = Don't know or doesn't apply; 1 = Strongly Disagree; 2 = Disagree; 3 = Agree; 4 = Strongly Agree.

2. The instructor is responsive to students.

   0 = Don't know or doesn't apply; 1 = Strongly Disagree; 2 = Disagree; 3 = Agree; 4 = Strongly Agree.

3. The instructor stimulates thinking.

   0 = Don't know or doesn't apply; 1 = Strongly Disagree; 2 = Disagree; 3 = Agree; 4 = Strongly Agree.

4. The instructor is able to get material across to the students.

   0 = Don't know or doesn't apply; 1 = Strongly Disagree; 2 = Disagree; 3 = Agree; 4 = Strongly Agree.

5. Overall, how would you rate the instructor in this course?

   0 = Don't know; 1 = Poor; 2 = Fair; 3 = Good; 4 = Excellent.

6. Overall, how would you rate this course?

   0 = Don't know; 1 = Poor; 2 = Fair; 3 = Good; 4 = Excellent.

Thank you for your participation. Please check to see if additional questions appear on the reverse side. If so, please answer them and then return all materials to the STUDENT in charge.

Office of Institutional Research                        Spring 1984

*FIGURE 3–1 (continued).*

2. *They are clearly worded.* During a personal interview, vague or confusing questions may be reworded and clarified. By contrast, when someone answers a questionnaire, no one will be available for comment and elaboration. It is crucial that the writer devise accurate, clear, and precise questions. One danger of imprecise questions is that the respondent will be uncertain about answering them. He or she may ignore them altogether.

3. *They are free of bias or misleading overtones.* Biased or misleading questions serve to limit the respondent's ability to provide truthful answers. Failure to offer enough flexibility in response occurs when questions elicit merely a YES or NO response rather than a series of choices or options. Avoid this kind of question:

Do you feel doctors' fees are too high?

        yes _____       no _____

4. *They focus on one idea.* Overly complex or detailed questions that concentrate on too many ideas will confuse the people attempting to answer the questionnaire. Follow a simple rule of thumb: One question; one idea.

5. *They do not suggest an answer.* The purpose of distributing a questionnaire is to evoke honest responses to specific questions. Suggestive questions counteract the chances for candid answers and ultimately hamper rather than advance an investigation. Pursuing the truth is essential to report writing. Avoid the following type of leading question:

Don't you agree that our new copier is the best on the market?

        yes _____       no _____

6. *They get to the point.* Ask straightforward questions that are precisely worded and as brief as possible. Indirect and excessively worded questions can hinder the accuracy of respondents' answers, or they can imply that the questionnaire requires more time than the respondents would care to spare.

7. *They are arranged in a logical order.* Often the best questions proceed from the general to the specific, and suggest an orderly progression or flow of thought. Questions can also be arranged according to priority and category, or arranged in any sequence that enhances their logical structure.

8. *They allow a flexible response.* Some questions may require more than a simple yes or no response. As such, the respondent should be offered the opportunity to express opinion, judgment, agreement, or disagreement.

9. *They provide space for additional comments.* Such comments

can often provide the unexpected helpful insight to difficult problems or issues that often contribute to a report's effectiveness.

10. *They invite consistent responses.* If the samples are to be valid, there must be some degree of consistency in interpretation and response. All respondents should interpret each question the same way. All questions, then, should be pretested to ensure consistency of interpretation. Rewrite them if they prove to be ambiguous or unclear.

The sample questionnaire shown in Figure 3–1 includes many of these features.

**SECONDARY RESEARCH**

When a report requires information beyond the writer's own knowledge, observations, company files, and personal contacts, it is necessary to conduct secondary research among printed books, journals, magazines, newspapers, and assorted reference materials available in public, private, or specialized libraries.

Although secondary research can prove rewarding, it can become tiresome and fruitless if the writer is not selective and methodical in approaching what may seem to be an overwhelming amount of available published material. Because libraries are as varied as the volumes on their shelves, it is important to focus on those which are most likely sources of information.

In general, libraries can be divided into two groups. The *general* library is an excellent starting point for gathering information. It has a variety of subject matter and is accessible for public use. The *specialized* library focuses on a particular subject area (business, fine arts, medicine) and tends to be selective in the materials it acquires. Specialized collections pertain to a profession as well as to a subject, and are sometimes housed in the administrative headquarters of trade and professional associations and societies, and in special interest organizations and unions. A number of these libraries are restricted to members. Specialized collections in corporations and in public and private foundations may be limited to use by employees, and those in universities may be open only to faculty and students. Nevertheless, very often these libraries will open their doors to those conducting serious research, and their staffs will provide cordial assistance. To locate a specialized library in a specific geographic location, the writer can consult one of these reference guides available in most general libraries: *Special Library Resources* (Special Libraries Association), *Special Libraries Directory* (Special Libraries Association), and *Directory of Special Libraries and Information Centers* (Gale Research Company).

After deciding which libraries will probably prove the best sources of information, it is essential to devise a plan that will further limit the research to the report's topic and concerns.

## PLAN THE RESEARCH

Carefully planned research enables the writer to focus on those reference and information sources that are relevant to the report's topic and purpose. Remembering to limit the research to a particular area will save hours of unnecessary searching and reading. One technique is to devise questions essential to the report's major points and scope.

For example, someone employed by a brokerage house is preparing to report on the reasons for the recent high turnover rate of bonds sales personnel in comparison with the turnover rate of managers in banking and advertising. The first step would be to consult company records for numerical data related to a specific time period, perhaps the last six months. Then, through interviews with personnel officers and supervisors, the writer might hear of several reasons for the frequent turnover rate among bonds salespeople. Secondary research would probably involve turnover figures for other brokerage firms and for banks and advertising agencies. Methodical preparation of questions about the information being sought will help the writer focus clearly and precisely on the available, and no doubt numerous, sources of information. Some questions might include the following:

1. What exactly is the turnover rate in my firm?
2. What factors influence turnover rates in general?
3. Why did so many bonds salespeople leave our firm?
4. How do the figures compare with other firms?
5. How do the turnover rates compare with those in banking and advertising?
6. In the last five years, what changes have occurred in bonds sales to warrant unusually high turnover rates?

Once the writer has formulated questions based on specific needs, it is much easier to concentrate on library reference sources most likely to provide answers.

## USING THE LIBRARY

Aside from special collections, library materials are placed either in a *reference* section or made available for *general circulation*. In either case, using a card catalog is a lot easier and productive than wandering among the stacks.

### Library and Reference Guides

Several books can provide orientation to using a business library and can help to locate various business information sources.

> Herbert Webster Johnson, *How to Use the Business Library*, 4th ed. (Cincinnati: South-Western Publishing Company, 1972).
> David M. Brownstone and Gordon Carruth, *Where to Find Business Information* (New York: John Wiley & Sons, 1979).
> Eugene Paul Sheehy, *Guide to Reference Books*, 9th ed. (Chicago: American Library Association, 1976).
> Lorna Daniells, *Business Information Sources* (University of California Press, 1976).

### The Card Catalog

To locate available books relevant to the report's topic, refer to the library's card catalog either under *Subject Listing*, if there is not an exact title in mind, or *Author/Title Listing*, if there is. All libraries arrange their card catalogs according to either the Dewey Decimal or Library of Congress classification system (see Table 3–1).

## REFERENCE SOURCES

Consulting general reference sources or guides will provide an overview of the information the writer needs to incorporate in the report. Here is a selected list:

> *Encyclopaedia Britannica*
> *Encyclopedia Americana*
> *Encyclopedia of Banking and Finance*
> *Accountant's Encyclopedia*

**TABLE 3–1.  Card Catalog Classification Systems**

| Dewey Decimal | |
|---|---|
| 000–099 | General Works |
| 100–199 | Philosophy |
| 200–299 | Religion |
| 300–399 | Social Science |
| 400–499 | Language |
| 500–599 | Pure Science |
| 600–699 | Applied Science |
| 700–799 | Fine Arts |
| 800–899 | Literature |
| 900–999 | History |

| Library of Congress | |
|---|---|
| A | General Works |
| B | Philosophy and Religion |
| C | History |
| D | History and Topography (except America) |
| E,F | America |
| G | Geography and Anthropology |
| H | Social Sciences |
| J | Political Science |
| K | Law |
| L | Education |
| M | Music |
| N | Fine Arts |
| P | Language and Literature |
| Q | Science |
| R | Medicine |
| S | Agriculture |
| T | Technology |
| U | Military Science |
| V | Naval Science |
| Z | Bibliography |

For facts and statistics, consult the following sources:

*World Almanac and Book of Facts*
*Historical Statistics of the United States*
*Handbook of Economic Statistics*
*Survey of Current Business* (U.S. Department of Commerce)
*Million Dollar Directory* (Dun and Bradstreet)
*Billion Dollar Directory* (Dun and Bradstreet)

*Economic Almanac*
*Poor's Register of Corporations, Directors and Executives of the United States and Canada*

***Biography.*** These directories offer factual biographical data:

*Who's Who in America*
*Who's Who in Commerce and Industry*
*Dictionary of American Biography*

***Specialized Business Reference Sources.*** The following sources include surveys, forecasts, report commentaries, and facts on specific business topics:

*Standard and Poor's Industry Surveys* (forecast reports and surveys of various industries).
*Business and Economic Books & Serials in Print* (R. R. Bowker Co.).
*U.S. Industrial Outlook* (U.S. Department of Commerce) (contains forecast reports for numerous industries).
*Moody's Manuals* (industry, banking, public utilities, transportation, government facts, statistics, analyses).
*Encyclopedia of Business and Information Sources* (Detroit: Gale Research Company, 1980).

***Indexes and Guides.*** There are innumerable annual indexes and guides to published material. These time-saving sources to information printed in books, magazines, professional journals, and newspapers include the following:

**Books**
*The Cumulative Book Index*
*The Library of Congress Catalogue*
*Books in Print*

**Periodicals and Specialized Journals**
*Business Periodical Index*
*The Reader's Guide to Periodical Literature*
*Bibliographic Guide to Business and Economics*

**Newspapers**
*The New York Times Index*
*The Wall Street Journal Index*
*The Times Official Index* (London)

**COMPUTERIZED RESEARCH AND INFORMATION RETRIEVAL**

Computerized data base research and information retrieval can save every report writer substantial time and effort. These systems provide access to the contents of newspapers, journals, magazines, encyclopedias, news wire service books, government publications, business reports, and indexes to specialized topics. For a nominal fee, the writer can gain access to data on a wide variety of topics through computerized information systems and centers operated by libraries, universities, government agencies, and private industry. While prices may vary, users are charged either by the hour or according to how much time is utilized on the computer. Some companies, such as DIALOG, also provide copies of abstracts or entire articles. Consult the reference librarian about possibly using such services as

DIALOG Information Services, Inc.
3460 Hillview Avenue
Palo Alto, CA 94304
(800)227-1927

COMPUSERVE
500 Arlington Centre Boulevard
Columbus, OH 43220
(800)848-8990
(614)447-8650

THE SOURCE
1616 Anderson Road
McLean, VA 22102
(800)336-3330

NTIS (National Technical Information Service)
U.S. Department of Commerce
Springfield, VA 22161

**COMPILE A WORKING BIBLIOGRAPHY**

During initial library research, it is helpful to compile a *working bibliography*, or list of books, articles, and other reference sources. Using either a notepad or 3″ × 5″ index cards, record the following publication facts for future reference (see Figure 3–2).

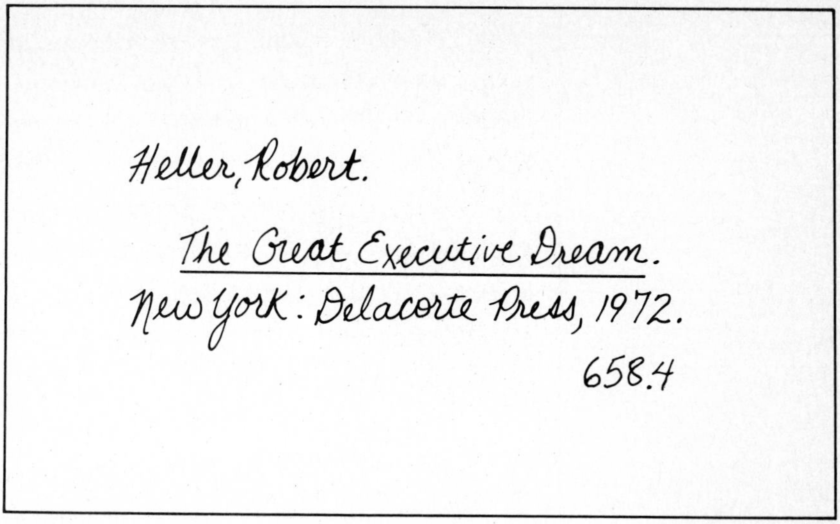

Heller, Robert.

The Great Executive Dream.
New York : Delacorte Press, 1972.

658.4

FIGURE 3–2.   *Record publication facts for a working bibliography.*

- Name of author or editor.
- Title.
- Place of publication.
- Publisher.
- Date of publication.
- Page reference numbers (articles).
- Library call number.

**RECORD THE INFORMATION**

After composing a working bibliography of potentially useful reference materials, the writer must then review each source. Any fact, opinion, or idea relevant to the report's purpose and scope should be noted carefully on index cards or notepaper. Information can be quoted directly or paraphrased (summarized in the writer's own words). Above all, record the page number on which the information appears. To avoid great confusion, not to mention the time wasted trying to remember just where the data appeared, it is helpful to record the author's name and source title on additional index cards in case the other cards become accidentally mixed up or lost. For example, see Figure 3–3.

> "The ideal worker, from management's point of view, does what he is told without argument; never makes mistakes; is punctual, clean, and tidy; produces maximum effort on a consistently rising scale; accepts any working arrangements his superiors ordain; and never demands more pay than the firm can afford (i.e. the minimum that the management thinks it can get away with.)"
>
> —Heller, *The Great Executive Dream*, p. 57.

FIGURE 3–3.   *Record relevant information from the sources listed in the working bibliography.*

## INCORPORATE RELEVANT RESEARCH DATA WITH THE REPORT

Research inevitably leads to the problem of selecting and incorporating relevant information into one's own writing. Quoting an expert can often reinforce an important point, support an idea, provide added insight to a problem, or reinforce opinions or judgments.

At the same time, it is best to avoid excessive use of quoted material, because the report should reflect the writer's ability to express an idea or analyze a situation. It is best to use quotations that precisely phrase or dramatically highlight a difficult concept. One problem arises when writers randomly present researched information with no regard to logic, organization, and idea development. To avoid this error, follow these steps:

1. *Separate* research sources and appropriate information according to probable placement in the report: Introduction, Discussion, Conclusion, Recommendations, Examples, Case Studies, etc.
2. *Decide* if the information explains, supports, exemplifies, describes or defines a particular concept or concern in the report.
3. *Select* information that will develop the report, not merely embellish it with extraneous, albeit interesting, details.
4. *Introduce* the information with expressions such as:

> According to . . .
>
> In Mr. Smith's opinion or view . . .
>
> Mr. Smith feels/believes/states/ thinks/notes/observes . . .
>
> This concept/idea/theory/feeling is supported by noted expert Charles Mature, who believes . . .

Framing quoted information with an opening phrase or expression enhances the reader's perspective and understanding of its importance to the report. The key to incorporating research material successfully, whether it is quoted or paraphrased, factual or opinionated, is to find exactly where it will best contribute to developing the report's ideas. This requires concentration, to decide exactly where supportive data can be inserted in the text without interrupting the reader's thoughts. Don't be afraid to use the cut-and-paste technique to decide on the most appropriate place for the information.

Above all else, the basis for incorporating research in a report is to provide added perspective and insight for the reader. One natural tendency after spending many hours gathering information is to feel that all of it has to be included in the report for no other reason than because the writer worked so hard to find it. Extraneous data can be included in an appendix at the end of a report, or consigned to company files for future reference. At worst, a writer should throw away information rather than risk boring the reader with unnecessary data.

Here is an example of how to incorporate information in a report:*

1. If the quoted information numbers four lines or less, it can be inserted into the body or text, provided it is distinguished and enclosed by quotation marks:

> Some observers, notably Mr. Harold H. Marquis, have concluded that "if there is one element in the corporate image program to which management should give its most careful attention, it is the annual report."

2. If the information is longer than four lines, it is standard practice to separate it from the text by leaving a double space above and below the passage as well as wider margins on each side of the page. Single-space rather than double-space the information. Quotation marks can then be omitted as in the following example:

---

* The passages that follow have been excerpted from Harold H. Marquis, *The Changing Corporate Image* (American Management Association, 1970), p. 86.

Some observers, notably Mr. Harold H. Marquis, have concluded that:

> If there is one element in the corporate image program to which management should give its most careful attention, it is the annual report. There is no doubt that this is the most direct and effective contact between the company and its present and potential stockholders. This document will be read more thoroughly than advertising or other publicity for the company, because it tells the reader how well his money has been invested. In effect, the annual report sums up the corporate image.

Recent interviews with a number of our firm's stockholders bear out this contention, and some have even suggested areas they would appreciate to be given wider coverage in our annual reports.

3. Often a writer encounters a long passage, yet wants to quote only fragments or particular phrases and sentences. To avoid quoting an entire passage or highlighting information out of context, the writer should acknowledge the break in the quoted passage by using ellipsis points or dots ( . . . ) to connect the words and sentences. Three dots indicate a space between words; four dots a space between sentences:

> In Mr. Harold H. Marquis' view of the importance of the annual report, "this document will be read more thoroughly than advertising . . . because it tells the reader how well his money has been invested."

or

> In Mr. Harold H. Marquis' view of the importance of the annual report, "there is no doubt that this is the most direct and effective contact between the company and its . . . stockholders. . . . In effect, the annual report sums up the corporate image."

4. Researched information can be paraphrased or summarized, and does not require quotation marks. While it is not necessary to acknowledge the reference source for known facts other than for the reader's convenience, a paraphrase of someone's ideas, opinions, or concepts should always include credit acknowledgement:

> Some observers, including Mr. Harold H. Marquis, believe that the annual report is a vital means of contact between corporation and stockholder, and sole reflection of the corporation's image.

Note that sometimes an error in spelling, punctuation, fact, or grammar occurs in the quoted passage. If the writer notices such instances, he or she should not correct them. Instead, the Latin term *sic* (thus) should be used to indicate that the error appears as such in the original source. Enclose *sic* in brackets.

For example:

The corporation grew rapidly in 1982, with a marked increase *[sic]* in production and manpower.

**USE OF FOOTNOTES**

Plagiarism involves taking false credit for someone else's ideas. Facts cannot be plagiarized, but theories and opinions can be illegally appropriated. Sometimes plagiarism occurs unconsciously when the author paraphrases ideas. It is common practice when incorporating information obtained from a reference source, whether quoted directly or paraphrased, to give proper credit through the use of a *footnote*, which contains essential publishing facts along with specific page reference numbers. A footnote, as the name suggests, is usually placed at the foot or bottom of a page. It bears information cited from a reference source. Sometimes footnotes are listed together on a separate page following the last page of the report. Here they are referred to as *endnotes, but they serve the same purpose.*

Footnotes are numbered consecutively throughout the entire report in small Arabic numerals. The numerals are placed both after the last word of the citation in the report's text and before the footnote at the bottom of the page. (See the examples on pages 52–53.)

**FOOTNOTE MECHANICS**

The following publishing facts are often cited in a footnote:

1. *Author's full name* in normal order (Jeremy Kane), followed by a comma.
2. *Title* of the work cited, underlined and followed by parentheses that contain the following:

*(Place of Publication: Publisher's Name, Date of Publication).*

        colon⟋        comma⟋

3. *Page number(s)* followed by a period.

Facts about publication can be obtained from the title page of a book and front cover of an article appearing in a magazine or professional journal. If the date of publication for a book is not listed on the title page, refer to the copyright page directly following.

**FOOTNOTE FORMATS**

Footnote format varies according to the type of reference source cited. While all footnotes contain publishing facts, there is a degree of variation among them, depending upon an organization's style and needs. The standard footnote formats listed at the bottom of this page are among those most commonly used in business reports:*

The *footnote* is placed three lines after the last line of text. The *first line is indented* three spaces, and the footnote is typed *single-spaced*. The *footnote number* is raised slightly above the line and is *not* followed by a period. Between footnotes, keep a double space.

**Examples**

The following examples illustrate the proper methods of footnote citation.

*Book*
[1] Salvatore J. Iacone. *Modern Business Report Writing* (New York: Macmillan Publishing Company, 1985), p. 28.

*Book by Two Authors*
[2] Leonard Silk and David Vogel, *Ethics and Profits: The Crisis of Confidence in American Business* (New York: Simon & Schuster, 1976), p. 20.

For books having three or more authors, simply list the first author's name, followed by a comma and the term *et al* (meaning and others) followed by another comma.

[3] Rudolph W. Schattke, et al., *Managerial Accounting: Concerts and Uses* (Boston: *Allyn* and Bacon, 1974), p. 30.

---

* For further reference see the following:
  *The MLA Style Sheet*, ed. William Parker, 2nd. ed. (New York: Modern Language Association, 1970).
  *MLA Handbook for Writers of Research Papers, Theses, and Dissertations* (New York, Modern Language Association, 1977).
  *A Manual of Style*, 13th ed. (Chicago: University of Chicago Press, 1982).
  Kate L. Turabian, *Student's Guide for Writing College Papers* (Chicago: University of Chicago Press, 1976).

### Edited Book
[4] William Rivers, ed., *Business Reports: Samples from the "Real World"* (Englewood Cliffs, N.J.: Prentice-Hall, 1981), p. 50.

### Article (magazine or journal)
[5] Arthur M. Louis, "The Hall of Fame for U.S. Business Leadership," in *Fortune*, March 22, 1982, p. 101.

In citing articles, the specific date of publication and volume number are noted. Do not list the specific publisher and place of publication.

### Newspaper Article
[6] William E. Blundel, "Confused, Overstuffed Corporate Writing Often Costs Firms Much Time—and Money," *The Wall Street Journal*, August 28, 1980, p. 21.

### Multivolume Work
[7] "Business Cycles," *Encyclopaedia Britannica* (1975) 3, 536.

When noting the volume number, omit the word "volume" or "vol.," and the "p." or "pp." before the page numbers.

[8] Victor Bondini, *Communicating Through Humor* (New York: Winston Publishing Company, 1983) I, 75.

**Subsequent Reference**

When a footnote contains a reference source that has already been cited, do not write the complete entry again. Three methods of abbreviation will save time and energy.

1. If a footnote refers to the same source as the preceding footnote, denote this by using the Latin term *Ibid.* (from *Ibidem*, in the same place) and cite the appropriate page number. For example:

[1] Salvatore J. Iacone, *Modern Business Report Writing* (New York: Macmillan Publishing Company, 1985), p. 100.
[2] *Ibid.*, p. 125.

2. For sources that are not consecutively repetitive, mention only the author's last name or title of the work. The term *Op. cit.*, mean-

ing "in the work cited," also indicates repetitive use of a previously cited source. However, this term is used with infrequency in recent years.

    [3] Mercatante, p. 10.
    [3] *Op. cit.*, p. 125.

    3. It is becoming increasingly popular among writers to avoid Latin expressions and merely use the author's last name or the source title for subsequent references.

    [1] *The One Minute Writer*, p. 25.

***Explanatory Footnotes***    Some footnotes serve to explain, define or present numerical data that would distract the reader or interrupt the flow of the narrative if included in the report's body. In such instances, use either an asterisk or a lower case letter to denote the information. For example:

    * A "marketing goal" is a specific marketing objective stated in such a way that it is measurable.

or

    [a] An "advertising goal" is a specific communications objective stated in such a way that it is measurable.

## THE FORMAL BIBLIOGRAPHY

The formal or final bibliography differs from the working bibliography in that it comprises the reference sources actually used in the research and final or finished draft. This bibliography is a listing of the books and articles the writer has consulted. The form and punctuation differ from footnote entries in the following ways:

1. No Arabic number precedes the entry.
2. All entries are arranged alphabetically.
3. The author's last name is listed first. When the author is not known, determine placement by the first word in the title.
4. The facts of publication are listed as in the footnote but are separated by a period rather than commas. No parentheses are used around place, publisher, and date.
5. The second line of the same entry is single-spaced.

6. Except in the case of articles, no page numbers are cited. With articles, the pages cited are inclusive of the entire run of the article. Specific pages are not highlighted.
7. The first line of the entry is typed next to the left-hand margin. Subsequent lines are indented three spaces.
8. For more than one entry by the same author, do not repeat the name. Simply introduce the entry by a single line followed by a period.

**Examples**     The following examples illustrate the proper methods of citing bibliographical references.

### Book
Iacone, Salvatore J. *Modern Business Report Writing*. New York: Macmillan Publishing Company, 1985.

### Book by Two Authors
Iacone, Salvatore J., and Judith Resnick. *The Reading Connection*. New York: Macmillan Publishing Company, 1983.

### Articles
Iacone, Salvatore J. "Investing in Rare Books." *Money Maker*, June/July 1981, pp. 46–48.
Bennett, Robert A. "Battling Over Bank Interest Rates." *The New York Times*, February 20, 1983, Section 3, p. 1.
"Accounting." *Encyclopaedia Britannica*. 14th edition.

**CHAPTER REVIEW**     **Questions**

1. Distinguish between *primary* and *secondary* research.

2. List the qualities of effective interviewing questions.

3. Outline the procedures to be followed when conducting an interview.

4. Discuss the value of using a questionnaire in surveying information.

5. How should the questions for a questionnaire be prepared?

6. What is a specialized library?

7. List five reference guides to specialized libraries and business information sources.

8. What is the function of a working bibliography?

9. Define plagiarism.

10. How does paraphrased information differ from a direct quotation?

11. What is a footnote? When are footnotes needed in a report?

12. How does a footnote differ from a bibliographical entry?


## Exercises

1. Select two of the following topics. For each of them, *list* three sources of information available in a library.
   a. Video Tape Equipment and Sales.
   b. Oil and Gas Drilling Projects in the United States.
   c. The Future of Railroads.
   d. Farm Equipment Production.
   e. Major Oil Company Profits for the Last Three Years.
   f. The Top Movie Box Office Attractions.
   g. Five Top Corporate Executives in Industry.
   h. The Largest Corporations in the United States.
   i. A topic of your choice.

2. From any one of the sources of information, note five articles.

3. Construct a working bibliography of at least ten reference sources for a report on any topic you choose.

4. Integrate the following quotations with the passage that follows.
   a. "Many companies are recognizing that manpower is a key resource and that success or failure of a company can depend more upon the effectiveness of its people than on any other factor."—Richard Smith

      During the 1970's, American business experienced a tight manpower situation. Essentially, this situation was brought about by an increase in new kinds of jobs, declining number of skilled unemployed, and continuing trends towards longer periods of education.

If a company is going to effectively build up and maintain its manpower resources it must be able to identify and develop potential management talent at an early age and have an idea of its future manpower needs so that young employees will know what they might expect in the way of advancement in the future. Otherwise, it will be difficult to retain potential management talent.

b. "The number of female employees in supervisory, technical and administrative positions increased on the average from 75 to 150."—Lester Johnson

If our company is to meet our commitment to equal employment opportunity, we must continue to give attention to providing jobs for women. Over the past decade, there has been a substantial increase in the number of women in business positions. If we continue our efforts, we should be able to develop additional numbers of women who can fill supervisory and other management positions. It appears that with increasing use of college women in clerical positions, we should be especially careful to insure that those among them with the ability are given the chance to advance to more challenging positions.

## Report Project

1. Decide if your report requires research. Is it necessary to conduct primary or secondary research, or perhaps both?

2. Conduct essential research.

3. Create a series of questions for an interview with someone who can contribute substantially to your report investigation.

4. Design a questionnaire that will support or expand the scope of the questions devised for the interview.

# CHAPTER 4

# Evaluating the Information

**EVALUATE THE INFORMATION**

At some point following research, the writer may well begin to wonder just what to make of all the data that has been gathered. What is important? What is not? How can the major ideas be readily distinguished from the minor ones? The surest way to impose order on what can easily become chaos is to evaluate and then organize the information according to its content's relationship to the subject and purpose of the report. Yet where does the writer begin?

The most logical and simple approach is to divide the information into primary and secondary categories. Distinguish between material that will support, explain, illustrate, or highlight major ideas and findings and that which is secondary or peripheral. The first step, then, in evaluating information is to select or discard data on the basis of how the material relates to the purpose and focus. From all the company files and records, personal thoughts and observations, library research, interviews, letters, memos, past reports, and other documents that have been collected, select only material that directly contributes to the development of the report. Someone who is preparing a report for an electronics manufacturer on the educational potential of computers may have gathered a great deal of information about the different types of computers, their purposes, advantages and disadvantages, limitations, costs, sales performances, and repair records. Additionally, assume that the writer has collected a number of market surveys that outline the potential needs in business and education for computers in the future, has interviewed educators or conducted mail questionnaire surveys among them, and has consulted and received written replies from engineers and designers about the technical possibilities for computers in relation to learning processes.

Keeping the report's purpose—the educational market potential for computers—in mind, the writer decides to construct the report around the needs and possible uses that were mentioned in the interviews and correspondence with teachers and designers. Subsequently, the writer will *not* focus on previous sales performance and incidence of repair records of computers, the different manufacturers and available models, and perhaps not even the cost, because this information is simply outside the focus of the report. While it may be painful to discard material that one has spent many hours gathering, the report will suffer greatly if it contains unnecessary information. One consoling thought is that any time spent collecting information is a learning experience that has enabled the writer to expand his or her understanding of a particular subject. Also, information that may seem of little value at one time may prove valuable at a later date for another report.

**ANALYZE THE CONTENT AND FUNCTION**

Information can be further evaluated by analyzing it according to its content and function. It is helpful to consider material in terms of its nature and role in presenting various ideas that include the following: *chronological development* or *time order, cause and effect, problem and solution, comparison, description, definition,* and *idea and example.*

A person who is writing a progress or status report on a project would consider which information best indicates development according to time and tasks accomplished. By contrast, someone preparing a feasibility study would select information that describes as well as indicates possible causes and effects (or the advantages and disadvantages of ideas and actions). Also, this writer may recommend a variety of alternative actions or solutions.

Determining which information would serve in an introduction, main discussion of findings, conclusion, summary, or recommendation is also helpful. Fact and opinion might also be separated. As each item is evaluated and analyzed according to its content and function, the writer can simplify matters further by placing the data in specially marked folders. This will enable the writer to feel in control of—rather than overwhelmed by—the material.

**JUDGE THE INFORMATION CAREFULLY**

Facts, along with opinions, statistics, and other data, must be interpreted and evaluated honestly and objectively. Even if the writer employs a computer—which saves time and insures a reasonable degree of accuracy in disseminating data—he or she must still personally judge both the value of those findings and how they are incorporated in the report. One problem that emerges is how to use one's experiences, knowledge, and viewpoints while simultaneously resisting the all-too-human tendency to allow feelings and personal beliefs to color, distort, or unduly influence the accurate interpretation of information.

Critical thinking varies from person to person. So too do experience and knowledge. Emotions can strongly influence one's critical perspective. Subsequently, perceptions of problems, issues, and solutions will differ radically unless the writer bears in mind the following guidelines for objective, and hence honest and accurate, critical thinking:

1. Avoid generalizations.
2. Avoid personal bias and pre-existing opinions.
3. Beware of unreliable data.
4. Beware of incomplete data.
5. Beware of unequal comparisons.
6. Beware of conflicting facts or evidence.
7. Do not assume something is true without proof.
8. Beware of drawing false conclusions about causes and effects.
9. Beware of misreading cause and effect patterns; an effect might not directly result from a previous action.
10. Beware of inferences based on personal feelings or emotional appeal rather than facts.
11. Beware of distorting evidence to prove a point.

In addition to these pitfalls, the writer should carefully examine the relationship of all collected data to the report's scope and purpose.

Experts' opinions should be compared and double-checked for consistency or strong variance. While the writer should note unique situations or circumstances and allow for alternative interpretations, the data should contribute to the formation of a clear picture of issues and problems addressed in the report. Some helpful questions to ask are as follows:

- Does the information support one or many interpretations? If so, which one(s) are correct?
- How does the information shed light on major concerns of the report?
- What conclusions tend to emerge repeatedly after the data is viewed in various ways?

**CRITICAL THINKING**    The ability to think critically is essential to the report writer who must frequently understand, analyze, and evaluate the various ideas presented in a business report. Facts may speak for themselves, but theories and opinions, along with conclusions and recommendations, must be carefully studied for validity and truth. In critical thinking, several modes of reasoning are involved.

*Induction*    Induction leads the writer to a general conclusion after he or she has studied evidence or details. The evidence must meet basic criteria:

1. *The evidence must be of sufficient quantity.* Enough cases must be considered to reduce the chances of a flawed induction. For instance, if someone concludes this next statement

> At two of our branch offices, each of which number ten employees, three have M.B.A. degrees. Therefore, 30 percent of the company's employees must have M.B.A. degrees.

the induction would be faulty because the two branch offices cited may contain a higher number of people holding advanced degrees than is true of other branch offices or the main office. Additional evidence is needed before the induction can be valid.

2. *The evidence must represent a true cross-section of a group.* In the previous example, the writer would have to consider all levels of management whose members hold advanced degrees.

3. *The evidence must be reliable and accurate.*

4. *Conclusions must be relevant to the evidence.* For example, to conclude that employees of one company receive the best health insurance benefits on the basis of how much money that company spends each year for employee benefits in general is not necessarily a relevant and, hence, valid conclusion.

**Deduction**    Deduction offers a conclusion that is then followed by supporting details and evidence. Deductive reasoning often involves three basic formats for argument, called *syllogisms*. Each syllogism consists of two premises or statements, and a conclusion.

**Categorical Syllogism.**    A categorical syllogism uses classes and categories and shows whether or not an individual case fits a particular category. It thus determines if the individual case has the same characteristics found in the larger group. The format consists of a *major premise*, or first statement about the relationship of two groups; a *minor premise*, or second statement about one individual and one group in the major premise; and a *conclusion*.

*Major premise:*    All great economists are geniuses.
*Minor premise:*    Adam Smith was a great economist.
*Conclusion:*        Adam Smith was a genius.

For this categorical syllogism to be valid, both premises must be true. In some instances, the premises either cannot be proven true or are debatable, in which case the conclusion may not be totally valid.

**Hypothetical Syllogism.**    A hypothetical syllogism poses an "if/then" premise and can be helpful in constructing cause and effect arguments. A *major premise* states a condition, while a *minor premise* states whether or not the condition exists. The *conclusion* indicates the consequence that follows both premises.

*Major premise:*    If a book wins a Pulitzer prize, it must be good.
*Minor premise:*    My professor's novel won a Pulitzer prize.
*Conclusion:*        Her novel must be good.

**Alternative Syllogism.**    An alternative syllogism uses an "either/or" premise in which one alternative is true.

*Major premise:* Bill is either in his office or at the club.
*Minor premise:* Bill is not in his office.
*Conclusion:* Bill is at the club.

Such a conclusion is valid only if the alternatives are mutually exclusive. In this case, Bill can be nowhere but in one of two places. If he can be elsewhere, then the conclusion is not valid.

## INTERPRETING THE INFORMATION

During the evaluation phase of preparing a report, it is often essential to interpret the information that has been collected. Usually this process involves the progression from general observations and inferences to specific statements, conclusions, and recommendations. Like an artist who begins a new work by painting broad brush strokes before applying fine details, the report writer moves from the general to the specific when interpreting information.

### Generalizations

As a primary step in evaluating and interpreting information, general observations enable the report writer to gain an overview of the findings and content. To be of any ultimate value, generalized interpretations should be supported by adequate evidence, such as facts, professional opinions, surveys, examples, trends, patterns, or other supportive data. Even though a generalization is merely the starting point for the writer's analysis, that judgment or viewpoint must have some form of substantiating basis. For example, if someone writing a quarterly sales report finds that sales figures have declined 25 percent from the last quarter, he or she can assert that business is down. Yet for the report to have greater range and substance, an analysis and understanding of the possible reasons for the decline in sales figures might be provided along with numerical data. At first, then, the writer may note the following

> There is indication that business is down. Last quarter's sales figures declined 25 percent from the previous quarter.

While the numerical evidence provides the writer with a factual basis for asserting that business is down, this general view is still a surface one because important details, in this case reasons for the decline in sales, have yet to be presented. While this generalized statement is fine for providing a topic statement to introduce the report, additional information must be given to develop the idea fully. Upon further analysis of available data, the writer might state more specifically:

> Last quarter's sales decline of 25 percent clearly indicates a downturn in business. According to sales personnel, this drop in sales can be attributed to inadequate marketing strategies and delivery procedures that were recently instituted. Further investigation with clients and major distributors support sales personnel's contention for declining sales.

Even though the writer will have to describe and comment carefully on the poor marketing strategies and methods of delivering the products, he or she has established a foundation upon which to develop specifically the report's premise concerning declining quarterly sales.

**Inferences**  Another method of interpreting data is to *infer*, or judge and draw assumptions on the basis of what is suggested rather than explicitly stated or supported by factual evidence. An inference is drawn from whatever information is presumed to be accurate and probable at the time by the writer. Inferences can be helpful in determining possible reasons or likely solutions for problems. For instance, if someone probing consumer reaction to a new soft drink learns that the demand from distributors is fast exceeding the supply, there would be a very good chance of being correct in inferring that the soft drink has become very popular among consumers.

Nevertheless, the writer must avoid imposing personal opinions or beliefs on inferences. A person who infers that because a particular new copier is efficient, the manufacturer will soon make a fortune in sales may be mistaken. Another mistaken inference results from assuming that a well-dressed woman sitting in a Rolls-Royce parked in front of the Plaza Hotel in New York is rich and powerful. While this may be true, there are little available facts other than appearances to support this notion. The woman may be a model, or could have rented the car for the day. Inferences, then, can have their pitfalls, and so they are to be drawn with caution.

***Conclusions***   Conclusions drawn from data should reflect a reasoned opinion and sound judgment. Interpreting information requires objectivity, integrity, and common sense. The writer must avoid the natural tendency to read trends and conclusions that are not in the findings. Additionally, no one can suggest with certainty that a series of similarities and differences in one situation will apply to all others. Nor can a valid conclusion be based on what the writer may feel rather than on what has actually been observed or verified. The facts must literally speak for themselves; there is little point interpreting conclusions on evidence that cannot be substantiated. For example, a report for an automobile manufacturer, analyzing which of two new models would have greater rental appeal to corporations, reveals that

1. a. Car *X* offers 23 miles per gallon of gasoline.
   b. Car *Y* offers 35 miles per gallon of gasoline.
2. a. Car *X* has a frequent repair record.
   b. Car *Y* hardly needs repairs.
3. a. Car *X* is uncomfortable on long distance trips.
   b. Car *Y* maintains a comfortable ride always.

One possible conclusion is that Car *Y* would be selected over Car *X* on the basis of fuel efficiency, repair records and comfort. However, this conclusion would have less weight if the choice were based solely on the writer's preference for color and styling. Then the supporting evidence would reflect someone's personal taste and preference, rather than any objective standard of measurement.

Another pitfall when drawing conclusions is to mistakenly assume the existence of a *cause and effect* relationship because of consecutive time order, or because one action directly follows another:

Ever since the company increased the number of part-time workers, productivity has declined drastically.

This erroneous conclusion had its roots in the writer's failure to consider other factors that might have affected productivity, such as the breakdown of equipment or late delivery of raw materials. Upon further examination of other possible influences, the conclusion can prove invalid.

Conclusions should not include broad generalizations, nor use words like *none, never, always,* and *all* to overstate an argument or belief. If a writer examines various brands of word processors in order to recommend one model for office purchase, and finds that the

ABC model breaks down more frequently than other models, he or she might conclude the following:

The ABC word processor always breaks down.

As stated, this argument could be disputed because it is based on the writer's limited personal knowledge and experience. For someone else, that particular model could prove superior to comparable machines.

Be especially wary of the following erroneous tendencies when drawing conclusions:

**1. *Non Sequitur.*** "It does not follow." A common error resulting from an assumption improperly drawn. For example:

- a. Automobile manufacturers are losing money.
- b. Toyota is an automobile manufacturer.
- c. Toyota is losing money.

The problem is obvious. As a result of what appears to be a logical argument, a company that may be an exception to statement (a.) is judged negatively and incorrectly (c.).

**2. *Begging the Question.*** Accepting a premise as being true before proving it. For example:

Should our firm invest in such a poorly managed company?

Further research may prove that the company in question encountered difficulties for reasons other than poor management.

**3. *Faulty Analogy.*** This occurs under two circumstances: (1) when two ideas are compared or equated even though they have little or nothing in common; and (2) when it is assumed that if two objects are similar in some ways they are equal in all. For example:

- a. American small cars may go the way of dinosaurs.
- b. Jack Wilson will make a fine bank president. He has been an accountant for twenty years.

The writer has mistakenly assumed that because Joe Wilson has been an accountant for many years, he will be a fine bank administrator. Yet what does one skill have to do with the other?

**STATISTICAL INTERPRETATION** In the 1980's, largely because of the proliferation of computers in business offices of all sizes, the report writer's task of manually interpreting statistical data may be lessened and perhaps improved. The science of statistics is concerned with the collection and analysis of numerical data. These data often constitute a substantial part of business reports. A basic understanding of the following statistical terms will aid the writer in interpreting data accurately.

1. The *mean* is the average reached by dividing the total figure by the number of parts or values. For example, to determine the mean sales of three leading audio equipment manufacturers, whose individual sales were respectively $10,000,000, $25,000,000, and $40,000,000, the total ($75,000,000) is divided by three, which results in $25,000,000 as the mean or average sales figure.

2. The *median* is the mid-value or number in a given sequence arranged in order of magnitude. In the above example, $25,000,000 would represent the median figure among the three companies.

3. The *mode* is the most common or frequently occurring value. In the sequence of 10–20–20–30–40–50, the mode is 20.

4. The *range* indicates the limits of variance of values or qualities in a given sequence. In a series of yearly salaries of $9,000, $12,000, $13,500, $18,000, and $22,500, the range between the highest and lowest figure is $13,500.

5. The *ratio* indicates a comparison of quantities usually expressed in a proportional relationship. Assume, for example, that a questionnaire requesting opinions concerning impending changes in annual meeting procedures is mailed to 10,000 stockholders of a large corporation. If 7,500 respond favorably and 2,500 do not, the ratio would be 3 to 1, because three times as many stockholders approved of the changes. In percentage terms, 75 percent approved; 25 percent disapproved.

**PROBLEM-SOLVING TECHNIQUES** Often the report writer is called upon to determine, analyze, and solve a problem or series of problems. Although the nature of the problems will vary, their solutions always require clear thinking and a methodical approach founded on principles that seek to perceive data objectively. The writer must also avoid the tendency to overlook information that is contrary to previously held notions and personal bias. When attempting to solve a problem, the report writer must offer the best possible solution in light of available evidence. Despite all the information-retrieval systems available in recent years, it is still difficult to acquire every bit of information required to solve a specific problem. Nevertheless, the following problem-solving techniques can aid in determining the surest solution to most problems an organization may encounter:

1. To *define the existing problem*, ask these questions:

- What is going wrong?
- Who or what is being affected by the problem?
- Why is the problem occurring?
- How can it be corrected?

2. To *decide if the problem has a major or minor cause*, ask these questions:

- Is the problem's cause simple or complex?
- Can it be easily corrected?

3. List the *possible solutions to the problem*. Few complex problems have single clear-cut solutions. Therefore, each corrective device or procedure must be carefully considered before the writer can conclude which solution seems best.

4. To *analyze the practicality of the solution*, ask these questions:

- Will the solution require a reasonable amount of time, money, or manpower?
- Can it be easily implemented?
- Is it legal?
- Is it operative immediately?
- Will the problem be resolved temporarily or permanently?
- Will there be any resistance on the part of management or labor?
- Will the solution indirectly create a further problem?

5. *Note each solution's advantages and disadvantages.* All possible solutions have their plus and minus sides. The advantages of any solution must outweigh its negative characteristics considerably if it to be fully usable. Otherwise, the writer risks offering a solution that may ultimately create more problems than it solves at the moment.

6. *Test the relationships.* Relationships represent the mode of connection between any number of items, ideas, objects, people, and procedures. In an effort to offer solutions to problems clearly, the

writer must establish a relationship between the variables under consideration. Basic relationship patterns include the following.

*Cause and Effect.*   Complex problems often have more than one cause. A series of forces are usually at work. The writer's difficulty is in truly identifying those causes and determining their effects or relationship to the problem under scrutiny. For example, consider this statement:

> Mark Duffy was promoted because he sold more computers than any other salesperson. His success was surely due to his good looks and sense of humor.

Yet what about Mark's ability to inspire trust, his energy and enthusiasm as a salesman, and his knowledge of the various uses of his company's product in unlikely situations? While Mark's physical appearance and personality could certainly play a large role in his success, they are not the only factors. In this instance, the reasons for Mark's success are numerous and related directly to one another. Also, these qualities can have more than one effect. Thus, Mark might be greeted more cordially than others, might earn a higher salary and bonus, might receive added benefits from his company, might be given greater responsibility, consulted frequently for advice, asked to train newly hired salespeople, and ultimately be promoted to sales manager.

*Sign Relationships.*   Sign relationships are indications rather than actual proof of causal patterns. To be meaningful, sign relationships should be consistent. For instance, if fewer homes are sold when mortgage rates are high, the sign relationship may be apparent in declining profits among businesses related to the housing industry, such as in steel, furniture, carpeting, lumber, and appliances. Yet the writer must take care to avoid misinterpreting or failing to consider signs that prove contradictory. Increases in new home and auto production may be signs of a healthy economy, but below-average retail store sales and rising unemployment suggest otherwise.

*Analogical Relationships.*   An analogical relationship theoretically suggests that if two or more items are similar in some ways they are similar in other ways. For example, if Harry and Joe are the same age, graduate the same year from the same college, obtain jobs in the same fields as their fathers with the same corporation, the conclusion seems to be that they will be equally successful. Perhaps. Yet there are other factors at work that determine success; among them are intelligence, drive, ambition, imagination, and integrity. The writer must ask three questions when considering an analogical relationship:

1. Are the similarities significant enough to warrant a connection?
2. Are the similarities relevant to the comparison?
3. Are there essential differences between the items being compared?

**EVALUATION CHECKLIST**   The following questions should help to simplify and facilitate the task of evaluating information.

1. How much of the information I have gathered is truly relevant to my report's purpose and scope?
2. Have I gathered enough material to address the major issues of my report effectively?
3. How reliable are the facts? Are they accurate? Have I double-checked the source of this information?
4. Are the facts recent or out of date?
5. Do the opinions expressed by various individuals through interviews, questionnaires or printed materials relate to the report's topic?
6. Is there any indication of personal bias? Were the opinions expressed by experts?
7. Have I carefully recorded pertinent information concerning my reference sources?
8. Have I carefully documented all information in terms of source and accountability?
9. Have I exhausted the major sources of information? Is my data complete?
10. Have I compared items that do not have a common basis?
11. Have I established the proper relationship between facts, opinions, other findings, and numerical data in terms of the total report?
12. How do the various bits of information fit to form an organized discussion?

13. Have I drawn faulty analogies or conclusions?
14. Have I overgeneralized?
15. Have I viewed the information from various perspectives in terms of its content and structural placement?
16. Have I discussed my observations and findings with others who may offer helpful advice?

The integrity and success of a report is directly related to the writer's diligent review of the raw data. The need to evaluate and interpret information carefully and critically is paramount to the success of the next step in the report writing process—organizing the information—which is discussed in the following chapter.

## CHAPTER REVIEW

### Questions

1. Discuss the need for evaluating information collected for a report.

2. What preliminary steps should be taken when evaluating data?

3. How should data be analyzed? List the possible methods.

4. When interpreting information, the writer should be aware of various pitfalls. List them.

5. Distinguish between a *generalization, inference, analogy,* and *conclusion.*

6. Define a *non sequitur.* Give an example.

7. Discuss the value and function of statistical interpretation.

8. Define these terms: *mean, median, mode, range,* and *ratio.*

9. List five problem-solving techniques useful to a business report writer.

### Exercises

1. Discuss the flaw in critical reasoning in the following statements:
   a. Hockey games always end in brawls.
   b. The best kinds of jobs are in banking and marketing.
   c. A course in business writing will help anyone get a promotion.
   d. Boys get better grades in science; girls do better in art.

  e. None of the doctors I know smoke. Doctors do not like smoking.

  f. Japanese technology is ahead of many Western nations because there are many scientists in Japan.

  g. Jack Watson has few scruples; his business advice is worthless.

  h. Charlie likes to have cocktails before lunch and dinner. He must have a drinking problem.

  i. Because the college has discontinued administering an admissions test, the academic quality of entering freshmen will decline sharply.

  j. Jane is a great speaker. She would make a great politician.

  k. Lucy Jones wears the latest clothing styles. She must have a lot of money.

2. Distinguish fact from opinion in this passage:

> Last year the Marlow Detective Agency was featured in ten newspaper and magazine articles. Sam Marlow, the principal partner, is a nice guy who has been in business twenty years. He must have many connections among reporters and magazine writers. That's why he always gets his name in the papers.
>
> Marlow once said that the trick to being a good detective is to investigate every lead and clue, no matter how trivial or absurd. He should know. He is one of the most famous private eyes in the world. He must be the best detective since Sam Spade.

3. Select a topic that allows for conflicting viewpoints—for example, *nuclear power plants, defense spending, use of preservatives in food, effects of sugar and salt in a daily diet, wine vs. hard liquor,* or *stocks vs. money market funds.* Then analyze and discuss each viewpoint according to the evaluative methods noted in this chapter.

4. From a printed source (book, magazine, journal, or newspaper) collect data on a specific industry. Write a forecast performance report.

## *Report Project*

Evaluate the information you have gathered thus far for this project, either through primary or secondary research (interviews, questionnaires, personal notes and observations, reference materials, etc.) according to the principles and techniques discussed in this chapter.

# CHAPTER 5

# Organizing and Outlining the Information

**ORGANIZE THE INFORMATION**

Effective organization of the content of the report can assure its success. The writer's problem is how to present that information in a suitable manner for the reader. Fortunately, a number of organization patterns can help the writer present information according to *time*, *space*, and *logic*.

**Time Order**

When the sequence of events or activities is central to a report's purpose, such as when the writer is narrating the background or history of a project, noting progress, or providing instructions, the information is best presented in time, or chronological, order. In such instances, the writer must simply remember to state first things first, or in their proper order of occurrence. Here is an example:

> *In March 1983,* Johnston Wingate, president of PBR, suggested that in-house training programs for management be expanded to meet the challenges and changes of the 1980's. *On April 1,* Mr. Wingate assigned the project to Thurston Martin, head of Human Resources, for analysis and implementation. *The next day,* Mr. Martin asked his assistant, Lucille Brennan, to prepare a report on the subject to be submitted no later than May 15. *By May 1,* Ms. Brennan's completed report, along with its many recommendations, was submitted to Mr. Martin, who after substituting his name for

Ms. Brennan's on the title page, presented his findings to Mr. Wingate. *The next morning,* a general memo was circulated throughout the company detailing Mr. Wingate's ideas and plans for the new management training program.

**Spatial Order**    If the report's focus is on physical description, the writer can help the reader see whatever is essential by using spatial organization. As is the case with someone using a camera, spatial description depends upon distance and the angle of vision. For instance, a room may be described spatially from left to right, while an object such as a television set might be described first by its outside or enclosed surface and then by its inner workings or parts. It is the writer's prerogative to select the best manner of visual presentation. Words such as *above, below, next, under, beneath, vertical to, horizontal to, to the left, to the right,* and *in the center,* to name only a few, will prove extremely helpful when a report is organized according to spatial order. For example:

> The general reception area is in urgent need of redecorating. *The entrance foyer* is so narrow that two people cannot pass each other at the same time. The various rugs scattered *on the floor* are soiled and tattered. *Above* the receptionist's desk, the yellowed white ceiling paint is peeling and often drops on someone's head, usually a visiting client. *Behind* the desk an open window permits anyone to see the messengers playing cards or watching television. *On the wall to the left* are blackframed portraits of deceased executives. *On a nearby table,* two stuffed fierce-looking eagles are perched in an attacking position, ready to prey on the nearest victim. *Along the right wall,* a brown leather sofa's torn areas have been patched with orange tape.

**Logical Order**    When the presentation of ideas or an analysis of issues is of paramount importance in a report, the writer must decide how to relate these thoughts to the reader. Surely one of the most logical and practical methods is to view the material in terms of which aspects would serve best in the beginning, the middle, and at the end of the report's discussion. Organizing a report according to an *introduction* (which serves to orient the reader to the purpose and scope), a *body* or middle (which discusses the findings and provides essential details), and a *conclusion* (which sums up major points and reflects a judgment based upon the related facts) is an excellent, and sensible, first step. An example of this method follows:

### *ABC* FIRST AID CREAM

*Introduction*

This report concerns *ABC* first aid cream. It also proposes that a recently discovered use for this product—the healing of detergent hands—be vigorously promoted to promote greater frequency of use, greater volume and to enlarge profit potentials.

*Body*

First aid cream was introduced as an external antiseptic to be used instead of iodine and mercurochrome in the home. While successful, the volume of sales for *ABC*'s first aid cream has been too moderate to warrant extensive promotion. Discovery last year of a new use for first aid cream, the healing of detergent hands, could provide it with greater volume and profit potential. A series of research projects to appraise the new use of first aid cream indicates real possibilities that have been confirmed by marketing studies.

*Conclusion*

This new use can be incorporated in an advertising and promotion program to develop an additional market for this product.

**SELECT A PATTERN TO DEVELOP IDEAS**

In organizing and developing the information according to *time order*, *spatial relationship*, or *logical arrangement*, a number of patterns are useful. These include patterns which: (a) use examples and details; (b) offer causes and their effects; (c) compare and contrast two or more aspects of the report's topic; and (d) analyze and classify the data.

*Citing Examples*

Providing examples and details to support arguments, assertions, premises, and theories is one of the best techniques a writer can use to prepare a convincing report. Using facts, opinions, numerical data, and other supportive material to illustrate and elaborate upon the report's central statement reinforces the writer's premise, argument or findings. The number of examples depends upon how much the writer feels is essential for the reader's understanding. Sometimes two or three details will suffice; at other times merely one. Here is a passage that includes details and examples to develop a central idea:

> Industry often responds to public problems by marketing new services. Public demand for increased crime prevention, *for example*, propelled the growth of the private security industry. The steady growth of profit-making

hospitals, and hospital management services, are other examples of market responses to public needs.

***Cause and Effect***    The notion that every action has a reaction certainly applies to developing many a report along a cause-and-effect pattern. The writer has the choice of presenting either the causes or effects first, depending upon which will have the greater influence on the reader. Whichever manner is selected, the writer must take particular care not to draw erroneous conclusions, to which all cause-and-effect relationships are prone. Instead, he or she must determine if one action will truly result in something occurring, as is true of the following passage:

> As American industry moves from the manufacture of labor-intensive goods to the provision of technology, services, and information, major changes are required in the work force. Among them: today's employees must have greater skills, while managers face greater demands to provide for employees' development and well-being.
>
> *As a consequence*, the role of the human resources executive has changed. It is both more complex and more important. Human resource executives must deal with a range of human and public problems—from alcoholism and drug abuse to the special needs of the working parent, the declining basic skills of youth, and spiraling health-care costs.

***Comparison and Contrast***    This method of development presents various ideas or provides information by noting their similarities and differences. This technique is particularly useful when the writer is highlighting the advantages and disadvantages of two or more products, ideas, or theories. Some examples include selecting a site among a number of possible locations for constructing a branch office building or plant, or considering which of two office stationery suppliers offers the best cost and delivery terms. In each instance, the writer would review each item according to comparative criteria. For instance, taxes, commuting convenience, and real estate values may be the bases for comparison in the former choice. Quantity, bulk discounts, and delivery speed would be crucial to the latter one. Here is an example:

> *In some areas*, corporations deal with certain problems because of governmental mandates on equal opportunity. *In other areas*, the failure of institutions creates a need for business to become active—for example, in the

provision of basic educational skills, and in the expansion of private security agencies. *In still other areas,* the corporation identified as the site of a problem and, therefore, as a requisite partner in its solution; quality of work and retirement issues are examples.

**METHODS OF ORGANIZATION**

*Induction and Deduction*

It is also helpful to consider using one of two classic methods of reasoning: induction and deduction. The inductive approach presents material in order of increasing importance. A problem or premise is often stated at the beginning and followed by a detailed discussion or analysis that leads to a conclusion. Consider the following example:

> Lightweight, 10-speed, racing-style bicycles accounted for some fifty-six percent of the total market in 1980, compared with seventeen percent only ten years earlier. Initially spurred by imports, the growth of this segment in recent years has resulted from increased utilization of bicycles by adults in search of cheaper transportation and exercise. While its share of the market will undoubtedly fluctuate from year to year, *the lightweight segment is expected to account for the largest percentage of the overall bicycle market in the years ahead.**

The deductive approach renders the conclusion at the outset; the statement is then followed by reasons and supporting data. Ideas are presented in order of decreasing importance. For example:

> *Industry sources are optimistic about the long-term growth prospects for the toy industry.* Some of this optimism is based on a possible reversal of a nearly twenty-year trend of declining births. In 1980, births totaled an estimated 3.56 million, some four percent above the previous year and the highest level since 1970. The Bureau of Census has projected that births will continue to increase to a level of about four million annually during the 1980's. This would enlarge the primary market for toys and games in the late 1980's and into the 1990's. The industry is also encouraged by the larger proportions of first-borns to total births, because parents (as well as other relatives) tend to spend more on toys for the first-born than they do for subsequent children.

Presenting information *deductively* offers the busy reader the chance to grasp conclusive findings and recommendations immediately. At leisure, readers can view the supportive material to enhance their

---

* This and the passage that immediately follows have been reprinted with permission from *Industry Surveys* (a Standard and Poor's publication), 1982, pp. L24, L26.

perspective of the content of the report. The following are a series of alternative methods of organization:

1. Background.
   Statement of problem.
   Analysis of problem.
   Description of possible solutions.
   Advantages and disadvantages of solutions.
   Conclusions and recommendations.

2. Background.
   Statement of problem.
   Description of equipment.
   Discussion of procedure.
   Statement of results.
   Discussion of results.
   Conclusions.
   Recommendations.

3. Recommendations.
   Conclusions.
   Possible solutions: advantages and disadvantages.
   Description of solutions.
   Analysis of problem.
   Statement of problem.
   Background.

4. Summary.
   Background.
   Statement of problem.
   Analysis of problem.
   Description of possible solutions.
   Possible solutions: advantages and disadvantages.
   Conclusions.
   Recommendations.

5. Abstract.
   Background.
   Description of problem or process.
   Findings.
   Conclusions.
   Recommendations.

The elements of any of these patterns of organizations can be varied to suit specific needs. Use these patterns as a guide, not as a straitjacket for ideas. Remember that each report is unique in content, even though it may be organized according to a standard structural format. Here is a report that incorporates aspects of these various patterns:

## A REPORT ON THE DEMAND FOR SPORTING GOODS*

*Summary and Background*

Sales of sporting goods and recreational equipment in 1981 are expected to total $15.23 billion, an increase of 9% from estimated consumer purchases of $13.92 billion in 1980, according to a survey prepared for the National Sporting Goods Association (NSGA). Totals for both years include sales of recreational transportation products. Excluding bicycles, pleasure boats, recreational vehicles, and snowmobiles, the projected growth rate for sales of sporting goods in 1981 would be 6% (to $9.09 billion), compared with a nearly 7% gain (to $8.58 billion) in the preceding year.

*Comparison and Contrast*

The less rapid increase in sporting goods sales, despite higher prices, reflects a sluggish economic background and the maturation of several product categories (most notably racquetball, roller skates, and cross-country skiing equipment), which experienced tremendous sales gains in the past few years. On the other hand, sales of recreational transportation products are seen rebounding from 1980's depressed level, which was caused by the recession, consumer credit controls, and concerns over the availability of gasoline.

The sporting goods industry produces a wide variety of equipment. The most important in terms of dollar volume, according to the NSGA, are pleasure boats, motors, and accessories; sports footwear; firearms and hunting equipment; bicycles and supplies; recreational vehicles; and exercise equipment. The remainder consists of items used in numerous other activities, ranging from archery, to snow and water skiing.

With few exceptions, the industry is mature, and year-to-year changes typically reflect gains and losses among the various segments. This fact is graphically illustrated in the NSGA data for 1979 through 1981. In 1980, the largest year-

* Reprinted with permission from *Industry Surveys* (a Standard & Poor's publication), April 1982, pp. L23–L26.

*Conclusion*

to-year sales gain (50%) was posted for roller skates; for 1981, that segment is projected to experience the steepest decline (50%). In addition, two product categories—basketball and golf—are expected to record sales gains in 1981, following declines in 1980, while several other product groups that achieved strong sales gains in 1980 are not expected to match those gains this year. The product categories (excluding recreational transportation products) projected by NSGA to register the sharpest sales gains in 1981 are exercise equipment (20%), baseball/softball equipment and sports footwear (12% each), and archery equipment and volley/badminton sets (10% each).

### Boating

Boating remains one of the most popular recreational activities in the U.S. More than 11.8 million pleasure craft are in use in the U.S., and during 1980, some 60.2 million individuals participated in recreational boating. The boating industry is not only large, it is also highly cyclical. Sales of pleasure boats, motors, and accessories are expected to climb some 18% in 1981 to approximately $3.2 billion, following the 25% decline (to $2.7 BILLION) experienced in 1980, according to the NSGA. *Boating Industry* magazine estimates that approximately $7.4 billion was spent at the retail level in 1980 on new and used equipment, services, insurance, fuel, mooring and launching fees, repairs, and boat club memberships; total boating-related sales in 1981, according to the publication, could rise to about $8.1 billion.

*Cause and Effect*

The boating industry was adversely affected in 1980 by the recession, inflationary pressures, higher fuel costs, controls on consumer credit, and a proposal (not implemented) by the Department of Energy that would have restricted weekend recreational boating. While the extreme ends of the industry—small nonpowered boats (such as canoes) and large yachts (purchased by affluent individuals not normally affected by economic downturns)—did fairly well during 1980 and sales of sailboats continued to rise, the middle market was the segment most severely impacted. Aided by the improved economic outlook, the increased availability of consumer credit (albeit at higher rates), more plentiful fuel supplies at relatively stable prices, and the release of pent-up demand by consumers who previously postponed purchases, sales of

*Problem and Solution*

boating products in 1981 are expected to rebound from 1980's depressed level.

Unit sales of both outboard boats and motors declined for the fourth consecutive year in 1980. Outboard boat sales of 290,000 units were down 10%, year to year, and nearly 31% below 1973's peak. On a nominal increase of 4% in the average retail cost (to $1,408), the retail value of outboard boats sold in 1980 fell 9.6% to $408.32 million. Sales of outboard motors during 1980 amounted to 315,000 units, down from 375,000 in 1979. Although the average unit price rose 10.7% to $1,760, the retail value of outboard motors sold declined to $554.4 million in 1980, from $596.6 million in the prior year. For the first time since 1975, the average horsepower of outboard motors dropped, slipping to 37.7, from 47.0 in 1979.

Sales of inboard/outdrive boats also declined in 1980. From a peak of 90,000 units in 1978, sales slipped to 89,000 in 1979, before plunging to 56,000 last year. At an average retail price of $11,000 (compared with $9,100 in 1979 and 1978, respectively), volume amounted to $616 million, down from $827.2 million in 1979 and $819 million in 1978.

*Time Order and Comparison*

### Golf

According to the NSGA, retail sales of golf equipment are expected to increase a nominal 3% in 1981 to $498 million, from the $483.4 million recorded in 1980 (which was slightly below the 1979 total). Price increases are likely to account for most of the anticipated sales gain. The market for golf equipment is mature, with limited growth potentials; while there are some 10 million golfers in the U.S., this figure has declined in recent years, and the National Golf Foundation predicts this total will grow by only $1% a year. In addition, golf is a relatively expensive participant sport, with the cost of green fees, cart rentals, and instruction on top of the price of equipment. However, the average golfer, who is typically older than participants in other sports, usually has a higher income.

*Problem and Discussion*

### Racquet Sports

Sales of tennis equipment in 1981 are projected by the NSGA at $341 million, virtually unchanged from the prior year's level. In 1980, sales declined to $340.6 million, from $343.4

million in 1979. Although there are some 24 million people actively playing tennis, growth in recent years has not been as rapid as it was during the first half of the year.

One of the sports that has emerged to compete with tennis is racquetball. There are currently an estimated 12 million active participants, playing at some 2,000 court clubs (all of which were built within the last 10 years), and this number is increasing rapidly. However, the NSGA estimates that sales of racquetball racquets in 1981 will total $65 million, 12% below the $73.8 million recorded in 1980.

### Bowling

The largest participant sport in the U.S., bowling attracted some 72 million people to 8,700 bowling centers in 1980. Even though the number of people participating in the sport is increasing and industry insiders predict that bowling has not yet reached its peak of popularity, sales of bowling accessories are not showing much growth. Sales of $94.9 million in 1980 barely exceeded the $94.8 million of 1979, and *Problem and* the NSGA projects only nominal improvement to $95 million in 1981; these figures exclude lineage fees paid in bowling centers. One explanation for this very slow growth is that many new bowlers are infrequent participants and do not feel the need to purchase their own equipment. Another is that regular bowlers might be using their equipment for longer periods.

*Problem and*
*Explanation*

### Sports Footwear

In its 1980 survey, the NSGA initiated a separate analysis of sports footwear; in previous years, sales of such items were included in specific product categories. The NSGA estimates that sales of this footwear in 1981 will approximate $1.82 billion, 12% above 1980's total of $1.62 billion. The largest segments in this area in 1980 were:

*Classification*

Gym shoes/sneakers, $400.6 million
Tennis shoes, $389.7 million
Jogging/running shoes $327.8 million
Basketball shoes, $143.5 million

While sales of these products are closely related to the relative consumer interest in the various sports, footwear products are often purchased by individuals for reasons other than participation in a sport.

***Ask Important Questions***

Applying a variation of the classic journalistic questions to reporting a story can help the writer more clearly organize collected data. The writer should consider the following:

1. WHO will read the report?
2. WHAT is my report's purpose?
3. WHERE should I begin my discussion?
4. WHEN, WHY, and HOW will the report be used?

These questions help the report writer focus on important considerations that can affect the manner in which information is presented. They can help the writer sort out and clearly arrange key ideas in order of priority and possible interest to the reader.

## OUTLINING THE INFORMATION

An *outline* is a working plan or blueprint of a report. It can consist of a series of simple informal notes or a formally arranged series of subject headings and subheadings. Outlining ideas on paper is often the surest way to sort and organize information. Outlines help the writer clarify, classify, and develop thoughts to be included in a report. Logical presentation of ideas is a direct by-product of an outline; its use permits the writer to indicate particular relationships as well as an overall view of the report's content. Outlines range from the simple to the complex, depending on the scope and content of each report. Yet all serve the same end: to help writers structure their ideas in an orderly fashion. When composing an outline, the writer should do as follows:

**1. State the Report's Purpose.**   In a single sentence or paragraph, state the purpose, thrust, scope, or main idea of the report. Consider what tasks must be accomplished and what ideas must be shown, explained, and developed.

**2. List Relevant Facts and Ideas.**   Note briefly the main points of the report, and how they will relate to the purpose and subject. These notes can include one's own thoughts and perceptions, data gathered from research, substantial facts, or opinions.

**3. *Eliminate Irrelevant Items.*** Next, cross out and eliminate any ideas irrelevant to the core idea or main point. Revise or add to the main idea any thoughts that may not have occurred to before.

**4. *Group Related Ideas.*** Reviewing the list, begin sorting the items into two or more groups that have obvious similarities. Sometimes it can be helpful to think in terms of primary and secondary material, or major and minor thoughts. Review initial notes to see if what was crossed out previously can now be added to one of the groups of ideas.

**5. *Balance or Relate the Groups.*** Think of headings or phrases that can precede the groupings of ideas. How are the items related to the core or main idea? Do they form a pattern? Try to devise headings broad enough to encompass similar ideas. Consolidating the information under appropriate headings and subheadings will add not only structure to the report but will also allow for smoother transitions of ideas.

**6. *Arrange the Groups According to Importance.*** Decide which groups should precede others. The order will depend on their relation to the main points of the report as well their intrinsic importance.

1. Heading (New York)         2. Heading (London)
   Item (Cultural Life)            Item (Cultural Life)
   Item (Mass Transportation)      Item (Mass Transportation)
   Item (Job Opportunities)        Item (Job Opportunities)

**7. *Write Consistent Topic Headings.*** In constructing an outline, be sure that the headings or captions include items of equal interest and importance in terms of subject matter. For example:

**UNEQUAL HEADINGS**

MAJOR BUSINESS SUBJECTS

  I. Accounting.

  II. Marketing.

III. Sales.

IV. *The Wall Street Journal.*

### EQUAL HEADINGS

MAJOR BUSINESS SUBJECTS

  I. Accounting.

  II. Marketing.

III. Sales.

IV. Public Relations.

**8. *Keep the Headings Parallel in Structure.*** Topic headings should be parallel or consistent in grammatical structure. Use either the topic word or sentence format to indicate topic variation. Do not mix both formats. For example:

### NON-PARALLEL FORMAT

 I. The U.S. Market
   A. Industry Trends.
   B. Role of Imports.
   C. The various factors that greatly influence market growth.
   D. Promotional Factors.
   E. A list of the strongest American competitors of our products.
   F. Marketing Strategy.

### PARALLEL FORMAT

 I. The U.S. Market
   A. Industry Trends.
   B. Role of Imports.
   C. Market Growth Factors.
   D. Promotional Considerations.
   E. Key Competitors.
   F. Marketing Strategy.

**9. *Avoid Solitary Headings.*** Each outline should have a minimum of two topic divisions. The following outline is incomplete:

HISTORY OF AMERICAN BUSINESS

I. 19th Century
   A. East Coast.

Rather, this outline should include at least a second major heading:

HISTORY OF AMERICAN BUSINESS

  I. 19th Century
    A. East Coast.
       1. Manufacturing.
       2. Banking.
    B. West Coast.
       1. Gold.
       2. Oil.

 II. 20th Century
    A. East Coast.
       1. Industry.
    B. West Coast.
       1. Industry.

## Standard Outline Format

A standard outline uses *headings* and *subheadings* to distinguish primary from secondary groupings of ideas contained in a report. It is customary to label an outline in the following manner:

TITLE

    I. MAJOR HEADING (denoted by large Roman numeral).
Indent ⟶ A. FIRST DEGREE SUBHEADING (denoted by large Arabic letter).
Indent ⟶ 1. SECOND DEGREE SUBHEADING (denoted by Arabic numeral).
Indent ⟶ a. THIRD DEGREE SUBHEADING (denoted by small Arabic letter).

    II. SECOND MAJOR HEADING
        A.

            1.

                a.

Here is a standard format for listing ideas in an outline:

OPENING STATEMENT OR MAIN IDEA

      I. MAJOR HEADING (denoted by Roman numeral).

Indent  ———→ A. SUBHEADING/TOPIC (denoted by large Arabic letter).

Indent  ———→ 1. NEXT SUBHEADING/TOPIC (denoted by Arabic number).

Indent  ———————→ a. MINOR SUBHEADING/TOPIC (denoted by small Arabic letter).

    II. SECOND MAJOR HEADING.

The extent of the outline depends on the nature and length of the report's content. Highly detailed reports may require detailed outlines; shorter or less detailed reports may use briefer outlines. While it is not necessary to follow this format precisely, any outline devised will surely contain some of these elements. The following is an example of a topic outline for a report on the advantages and disadvantages of investing in money-market funds.

MONEY-MARKET MUTUAL FUNDS

What are the advantages and disadvantages of investing in money-market funds?

   I. Money-Market Mutual Funds
     A. How They Work.
        1. Contributions of individuals pooled.
        2. Actual yield.
        3. Management fee.
        4. Minimum investment.

  II. Comparison to Passbook Savings Accounts
     A. Advantages of Money-Market Funds.
        1. Low-risk.
        2. Liquidity.

        3. No withdrawal penalty.

        4. Higher interest rate than savings account.

    B. Disadvantages.

        1. Fluctuating interest rate.

        2. Uncertain long term return.

III. Conclusion

Here is the same outline expanded into a sentence outline:

MONEY-MARKET MUTUAL FUNDS

Should someone invest in money-market funds? What are the advantages and disadvantages?

  I. Money-Market Mutual Funds

    A. Money-Market Funds Contain Unique Characteristics.

        1. Money funds pool individual contributions to buy short-term notes or IOU's.

        2. The fund pays the investor the actual yield on its portfolio.

        3. The management fee is typically less than 1 percent yearly.

        4. Minimum investment for most funds is under $1,000.

  II. Comparison to Passbook Savings Accounts

    A. Money-Market Funds Have Several Advantages over Traditional Passbook Savings Accounts.

        1. Money funds are low-risk investments.

        2. Investor's capital is liquid. Checks can be written against the account.

        3. There is no withdrawal penalty.

        4. Money funds pay much higher interest rates than passbook accounts.

    B. Money-Market Funds Have Some Disadvantages.

        1. Money fund interest rates can fluctuate daily.

        2. Small-saver bank certificates can offer high interest rates and protection.

        3. Return on capital over a long term is uncertain.

III. Investor Must Decide

    A. In conclusion, each investor must decide whether or not to invest in money-market mutual funds.

A sentence outline represents a more fully developed structure of ideas. Very often, these key sentences will serve as topic sentences or springboards for developing your thoughts and expanding various details into paragraphs. Think of a *topic outline* as a sketch of the subject; the *sentence outline* as a line drawing which includes more developed details. The paragraphs that develop ideas are comparable to the first layer of paint applied to a drawing. Soon both the scope and tone of the report begin to take shape, and a sense of organization and development begins to emerge.

Here is the result of these outlines, fully expanded to include additional details.

## WHAT ABOUT MONEY-MARKET MUTUAL FUNDS?*

Since 1979, money-market mutual funds have been, for many consumers, an attractive alternative to traditional bank accounts. Money funds pool the contributions of many individuals to buy short-term debt obligations (in effect, interest-bearing IOU's) issued by government agencies, banks, and corporations.

The fund pays you the actual yield on its portfolio, less a management fee that is typically less than 1 percent per year of the fund's assets. The minimum initial investment at many funds is $1000, but you may later be allowed to withdraw part of your initial investment.

Money funds are low-risk investments. Like a passbook savings account, but unlike a certificate of deposit, a money-market fund lets you withdraw your funds at will, without penalty. Withdrawals can be made by written request or, with many funds, by telephone request. Many funds also allow you to write checks against your fund account, often with a minimum of $500. Some people have experienced delays in making withdrawals, but on the whole the funds provide almost as easy access to your money as a passbook savings account would.

Money funds pay much higher interest than passbook savings accounts. Indeed, during the past couple of years, they've paid higher interest than was generally available on certificates of deposit—that's why they've been so popular. The funds have had that edge because short-term interest rates, in contrast to historical patterns, have been higher than long-term rates. If that relationship were to change, as it gave signs of doing last fall, the funds might not be able to maintain their edge.

Last November (1981), both small-savers certificates and money funds were yielding around 14 percent a year (before compounding). Since interest rates can be volatile, you'll want to check yields carefully before putting your money into a money fund or certificates of deposit. Keep in mind that while certificate rates stay fixed for the term of the certificate, the money-fund rate can fluctuate daily.

Proper outlining and organizing procedures are indispensible to a logical arrangement of the writer's thoughts. Though such methods can be somewhat painstaking, the benefits derived for both writer and reader will prove immeasurable in the end.

## CHAPTER REVIEW

### Questions

1. List three patterns of organization.

2. Describe four methods of developing a report's ideas.

3. Distinguish *inductive* from *deductive* reasoning.

4. What is the value of an outline? What is its function?

5. Define three types of outlines.

6. List the characteristics of an effective outline.

7. How is a simple informal outline different from a formal one?

8. What is meant by parallel structure?

9. How should topics be arranged in an outline?

### Exercises

1. You have gathered the following information for a report on cable television.* Now it must be organized in terms of *background, description of current situation,* and *future prospects for growth.*

   The cable television industry enjoyed a year of substantial growth and progress in 1981. The number of subscribers to basic cable television service increased an estimated 2.4 million to about 20 million at the end of the year. Basic cable service revenues reached an estimated $2 billion, up 20 percent for the year. Of these basic cable subscribers, an es-

---

* From *U.S. Industrial Outlook, 1982,* "Broadcasting," pp. 364–370. Department of Commerce, Bureau of Industrial Economics.

timated 11 million also paid an additional fee for one or more tiers of premium pay cable service. Revenues for this premium service—primarily motion pictures and sports—amounted to about $1 billion. These pay cable revenues are shared by the cable systems, program syndicators, motion picture and program producers, and organized sports.

The cable TV industry should experience a year of continued expansion in 1982. Any dampening effect of the general economic slowdown is expected to be offset by the consumer's perception of cable TV as a low cost form of family entertainment. The number of basic subscribers is expected to increase 2.1 million to a year-end total of 22.1 million. Basic revenues are expected to rise 20 percent to approximately $2.5 billion for the year. The number of premium pay cable subscribers should reach 13.5 million. Corresponding premium pay cable revenues are projected to total about $1.4 billion, up 35 percent for the year.

Basic cable service began in small communities which had no local television stations and where reception from distant stations was poor or nonexistent. Later, cable service was introduced in suburban areas and a few cities where it added the programs of one or two distant stations to those available from the local stations. The higher cost of installing cable in large cities, coupled with the greater variety of local TV programs readily available, kept cable systems out of many urban markets.

Cable television will continue its penetration of TV households during the decade of the 1980's. By the end of 1986, basic cable subscribers are expected to number about 32.9 million for a 39 percent share of total TV homes, and to provide about $5 billion in basic cable revenues. An estimated 22 million of these basic subscribers will be paying an additional subscription fee for a second tier of premium program service, and adding revenues of $2.8 billion. By 1990, the number of basic cable subscribers could reach 47 million, and provide $8.5 billion in current dollars of revenues. Pay cable revenues could provide an additional $5.8 billion from 32 million premium subscribers in 1990.

Domestic communications satellites revolutionized the cable TV industry by making possible low cost distribution of programing to independent cable systems throughout the country. Cable program services such as Home Box Office, Showtime, The Movie Channel, Home Theater Network, and numerous others were established to provide premium programing. Toward the end of 1981 there were nearly 50 cable programing services on the satellites; of these, thirty-seven were video services ranging from a few hours a week to 24 hours a day.

The large number of channels available on cable systems and the growing number of cable program services are placing increasing demands on the suppliers of programs. Motion pictures, supplemented by sports, have been the mainstay of pay cable but these sources are not inexhaustible. Program suppliers are looking for new sources of entertainment programing and other video fare. Producers of motion pictures and other entertainment forms will benefit from the added demand and competition for their products. The already high production costs of feature programing for TV—which at present are recovered through network, syndication, and overseas release—will be even more costly if intended primarily for cable. Cable program suppliers will also seek to increase the variety of special interest programing appealing to specific demographic or other groups.

At present the amount of advertising on cable is small. But as the cable audience increases during the 1980's, cable will become a significant advertising medium. It will begin to share video advertising expenditures which, heretofore, have gone exclusively to broadcasters.

2. Rewrite the following headings so that each is grammatically consistent:

Computers for Personal Use
How to Invest in Computer Firms in the U.S.
Foreign Trade in the 1980s
Competition from Foreign Manufacturers
The Use and Value of Computers in the Modern Office
How to Compare Computers in Terms of How Much They Cost

## *Report Project*

1. Construct a topic outline of the subject selected for your report.

2. Transform the topic outline into a sentence outline.

3. Decide if any important elements of the report have been omitted.

4. Eliminate irrelevant ideas or details from the sentence outline.

5. Organize the information into a suitable pattern or format.

# CHAPTER 6

# Report Formats and Elements

**REPORT FORMATS**   Once the writer has gathered, evaluated, and organized the information for the report, this material must then be presented to the reader, or "packaged," in a suitable format. Although there is no one standardized format due to the great variety of reports, the majority that are written for business share common elements or components that convey the findings in either an *informal* or *formal* manner.

*Informal Reports*   The difference between an informal and a formal report rests neither in the depth nor quality of the content and writing, but in the distinction between their physical make-up and the writer's tone of voice. In general, informal reports tend to be less complicated than formal ones in terms of structure, and the writer's tone is usually familiar and conversational. At the same time, there is no law that insists that informal reports should be always expressed in a familiar tone of voice, or that formal reports should always reflect greater seriousness or distance between writer and reader. Nor too is length a constant distinguishing factor between an informal and a formal report.

Rather, the difference between the two is often determined by the report's purpose and probable audience. Reports written on a routine basis, such as field trip or test reports, may be expressed informally on a *printed form* or in a *memo* or *letter*. However, special reports designed to treat a subject extensively or that are prepared for a select audience, such as for a board of trustees or a Congressional committee, are accorded a formal status.

Informal reports often assume a particular understanding or relationship between writer and reader, and the importance of audience analysis becomes an apparent factor in the writer's decision to present findings informally or formally (see Figure 6–1). If a writer is aware of the readers' background and needs, he or she can add or delete technical or specialized information, or provide supporting data according to what is known or can be assumed about the reader.

An informal report expressed in a one-page memo from one executive to another in the same office could be thorough in content yet casual in tone; a letter report might include a background summary or include a letter of transmittal to help the reader place the report in the proper perspective. Generally, memo reports circulate internally and letter reports are addressed to those outside an organization. In the end, a report's informality is determined by the writer's understanding of the subject matter, relationship to the reader, and the manner in which the subject is best presented.

*Formal Reports*    Complexity and depth are often associated with formal reports because of the style and tone of the writing and because of additional structural elements not generally associated with informal ones. Formal report elements include the following:*

1. Letter of Transmittal.
2. Title Page.
3. Circulation/Distribution List.
4. Contents Page.
5. List of Illustrations.
6. Summary or Abstract.
7. Introduction.
8. Body or Discussion of Findings.
9. Conclusions.
10. Recommendations.
11. Bibliography.

* Examples of formal reports can be found in Appendix B.

Memorandum Report

DATE:    July 15, 1984

TO:      Sid Halfrey

FROM:    Bert Miller

RE:      Workload - Amanda Elliot, Investment Division


Problem:    There has been a significant increase in the workload
            of Ms. Amanda Elliot, supervisor of the Investment
            Division, which requires immediate attention.

            Specifically, there has been a marked increase in the
            volume and types of securities traded.  An analysis of
            these transactions shows a 440% increase from last year.
            Since such trading activities require special handling
            this figure does not take into account additional
            responsibilities, such as brokers settlements, delivery
            instructions, bookkeeping tickets, accruals, and
            telexes.

            All these activities are being handled by Ms. Elliot
            alone, and despite the intense pressure in carrying out
            these tasks, her performance has been exceptional.

            Nevertheless, I feel it is essential to relieve some of
            the strain of her responsibilities and also acknowledge
            the fine job she has been doing.


Solution:   One way to alleviate pressure from Ms. Elliot is to
            assign additional personnel to her staff.  In recogni-
            tion of her exceptional performance, I suggest that
            Amanda Elliot receive an increase in salary commen-
            surate with her responsibilities.

FIGURE 6–1.  *An informal memo report characterized by a simple structure and conversational tone.*

12. Glossary.
13. Illustrations.
14. Appendix.

Unless an organization insists on a particular format, the report writer generally is free to select only those elements that are relevant to the assignment. For instance, a brief informational or descriptive study need not include an abstract, a series of recommendations, or numerous appendices. Yet it would certainly contain a title page, an introduction followed by a thorough discussion of major issues of interest to the reader, and possibly an illustration or two.

By contrast, a long and highly detailed report that addresses several issues or difficult concepts would probably be more effective, and readable, if it were divided into separate sections, if it contained a contents page, an abstract or summary of important ideas, conclusions, recommendations, and a glossary of unfamiliar or specialized terms.

Selecting the best format for a formal report depends on the writer's awareness of the reader's needs and a clear understanding of which elements would best convey the writer's thoughts and observations. The report should include only those elements that will highlight the logical development of ideas. The elements that the writer selects should, in a word, impose structure and order on what could easily become chaos.

## BASIC REPORT ELEMENTS

Whether expressed in a memo, letter, or a formally structured format, all reports generally follow traditional guidelines, and therefore contain four basic elements—a *title*, a *beginning*, a *middle* and an *end*. Bearing these minimum requirements in mind will help the writer organize his or her thoughts in an orderly fashion.

Each part has its particular demands. A *title* should be exact and should clearly point out the subject under discussion. An *introduction* should state the report's purpose, need, scope, essential background information, and possibly conclusions. The *middle* or *body* must present adequate details and examples essential to the development of the report's topic (arguments, facts, opinions, etc.). The *end* or *conclusion* should truly sum up all that has preceded it.

There are occasions, however, when the complexity and depth of the subject, or the reader's needs, require structural elements in addition to the basic ones, such as summary, contents page, and recommendations.*

**Letter of Transmittal**

In general, a letter of transmittal is written in a cordial conversational style, making full use of such personal pronouns as *I* and *you*, and is often directed to the individual or group that has requested or authorized the report. This letter should be concise, yet it should offer an adequate overview of the report's purpose, along with some mention of key findings and conclusions. The letter of transmittal should include any information that may enhance the reader's perspective, and it should provide acknowledgement of appreciation for assistance the writer has received while preparing the report. (See Figure 6–2.) All conventional stylistic formats are acceptable (block, variation of block, or indented).

Some writers also use a letter of transmittal to indicate limitations, such as time and money, that may have influenced the report's effectiveness. So too can the writer refer to previous studies and reports relevant to the topic. He or she can explain criteria or the method of investigation, summarize recommendations, and urge action.

**Title**

Report titles should be brief and accurate, composed of key words that clearly describe the content and focus of the study. Titles are *clues* to content. The reader should not be confused or misled by vague, inappropriate or inexact titles. Notice the difference in exactness and clarity among these titles:

**General/Vague/Unclear Titles**
- The Electronic Industry
- Training
- Job Knowledge Essential

**Exact Titles**
- Sales Trends in the Electronic Industry
- Management Training Objectives and Procedures
- Essential Skills for Executive Assistants

---

* For examples of these report elements, refer to the Status Report in Appendix B, titled "Basic Skills in the U.S. Work Force," pp. 310–335.

# Putnam-St. Clair Marketing Services, Inc.

135 Madison Avenue
Englewood, N.J. 07631
(201) 569-3020

April 30, 1984

Mr. Henry A. Thompson
Vice President
Chary and Buck Ltd.
Dutch Mill Road
Dellwood, New Jersey 07000

Dear Henry:

   With today's submittal of the Market Analysis of the Defense,
Aerospace and Governmental (Non-Defense) segments, and the accompanying source documents for ongoing monitoring, the first two
assignments are complete, save any revisions that may be requested.

   Assignment #1 (Analysis of the Architectural Markets) is
composed of 81 pages (excluding charts), plus 64 annotated source
documents and 24 addenda sources.

   Assignment #2 (Analysis of the Defense, Aerospace and Governmental (Non-Defense) is composed of 77 pages (excluding charts and
exhibits), plus 54 annotated source documents and 3 addenda sources.

   In addition, there is an Action Step Outline for each of the
market segments in the two analyses, plus a possible organizational
approach you may want to consider.

   Master copies of each analysis contain an explanation of
methodology used in annotating source documents and identifying
original sources of charts.  All original source data, as received
from the various publications, agencies and associations, have
been delivered to your staff.

   Also enclosed are final invoices for both assignments, with
the exception of out-of-pocket expenses, which are now being
assembled.

   We hope that you are as pleased with the final results as we
are in submitting them to you and your associates.  We look forward
to working with you again on subsequent assignments.

                                        Sincerely,

                                        *R. J. Putnam*

                                        R. J. Putnam
                                        President

RJP:ds
encl.

FIGURE 6–2.  *A letter of transmittal that outlines the report's content and purpose.* [Reprinted with permission of Putnam-St. Clair
Marketing Services, Inc., Englewood, N.J.]

With a little thought about the report's subject and purpose, a writer can devise titles that are precise and clear. Avoid abbreviations and confusing words and phrases. Titles are similar to first impressions; they must be good. Title pages usually contain the following:

1. Title.
2. Author.
3. Organization or agency that requested the report.
4. Address of organization or agency.
5. Submission or publication date.
6. Project identification number (for reports filed under such a system).
7. Library identification number (for reports deposited in a corporate library).
8. Security notice (if applicable).

***Circulation or Distribution List***  If the report is to receive limited distribution, the writer should list the recipients' names on a separate page. Should the report contain classified or confidential information, include a restriction notice on or before the title page. For reports distributed publicly, there need be no mention of specific names. However, if the report has been prepared for a particular organization prior to general distribution, the name of the organization should appear on the title page.

***Contents Page***  For long reports, the contents page is a guide to topic headings and section divisions. Report topics are best arranged in column format beneath precise caption headings. They should include appropriate page reference numbers. Major headings are denoted by Roman numerals; primary subdivisions are noted by upper-case Arabic letters. Secondary subdivisions of subject matter are distinguished by Arabic numerals or lower-case Arabic letters.

I. MAJOR TOPIC
    A. Primary topic subdivision.
        1. Secondary topic subdivision.

Prefatory or introductory material can be distinguished from the major discussion by small Roman numerals:

Alternative numbering systems include the following:

**THE CENTURY-DECADE UNIT SYSTEM**

**100.** MAJOR TOPIC
  **110.** Primary topic subdivision.
  **111.** Secondary topic subdivision.

**200.** MAJOR TOPIC

**THE MULTIPLE DECIMAL SYSTEM**

**1.** MAJOR TOPIC
  **1.1** Primary topic subdivision.
    **1.1.1** Secondary topic subdivisions.
    **1.2.2** Secondary topic subdivisions.
    **1.2.3** Secondary topic subdivisions.

**2.** MAJOR TOPIC
  **2.1** Primary topic subdivision.
    **2.1.1.** Secondary topic subdivision.

Although the report writer can select from any of these standard notation systems, the captions or headings must be worded exactly as their corresponding sections in the text to avoid confusing the reader.

***List of Illustrations***   As is true of topic elements, illustrations are listed at the beginning of the report following the contents page. Because illustrations include graphs, charts, drawings, tables, and photographs, each graphic aid must be numbered (Roman or Arabic), and titled. They should also include specific page reference numbers. Headings and captions should be complete yet concise. For example, the heading "Comparable Word Processors" is preferable to "A Table Showing Different Kinds of Word Processors."

## LIST OF ILLUSTRATIONS

**Abstract or Summary**

An abstract is comparable to a summary because both elements briefly highlight the key ideas, conclusions, and recommendations of the report. Use an abstract when a report is long and complex, and the busy reader will surely benefit in terms of time and comprehension. Abstracts can *inform* or *describe*, depending on the nature and purpose of the report. The amount of detail included in an abstract or a summary depends upon the length of the report. A relatively short report (five–ten pages) may require one separate page of condensed information; a longer report (twenty-five or more pages) might require two or three pages. Traditionally, an abstract represents 10 percent of the total report length.

Abstract or summary pages are usually not numbered and do not include illustrations. They are typed single-spaced only *after* the entire report is written and fully revised. (See Chapter 10 for a more detailed discussion of how to write an abstract.)

**Sample Abstract**

### AN ANALYSIS OF INTEREST-RATE EXPECTATIONS*

This report presents results of a survey of investors' forecasts of future interest rates and their evaluations of the maturities of government issues they regarded as "particularly attractive" for investment. The following information was collected by questionaires from a sample of institutions who are important participants in the market for government

* Adapted from the *Journal of Economic Abstracts*, (March 1963), p. 139.

securities. The survey results suggest a number of conclusions relevant for the conduct of monetary policy:

1. While many investors seem to formulate specific interest-rate expectations, others do not. Significantly, differences in the willingness to predict follow institutional lines. In particular, banks are more likely to venture predictions than other institutions.

2. The theory that investors hold a uniform set of expectations of future interest rates is contradicted by the data.

3. Both the willingness to predict and the extent of disagreement vary with the futurity of the rate being predicted.

4. The data suggest that investors are influenced by their expectations in deciding which maturity areas are attractive for purchase.

5. Investors appear to exhibit varying degrees of risk aversion in their appraisal of the attractiveness of securities.

## The Introduction

If someone enters a theater twenty minutes after a play begins, he or she cannot help feeling disoriented and somewhat bewildered about what is happening on the stage. A report without an introduction can have a similar effect on the reader. A good introduction outlines the writer's purpose, focus, method of collecting information (interviews, research, questionnaires), approach toward the subject matter, and some background about the need for the report.

An introduction lends continuity of thought to the report's development. At the same time, an introduction is *not* an abstract of the entire report, and should not contain an excessive amount of detail. Rather, it is a graceful beginning.

All introductions need not include the same elements. Some are short, others long. Also, it is customary in some organizations to regard the introduction as being separate from the text. However, the report writer can choose to include it with the body of the report. If this is the case, the introduction would be numbered *page 1* on the contents page as well as in the text.

## Body or Discussion of Findings

In the body of the report, the writer discusses in detail the findings, analyses, problems, solutions, procedures, costs, nature of equipment, and all other observations that relate to the subject and purpose. Any detail that can explain, illustrate, prove, or otherwise elaborate on major ideas and points should be included in this section. The body of the report is its nerve center that activates all other aspects or elements of the report. In this section of the report, the writer can fully discuss the nature of a particular procedure, analyze a problem, compare one method with another, or comment on the feasibility of a future project. The potential, advantages, and possible drawbacks of a new product can be scrutinized as carefully as last year's sales figures.

For the body of the report to be complete and comprehensive, the writer must distinguish between major and minor thoughts and findings. Ideas should be presented in order of importance and relevance to the central theme of the report. Applying the questions *Who? What? Where? When? Why?* and *How?* to any problem, project, test, analysis, situation, or issue will further enable the writer to produce thorough, clearly written business reports.

*Conclusion*  A valid conclusion reflects the writer's judgment drawn from facts, opinions, analyses, and other observations discussed in the report.

A conclusion should bear a logical relationship to the data that precedes it. This outcome should seem natural and should be stated directly and often without comment or discussion. If the conclusions are listed either in order of importance or in the order that they appear in the text, and if they are supported by a summary of the evidence that led to them, the reader will clearly understand *how* the writer arrived at them.

Placement of conclusions depends on the readers' interests, needs, and background. If the writer knows that most readers will be too busy to absorb every detail of a report's findings, the conclusions should be placed at the beginning of the discussion. If the report requires a careful understanding of bases for arriving at the conclusions, they should be placed at the end of the discussion. Wherever they are listed in a report, the conclusions should clearly express the writer's ideas, and emphasize their importance.

*Recommendations*  Recommendations suggest a course of action based on previous observations and conclusions. Sometimes conclusions and recommendations can be combined, though each serves a distinct purpose. Recommendations should be clearly worded and presented in the same order as the conclusions that lead to them. At times, however, not every conclusion will lead automatically to a recommendation.

Recommendations should be direct and emphatic; otherwise, the reader may feel confused about the best course of action. On some occasions, due to insufficient evidence or contradictory findings, the writer may recommend further investigation before urging a specific course of action.

Note that for informational reports that do not contain conclusions and recommendations, the writer should summarize the key ideas at the end of the text.

**Bibliography**   As discussed in Chapter 3, a bibliography alphabetically lists reference or research sources. These include the following:

- Books.
- Magazines.
- Professional or specialized journals.
- Newspapers.
- Encyclopedias.
- Dictionaries.
- Dissertations.
- Previous studies and reports.

**Glossary**   A glossary is a list of definitions of words, phrases, and terms that may be unfamiliar to most readers. The best approach to composing a glossary is to assume nothing on the readers' behalf regarding specialized or technical vocabulary if the report is to be publicly or generally distributed.* The glossary's technical, trade, or otherwise unique expressions are listed alphabetically and placed either before or at the end of the text. While it is not necessary to number the items listed in a glossary, the expressions can be highlighted by typing them in capital letters.

### Glossary of Banking Terms

BASIS POINT   the equivalent of one one-hundredth of one percent (0.01%). This unit is generally used to measure movements in interest rates.

---

\* If the probable audience for the report consists of one particular profession (doctors, engineers, scientists, stockbrokers, bond analysts), the writer should be careful to avoid constructing a glossary of commonly known terms. To do so might unintentionally cause offense.

**BOOK VALUE** the value of a share of common stock, determined by dividing total shareholders' equity at the end of a period by total number of shares outstanding at the end of that same period.

**CAPITAL** in addition to equity capital, regulators allow certain categories of subordinated debt (under certain conditions) to be included as capital.

**CLEARING HOUSE** an institution where mutual claims and accounts are settled, as the reciprocal exchange of checks and drafts between banks.

**CORE DEPOSITS** the total of demand deposits (checking accounts) NOW accounts and consumer time deposits. Consumer time deposits consist of savings certificates and regular passbook and bonus savings accounts.

**DISCOUNT RATE** the interest rate charged by the Federal Reserve banks on secured borrowings by member banks.

**EARNING ASSETS** interest-bearing financial instruments, which are principally commercial, real estate, and consumer loans; investment securities and trading account securities; money-market investments; lease finance receivables; and time deposits placed in foreign banks.

**FEDERAL FUNDS** purchase of member bank deposits at Federal Reserve banks, usually for one day, at a specified rate of interest. Such purchases are made in order to achieve mandatory reserve levels.

**HEDGING** the process of trying to minimize foreign exchange risk by purchases or sales of forward contracts, or by borrowing or lending in other currencies to cover exposed foreign currency positions.

**INTEREST-RATE SENSITIVE** interest earning assets or interest bearing liabilities on which interest rates are adjustable within a short period of time (under one year) as a result of maturity or contractual terms. The rate adjustments usually relate to changes in prevailing short-term money market rates.

**MARGIN** net interest income divided by average earning assets.

**NET INCOME** net operating income, plus realized capital gains or losses (after taxes), arising from the sale of investment securities.

**NONACCRUAL LOANS (cash-basis loans)** loans or other assets whose income is recognized uon the actual collection of cash, rather than through the standard practice of accruing rights to that income. In certain situations, all cash receipts from these assets are credited directly to principal.

NOW ACCOUNTS   interest-bearing checking accounts written on time deposits. Technically, 30 to 90 days' notice is required before funds can be withdrawn. In practice, prior notice is not needed, and the negotiable order of withdrawal works like a check.

PRIME RATE   the interest rate charged the largest and most creditworthy corporate customers of the bank for short-term borrowing.

RETURN ON ASSETS (ROA)   used as an indicator of earnings efficiency. Calculated by dividing net operating income by total average assets.

TAXABLE EQUIVALENT INCOME   income from tax-exempt securities and certain other tax-exempt assets including leases, which for comparative purposes has been increased by an amount equal to the taxes which would have been paid if this income was taxable at statutory rates.

*Illustrations*   Illustrations are added to clarify, not to clutter, a report. They should be used with discretion and can be inserted either in the text or on separate pages opposite the corresponding material. Refer to Chapter 8 for a detailed discussion of the various types and uses of illustrations.

*Appendix*   Material that is supplementary to the report's findings and purpose is included in an appendix at the end of the report. Charts, letters, copies of contracts, questionnaires, memos, transcriptions of interviews, calculations, company files, field notes, previous reports, and any information that is relevant but not essential to understanding the report can be contained in an appendix.

*Selectivity* is the key to compiling a useful appendix. Avoid adding material that is repetitive or only remotely related to the report. Extraneous bulky material will add to the cost of producing the report and result in awkward handling for the reader. Quality and relevance should be the bases for choosing data for an appendix.

On some occasions, more than one appendix is necessary to supplement the discussion of the report. For example, one appendix might include examples of questionnaires used to gather information, or photographs to support a major point. A second appendix might include selections from past reports, and a third a list of financial statements. In such instances, distinguish the appendices by labelling them with letters or numbers ("Appendix A," "Appendix B," or "Appendix 2").

**SUMMARY**   Before selecting the report's elements, ask these questions:

1. Will the subject of the report be simple or complex?
2. Will the reader find it helpful and convenient to refer to a contents page and a summary or abstract?
3. Should illustrations be added to support or help clarify the central discussion?
4. Is a bibliography necessary? Should the reader be aware of the reference sources consulted during the investigation?
5. Are there any difficult or highly specialized terms that should be listed in a glossary?
6. Which information is primary? Which is secondary? Could the secondary material best be presented in an appendix?

Selecting the best format for a business report is relative to a number of considerations: subject matter, purpose, scope, audience, and individual organization report procedures. For this reason, the correct format will vary among report assignments and organizations. Bearing this fact in mind will help the writer appreciate the flexibility afforded in preparing reports as well as the diversity offered by each assignment.

**CHAPTER**   *Questions*
**REVIEW**

1. Discuss the relationship between a report's purpose and format.
2. Distinguish between informal and formal reports.
3. What factors often determine the writer's choice of format?

4. When is a formal style and format appropriate? Under what circumstances can a report be informally written?

5. List the elements that are basic to all business reports.

6. List the components of a standard formal report format.

7. Define each of these terms: *glossary, abstract, appendix.*

8. What is the purpose of a letter of transmittal?

9. Contrast an abstract with an introduction to a formal report.

10. When should a report include a bibliography?

## Exercises

1. Which of the following reports could be written and presented informally?
   a. A trip report for a sales manager.
   b. A study of college students' buying habits, written for a federal government committee.
   c. The latest information about word processors to be circulated among office staff.
   d. An audit report for a large corporation.
   e. A marketing survey for a small advertising firm's executives.
   f. A study of comparative prices and services of hotels in Los Angeles for your company's budget director.
   g. An annual report for a nonprofit organization.
   h. A description of in-house seminars for all managers.
   i. A status report for your supervisor.

2. Write a memo report on any of the following:
   a. Topics to be covered at the next sales meeting.
   b. Changes in vacation schedules due to unexpected orders for goods or services.
   c. Storage of past files, catalogs, and annual reports.
   d. A product or service urgently needed by your report-writing staff.
   e. New courses for your college's business degree programs.

## Report Project

1. Decide which formal structural elements should be included in your report.

2. Write a letter of transmittal.

3. Determine which information is best placed in an appendix.

4. Explain your choice of report components in terms of the scope, purpose, and probable reader of your report.

# CHAPTER 7

# Writing the Report: The First Draft

**THE NATURE OF WRITING**

Good writing requires *time* and *discipline*. Very often, the writer is anxious to put down on paper all he or she has observed and learned about a subject. Yet as writing is an expression of thinking, and because it manifests otherwise invisible ideas and thoughts, the writer must patiently explore the best ways to express the variety of personal impressions and factual information that will constitute the report's content.

The first step is to probe one's feelings about the subject. Ask the following four questions: (1) What seems most important or will have the greatest effect on the reader's attitude toward the subject? (2) What is the best way to state the findings, conclusions, and recommendations? (3) How should the ideas be related, and in what order or through what means? (4) Which words will state the ideas simply and clearly?

In addition to these considerations, the writer must cope also with the anxiety of completing the assignment on time. To lessen such tension, the writer must learn to relax by going for a walk, visiting a gym, riding a bicycle, taking a swim, watching an old movie, or simply enjoying a cup of coffee or tea. Very often, while the writer is in-

**113**

volved in other activities, ideas will emerge unexpectedly. It is therefore a good idea to carry a small notebook to write down thoughts, observations, words, phrases, and even sentences as they occur. By understanding the important roles relaxation and diversion play in unlocking and releasing thoughts, the writer can avoid unnecessary frustration and anxiety. Because writing often involves more perspiration than inspiration, the writer must approach the report assignment with a degree of patience, common sense, and discipline.

One of the greatest literary figures of the eighteenth century, Samuel Johnson, wrote the following: "What is written without effort is read without pleasure." As a writer, Dr. Johnson knew that good writing best resulted from discipline and hard work. In fact, even when it appears to be going well, writing isn't easy. Very few people can sit down and clearly relate their precise thoughts on paper at the first attempt. This is true for professional writers as well, because the writing process involves three unavoidable stages: *planning*, *actual writing*, and *revising*. All writing requires one or more drafts before rough thoughts can be transformed into polished ones. Understanding the need for discipline allows the writer to develop a realistic attitude to the demands of transforming the seemingly jumbled mass of data, observations, research, and notes into a well-written report. Otherwise the writer may feel overwhelmed by the sheer amount of information that business reports can often convey. Outlines, summaries, and standard formats can help the writer structure and organize the material. Yet first, the sentences must be composed to convey those thoughts. If the most difficult question the writer asks is "Where do I begin?" the most likely response is "In the rough draft," where thoughts begin to crystalize, and all writing originates.

## THE WRITER'S ENVIRONMENT

Before working on the rough draft, it is important to establish an environment conducive to writing. Environment can affect the writer's ability to concentrate. However, there is no one environment for writing that is best. Personal preference and habit play too great a role in the places writers choose to work. For some, complete privacy and silence is essential. A private office, library, empty conference room, park bench, deserted beach, or quiet garden can best stimulate ideas. For others, the best place to write may be on the train or bus to work, in a taxi cab traveling precariously through traffic, in a restaurant, or perhaps while listening to music at home. Some people are able to focus their minds best amid noise and diverse distractions; others need absolute silence. The trick to establishing the proper writing environment is to find a place that feels most comfortable.

In addition to finding a suitable place to work, the writer must determine the best time to work on the rough draft. Due to such routine distractions as telephone calls, meetings, lengthy business lunches, and unexpected problems, finding the time to write at work can be difficult unless specific hours are deliberately set aside. The writing process, if it is to be fruitful, must become a real and important aspect of the writer's daily life. It must not be regarded as an activity to fill free time. Perhaps for some it becomes necessary to hold all phone calls except for emergencies during certain hours. These people should reschedule meetings, lock themselves in their offices, ask their secretaries not to disturb them, and even arrive early or leave later in order to allow time for writing. The chances for successful writing increase if the writer can control or determine the proper environment, and then establish a work schedule. Writing thus becomes a challenging habit rather than unwelcome drudgery.

## GETTING STARTED

There are two factors that often inhibit the writing process. One is the fear of criticism and failure. The other is uncertainty about the kind of writing that will make the best impression.

The sense of permanence associated with committing ideas to paper often produces anxiety and procrastination. Like the movie star who winces at the memory of an inferior performance years ago, the writer often fears that what is written today can surely haunt him or her tomorrow. No one enjoys being criticized negatively. Writing is especially prone to criticism, whether from one's peers, supervisors, teachers, or unknown readers. For this reason, it is no wonder that the freedom of expression and spontaneity so essential to the writing process is so vulnerable to being stifled.

One way the writer can overcome this fear is to accept the fact that there is no such thing as perfect writing. Even if there were, someone would find fault with it. Yet this is little reason to ignore the reader or to develop a cavalier attitude to writing. One must try instead to disregard the possibility of criticism until the rough draft has been written. Then the writing can be revised and improved. Once the writer is familiar with the essential writing skills and goals of clear writing—simplicity and precision—he or she can become his or her own best critic.

As to what kind of writing makes the best impression, there is only one kind: the kind that communicates clearly. The notion that the only acceptable writing is either the kind that appears in textbooks, newspapers, trade journals, magazines, and other reports prevents the occasional writer from getting started on the rough draft. For some people, the mere publication of an article or essay is proof of a well-written work, or a model of what effective (or professional) writing should sound like. Though editors have very high standards about the writing they publish, they are not impressed by the fact that one writer uses obscure vocabulary terms and another the simplest language. On the contrary, it is the way the words are put together that counts, as well as the writer's skill in presenting the subject matter.

## THE WRITING PROCESS

Generally, all writing can be divided into three stages: (1) Prewriting or planning, (2) actual writing, and (3) rewriting or revision.

### Prewriting

Misdirected writing can be as wasteful and time-consuming as taking a wrong road on the way to an important meeting. The report writer must have a clear idea of the major concerns of a report. Before writing, ask the following questions to help focus random thoughts:

1. What do I want to say about my subject?
2. What is the purpose of my report?
3. Which ideas are most important?
4. Who will read this report?

Then jot down simple notes (words, phrases, sentences) that list the central ideas.

For example, a person may be asked to write a brief memo report about the importance of corporate cash flow. Drawing on personal thoughts, discussions with others, or research, he or she jots down several points and observations about the topic. Among them are the following thoughts and expressions:

- Cash flow importance.
- Analysis of cash availability.
- Twenty-day operating costs.
- Tight money markets.
- Economic downturn.
- Ability to borrow.
- Emergencies.
- Asset value of cash.
- Keeping cash to a minimum.

The next step is to fashion these ideas into substantial sentences that will mark the transition from the planning phase to actual writing.

## FACING THE BLANK PAGE: OVERCOMING WRITER'S BLOCK

In a rough or first draft—during the transition from the planning to the actual writing stage—it is best to get ideas down on paper quickly, without concern about style, grammar, punctuation, and even spelling. Otherwise, the initial encounter with the blank page may lead to what is known as *writer's block*, the inability to begin or to continue developing ideas that need to be expressed. Every writer is familiar with this frustrating experience. It therefore is important, and somewhat comforting, to accept the fact that the writing process is a delicate one in which the writer's thoughts can be easily inhibited or blocked at times.

Any number of reasons can lead to writer's block. The causes range from being troubled about some personal or job-related problems, to fearing criticism from others, or from physical illness. Whatever the cause, the writer *can* and must overcome writer's block, either to get started or to continue committing ideas to paper. Here are some suggestions:

1. Do some *free-writing*. That is, write down everything known at the moment about the report's subject. Describe any particular feelings about the subject. Try to focus on one main point at a time. Ask

this question: What is important about this point? During this stage, set a time limit, perhaps twenty minutes, and don't stop writing until the time is up. DO NOT STOP to cross out awkward phrases, to correct spelling or punctuation, or to reread the writing.

2. After initial thoughts are set down, review and select sentences and ideas that appear most relevant to the report's purpose and development. Look for important details that may be missing. Verify that enough examples and details have been provided. One helpful technique is to use a red pen or pencil to underline important phrases and sentences. Another method is to compose one or two summaries of the major ideas listed, remembering to look for key points.

3. It is not important when doing free-writing to begin actually at the beginning. Start anywhere. The idea is to get as many thoughts down on paper as possible within a given time frame. Then rearrange and edit them later.

4. If it becomes very difficult to get started or to do free-writing, use instead these lead-in phrases: "I can't get started on this assignment because . . ." or "What I really want to say here is . . ." or even "I don't feel like writing this report because. . . ." These expressions have helped many a blocked writer fill a number of what seemed to be impossibly frustrating blank pages.

**Actual Writing**   Transforming notes and observations into sentences and paragraphs that will form the first draft becomes an easier task by following these principles of organization:

1. Begin with a *topic* sentence or paragraph that will tell the reader *what* you want to say and *why*. This is also known as a headline or main idea statement that helps orient the reader to the specific subject and purpose.

For example, from the notes concerning the management of cash flow, develop a topic sentence that will best introduce key ideas as well as highlight supporting details and conclusions. Although it is possible to begin with general sentences such as these examples

A company should not run out of money.

A company must anticipate unexpected cash flow problems.

the final topic sentence form might read

> The cardinal sin of any company is to run out of cash and cash availability.

With this sentence, the main idea has been refined to include mention of the importance and danger of monitoring cash flow.

2. Next, provide *details* to support, explain, or illustrate the topic sentence. These details can be facts, opinions, statistics, and any other information that will be relevant to the central message.

It is helpful to refer to notes for crucial points and to help anticipate any questions that may arise in the reader's mind about the arguments, findings, assertions, and conclusions. Next, answer those possible questions in the order that they will probably occur to most readers. Then, the details that have been expressed in previous notes must be transformed into sentences. At first, the sentences might not be written in a particularly logical order. Therefore, number and then reorder the sentences after double-checking their content for precision and relevance. For example:

1. Unknown factors include tight money markets, unfavorable business conditions, lower demand for products or services.
2. Enough cash should be available to absorb a 20 percent downturn in a business on a month-to-month basis for a minimum of three months.

*4.* ~~3.~~ Cash itself is a nonearning asset.

*3.* ~~4.~~ Develop a program to identify major cash flow fluctuations.

5. Cash on hand should be kept to a minimum.

*Combine with # 4.*

3. The *conclusion* should result directly from the previous details and findings. It serves to tie the details and topic sentence together, and it lends a sense of unity and completeness to your presentation. The conclusion should not introduce any ideas and findings outside the scope of the topic sentence and supporting details.

From the list of brief details in the last example, this concluding sentence might be fashioned:

> Cash itself is a nonearning asset, and as such, should be kept to a minimum needed for normal operations.

While the writer decides which thoughts to place in the introduction, body, and conclusion, one helpful technique is to perceive and organize the ideas in a visual pattern.

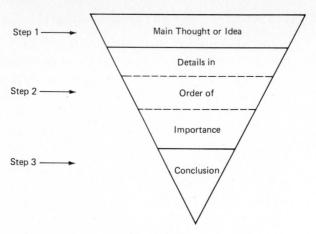

*FIGURE 7–1. Writing structured as an inverted pyramid.*

**VISUALIZE THE WRITING**   In visual terms, writing can be depicted as an upside-down pyramid, with the base containing the topic sentence, followed by supporting details and findings in order of importance and then a conclusion at the bottom tip. For reports that lack a formal conclusion, the tip can represent a summary of key ideas (see Figure 7–1).

The following is an example of the completed brief report:

## CORPORATE CASH FLOW

*Main Thought* { The cardinal sin of any company is to run out of cash and cash availability. Unknown factors such as tight money markets, unfavorable business conditions, lower demand in the product or service area a company operates in, and any other adverse condition must be considered in determining the scope, source and amount of cash reserves. A program to *Details* { identify and anticipate major cash flow fluctuations on a timely basis should be developed. In general, sufficient cash should be available to absorb a 20% overall downturn in business on a month to month basis for a minimum of three months for overhead. This amounts to about 20 days of average expenses. Consolidated borrowing power will be continuously monitored and forecasted. Cash itself is a non-earning asset, *Conclusion* { and as such, should be kept to the minimum needed for normal operations.

**WORDS**   Polonius: . . . *What do you read, my lord?*
Hamlet: *Words, words, words.*
　　　—II, ii, 193–194

As Shakespeare well knew, words are the building blocks of our language. Yet all too often people seem to forget that the purpose of words is to enable *clear* and *precise* communication. Nevertheless, some unfortunate individuals actually believe that to make the proper impression on the reader words have to be ten letters long and strung together in groups of twenty or more in a sentence. They confuse quantity with quality. They are like the colonel who would send a report to Washington only if it reached the minimum weight on his scale. As James Thurber once observed "A word to the wise is not sufficient—if it makes no sense."

Writers must avoid thinking like the colonel and others who associate length with depth, or who equate complex words with intelligence and sophistication. All good writers know better—they have learned that communication is best achieved through words that precisely and simply express their thoughts.

Here is an example of an overworded sentence:

> We are at a loss to know if a suitable time period has passed in order to inform us as to whether a favorable decision has been ascertained with consideration to our recommendation. (33 words)

The sentence sounds long-winded and confusing. Note this revision:

> We last heard from you on June 24. Have you decided to follow our recommendation? (15 words)

The significant difference between the two sentences rests less in the number of words used than in the choice of words and the way they are put together. The sentence wasn't shortened merely to eliminate words, but to convey the essential thought through simpler and concise words. However, the writer must not construct incomplete sentences merely to avoid writing longer ones. If for instance, someone receives a memo asking for further information in this way—"Your report does not contain all the required information"—he or she would not know what specific information is needed. Additionally, when attempting to be concise, the writer must avoid sounding curt or abrupt. It is far better to write, "Please submit your report by the end of the month" rather than "Report due me end month." Although both sentences transmit the same message, one does so with smooth precision; the other reads more like a telegram.

The following is a list of some common wordy expressions and their concise counterparts.

| Wordy | Concise |
|---|---|
| accounted for by the fact that | because |
| along the lines of | like |
| I am of the opinion | (I) believe, feel |
| at an early date | soon |
| based on the fact that | because |
| concerning the matter of | about |
| due to the fact that | because |
| during the time that | while |
| for the purpose of | for, to |
| for the reason that | for, since |
| in a position to | can, able |
| in addition to the above | also |
| in the event that | if |
| in view of the fact that | since, because |
| is predicated on the assumption | assumes |
| in the neighborhood of | about |
| is similar to | like, resembles |
| one finds it necessary to | (I, we) must |
| prior to | before |
| raise the question | ask |
| render every possible assistance | help all we can |
| subsequent to | after |
| the foregoing | these, those |
| the question as to whether | whether |
| through the use of | by, with |
| we are in receipt of | we have |
| will you be good enough to | please |
| with a minimum of delay | as soon as possible |
| with a view to | to, for |
| with reference to | concerning, about |
| with the exception of | except |
| with the result that | resulted in |

This list and the others that follow are not intended to inhibit writers from using wordy expressions in every case. Habits are difficult to break. Rather, the purpose is to point out the obvious advantages to clarity these simpler words can offer.

**Mock Legal Jargon**

Another trouble spot in selecting precise words is the tendency to use legal jargon. Many people believe that it sounds impressive, but this kind of language is best left to lawyers. Familiar words communicate thoughts more clearly, and hence faster, to the reader. The following is a list of some commonly used legal jargon and the more appropriate alternatives.

| Mock Legal Jargon | Clearly Worded |
|---|---|
| attached hereto/herewith | attached |
| herein set down | listed here |
| in connection therewith | connected with |
| in lieu of | instead of |
| in reference to | regarding |
| interpose no objections | agree with, approve |
| predicated on | based on |
| pursuant to | according to |
| thereby | by that |
| therein | in that |
| thereto | to that |
| until such time that | until |

**Euphemisms**

Euphemisms are formal words or expressions that serve to transform a seemingly simple term or idea into an overly and unnecessarily complex one, or to disguise or dress up an embarrassing or awkward situation. At a party, if someone approached a guest and asked

"May I bring you a libation?"

that person would probably laugh or shift about uncomfortably. Why? Because the term sounds pretentious. The guest would feel a lot more relaxed if asked

"Would you like something to drink?"

The following is a list of some common euphemisms and their meanings. For an up-to-date list, consult a newspaper or the wording of an official announcement, be it corporate, political, academic, legal, military or social. ("On the twenty-fifth day of July, you are invited to partake. . .")

| Euphemism | Meaning |
|---|---|
| net profits revenue deficiency | loss |
| altercation | fight |
| directive | order, memo |
| memory garden | cemetary |
| facility | building |
| visual surveillance | spying |
| initial | first |
| perpetrator | criminal |
| patron | customer |
| sanitary engineer | garbage collector |
| peruse | read |
| transpire | happen |
| inner city | ghetto |
| access controller | doorman |

**SENTENCES**  In a first draft, construct short, simple sentences, each expressing one idea. Later these sentences can be transformed into longer or more complex ones. The benefit of limiting one idea to as brief a sentence as possible will help the writer avoid confusing or over-wordy statements in the first draft.

Instead of this sentence

> To make a business report as well written as possible, a writer should, before he or she begins to write, review all of the collected information to evaluate the facts so he may decide how to properly emphasize the points that are most important.

write the following:

> For an effective report, a writer should first review the collected information. Then he or she should evaluate the facts to decide how to emphasize their relative importance.

***Vary Sentence Length***  Effective sentences are often varied according to length and construction. All sentences should not begin with *the, a, an, it is* and *there are,* because the reader will soon weary of the repetition. Good sentences average ten–fifteen words, and these can be a mixture of simple and more elaborate constructions interwoven to create a graceful rhythm within each paragraph. Repetition makes for dull reading. Variety, as applied to sentence structure, can truly enhance any report. Listen to the writing. Read the sentences aloud to hear and judge the rhythmic pattern. Keep it alive and interesting. For instance, dull writing sounds like this:

> It is recommended that our department consider remodeling. It is a good idea to modernize the office. An office should be modern and up to date with the latest in furniture, equipment, and design features. An office is a reflection of how well a company is doing in the marketplace and an indication of being successful.

This passage is a bit livelier, due to sentence variety:

> Our office should be modernized in terms of the latest design, equipment and furniture. The modern business office of the 1980s should reflect success in the contemporary marketplace.

**Combine Sentences**

Combine short, choppy sentences into graceful ones by eliminating unnecessary words and repetitive phrases and expressions. These sentences are choppy:

> Tom Doyle is an executive. He is with the ABC Book Company. Tom's job concerns sales.

They are more effective when combined:

> Tom Doyle is a sales executive with the ABC Book Company.

**Consistent Verb Tense**

Avoid confusing the reader's perspective of events and procedures by keeping verb tenses consistent:

> Mixed Verb Tense
> Managers *received* a bonus when their divisions' sales *increase*.

> Consistent Verb Tense
> Managers *received* a bonus when their divisions' sales *increased*.

The first sentence mistakenly combines past and present tense verbs, thus resulting in an awkward time frame. The second sentence clearly states that the action occurred in the past.

**Sentence Structure**    The writer can generate stronger and more effective sentences by avoiding the following pitfalls in structure.

**Avoid Pretentious Sentences.**    Sentences that use complex terms or wordy expressions for their own sake often confuse rather than clarify thoughts. Only clarity truly impresses the reader.

> The nature of the material is such as to *negate fully* the *feasibility of mass production*.

Write instead:

> This material cannot be mass-produced.

**Avoid Sentences Containing "Roundabout" Expressions.**    Both the content and structure of a sentence are improved by avoiding redundant or unnecessary words.

> He presented his report *at the time* of the final meeting.

Write instead:

> He presented his report at the final meeting.

**Avoid a Pompous or Arrogant Tone.**    Sentences that exhibit a gracious diplomacy usually prove more effective than abrasive ones, which only alienate the reader.

> In the future *see to it that it is not necessary for this office to remind you* to present your report on time.

Write instead:

> In the future, *please submit* your report on time.

**Avoid Seeming Indifferent.**    An indifferent attitude will often seem offensive and can anger the reader.

> The responsibility for administering the new program belongs to the Human Resources Agency. This department is only interested in matters concerning previous programs.

Write instead:

> The Human Resources Agency is responsible for administering new programs. Our department is restricted to administering programs that have been in effect for two or more years.

***Avoid Being Offensive.*** No reader appreciates being offended either unconsciously or intentionally.

> You totally misunderstood my memo for implementing new office procedures.

Write instead:

> Because some confusion has occurred regarding my memo concerning new office procedures, please refer to it again to avoid future misunderstanding.

***Avoid Being Insulting.*** While candid expressions of feelings may satisfy the writer for the moment, they can hamper future relations.

> Obviously, your thinking on this matter is so ridiculous I am completely baffled. It is clear that only a confused half-wit could offer such an absurd suggestion.

Write instead:

> There are some points in your suggestion that I found confusing. Perhaps you can clarify matters by answering this brief list of questions.

***Avoid Misplaced Words.*** Correct word order is crucial to the reader's understanding. Misplaced words and phrases intensify confusion.

> Harry asked the publicity director about changing advertising agencies, which his boss had suggested.

(Did the boss ask that Harry speak to the publicity director or that there be a change in advertising agencies?)
Write instead:

> The boss suggested that Harry ask the publicity director about changing advertising agencies.

**PARAGRAPHS** Paragraphs expand or develop ideas. There are, however, different ways to state the main ideas in a paragraph. The easiest method is to state the main idea in the first sentence of the paragraph, and then to provide details to support, illustrate, or explain that idea.

> *Rare book collectors usually seek books ranging from good to near-perfect condition.* In most instances, a book's covers shouldn't be badly scratched,

cracked, detached; nor should the binding be soiled, shredded, or faded due to excess exposure to sunlight. The pages shouldn't be torn, spotted with ink, or burned by ashes. Above all, there must be no missing pages, especially the title page.

The details that support the main idea concerning rare book collector's standards are clearly presented. Yet this same main idea could also have been stated at the conclusion of the paragraph.

In most instances, a book's covers shouldn't be badly scratched, cracked, detached; nor should the binding be soiled, shredded, or faded due to excess exposure to sunlight. The pages shouldn't be torn, spotted with ink, or burned by ashes. Above all, there must be no missing pages, especially the title page. *Rare book collectors, therefore, seek books ranging from good to near-perfect condition.*

The main idea can be stated in the middle of the paragraph as well:

In most instances, a book's covers shouldn't be badly scratched, cracked, detached; nor should the binding be soiled, shredded, or faded due to excess sunlight. *Rare book collectors will seek books ranging from good to near-perfect condition only.* The pages shouldn't be torn, spotted with ink, or burned by ashes. Above all, there must be no missing pages, especially the title page.

## Introductory Paragraphs

A good introductory paragraph provides the reader with an idea of what is to follow in the discussion, or body of the report. Introductory paragraphs should be interesting, relevant, and concise.

The Investor Relations Program at Acme should be based on the simple premise that we are always available to security analysts and the financial community, that we communicate all information that investors might require, and that we transmit all information within the letter and spirit of the SEC and NYSE regulations. There are reasons for this attitude.

Of course, the rest of the report would discuss in-depth the details and reasons supporting the company's position.

## Paragraph Length

Paragraphs vary in length and organization, depending on the nature of the material and the amount of detail required. The question often asked is "How many sentences form a paragraph?" There is no general rule concerning the number of sentences each paragraph should contain. It stands to reason, of course, that a short simple sentence does not really constitute a paragraph. The primary guideline is that each sentence be relevant to the topic sentence or main idea of a paragraph, because paragraphs are in fact individual units of thought linked by a central idea. For some, six–nine sentences might represent maximum paragraph length; three–four sentences the minimum.

For a paragraph to be effective, the ideas must flow smoothly from the opening sentence through the middle and concluding ones. No better example of the maxim that "the whole is the sum of its parts" exists than in the relationship of one paragraph to another. Continuity of thought can be more easily achieved if the writer uses transitional words and phrases, which serve as signs or guidewords throughout the report.

***Transitional Words and Phrases***

The following lists of transitional words and phrases are intended to aid the writer in constructing effective paragraphs.

1. To indicate *reversal* or *limitation* use:

| | |
|---|---|
| But | Otherwise |
| However | At the same time |
| Nevertheless | On the other hand |
| Although | On the contrary |
| Though | Yet |

2. To indicate an *example* use:

| | |
|---|---|
| For example | For instance |

3. To indicate a *conclusion* use:

| | |
|---|---|
| Therefore | In conclusion |
| So | As a result |
| Finally | In summary |

4. To indicate *continuity* use the following terms to link sentences:

| | |
|---|---|
| Also | In the same manner |
| And | Too |

| | |
|---|---|
| Moreover | Again |
| In addition | Nor |
| Another | Then |
| Similarly | In fact |
| Likewise | Besides |
| Further | Consequently |
| Furthermore | Accordingly |

5. To indicate *time order/chronology* use:

| | |
|---|---|
| First | Here |
| Second | There |
| Last | Eventually |
| At this point | Soon |
| Meanwhile | Later |
| Next | Before |
| Afterward | As a result |

**Concluding Paragraphs**   An effective concluding paragraph must be based on what has preceded it. It should not offer irrelevant conclusions or new ideas that have not been previously discussed. Concluding paragraphs should be neither abrupt nor long-winded, but concise and exact. Among the things that conclusions present are the following:

- A Summary.
- A Final Generalization.
- A Final Inference.
- A Call to Action.
- A Forecast or Prediction

Example:

Therefore, proper cash and debt management requires updated quarterly forecasts of asset and liability changes.

**STYLE**   Style marks a person's individuality in every aspect of life—dress, ideas, ability to communicate, the choice of restaurants, travel plans, leisurely interests. In short, style is the essence of someone's personality. In writing, style has to do as much with craft as with personality. Style can be constrained or given free rein. It depends on the words the writer chooses and how he or she arranges them.

Selectivity is as crucial to writing as it is to choosing a wardrobe. Appeal often depends on simplicity, good taste, and tailored precision. Style varies. Some people write short precise sentences. Others take a long time to think about what they want to say, and fill many sheets of paper to state the simplest ideas. Still others feel that writing should reflect one's sense of self-importance; appropriately, their writing tends to be stilted, pompous, and overwordy.

Although content is most important, there is nothing wrong with trying to infuse the writing (especially if the subject is a dull one) with a degree of liveliness and color that clearly reflects the writer's personality. After all, style in a report represents particular thinking, and it is indicative of who the writer is in the first place.

## MAKE THE REPORT INTERESTING

People work best at what they enjoy most. In daily business activities, not every task is challenging and exciting. This is especially true of a report-writing assignment. The writer will never be equally interested in all topics. Yet energy and enthusiasm are the impetus behind a forceful and dynamic report. The first step in approaching an assignment is therefore to try to find something appealing about it. Otherwise, the result will be a monontonous report characterized by lifeless sentences.

Next, convey that sense of importance and appeal to the reader. Get excited about the topic. Add an anecdote and perhaps an illustration or two. Readers will sense immediately either enthusiasm or lack of it. Attitude is crucial to interest. If a writer is interested, somehow it will be reflected in the writing.

Remember, drudgery in writing leads to drudgery in reading. All writers should regard their subjects as highly as their own careers. Each will surely affect the other.

## BE CONCISE

The idea that *less is more* can certainly be applied to report writing. The ability to express thoughts clearly and completely, yet concisely, will be appreciated by readers, even if they have the time or the inclination to read a longer report. Whenever possible, use the following guidelines:

- *Reduce* sentence length by eliminating unnecessary words.
- *Combine* very short ideas and repetitive ones.
- *Shorten* paragraphs.
- *Discard* irrelevant thoughts and points.
- *Focus* on the essence of your ideas.

Being concise is as vital to successful report writing as brevity is to wit. The writer has an obligation to the reader—to be clear. Concise expression of ideas not only fulfills this obligation, but allows the writer to know he or she has truly communicated the ideas at the heart of the report's purpose.

## BE OBJECTIVE

Achieve an unbiased tone by selecting words that do not connote personal viewpoints (unless called for) but rather that suggest impartiality and objectivity of judgment. In memos and letters, familiar pronouns (I, you, we) are freely used. Yet in formal reports, some organizations frown upon their inclusion because such use sometimes detracts from the clear, cool and unbiased perspective essential to objective reports.

Such expressions as *I, this writer, this observer, you will note*, and *we believe* are often subordinated to such passive and anonymous phrases as *it is recommended, it has been found*, and *the findings disclose*. These phrases maintain a sense of distance between the writer's observations and feelings and the content. Paradoxically, distance is preferable to personality or subjectivity in constructing an objective report, despite the obvious loss of immediacy and style.

## A FINAL NOTE

It should be apparent now that the first or rough draft is the testing ground for transforming the writer's initial ideas and observations into written form. Therefore, the writer's primary objective is to put into words and sentences the myriad of facts, opinions, statistics, and other findings that will constitute the heart of the report.

While consideration is given to word choice, sentence structure, the logical development of ideas and paragraphs, tone, and style, the rough draft is not a finished product. Rather, it is a means through which the writer finds his or her way to a well-written report. Only through careful editing and revision can the finished report truly represent an example of fine architecture built by words.

## CHAPTER REVIEW

### Questions

1. Discuss the three stages of the writing process.

2. Describe the importance of a report writer's environment.

3. What factors often inhibit a report writer from getting started on a first draft?

4. List the steps that often prove helpful in overcoming writer's block.

5. Discuss the relationship between a topic sentence and the details that follow.

6. Give five examples of overwordy expressions.

7. Define *euphemism*. Give three examples.

8. What characteristics should sentences *not* contain?

9. What is the function of transitional words?

10. Discuss the role of style in business reports.

### Exercises

1. Review any previously written report or the first draft of one in preparation. Eliminate wordy or outdated expressions and improve sentence and paragraph structure according to the guidelines outlined in this chapter.

2. For the same report, supply transitional words and phrases where they will be most helpful in developing your ideas.

3. Describe the environment in which you write. Note advantages and possible disadvantages.

4. Select any topic and write freely on it for five minutes. Then choose the phrases or sentences that would be most useful in writing a first draft. Write a brief report.

5. Eliminate wordiness in each of the following sentences.
   a. It has been decided that this company will no longer be providing coupons on its cereal boxes.
   b. The writer wishes to state that it is not practical for our corporation to become involved with issues of a controversial substance.
   c. Mr. White wishes to render it necessary that personnel be less extravagant with telephone calls of a personal nature and expenses charged to corporate accounts.
   d. A bank is a very interesting place to work because of the varied and different kinds of business transactions that take place there in the course of an average business day.
   e. It is recommended that you refer to those sections of the report that are important and essential and are contained on pages 25–40.
   f. Mr. Thomas Jones, a specialist in marketing, will assist the new marketing expert to be hired as a consultant on all matters concerning marketing activities to be carried out during the first year of the new product's introduction.
   g. This study contains information of a confidential background and nature.
   h. An investigation of the number of available ambulances in the city was made by the office of Governor Harris.

6. Correct the inconsistent verb tenses in these sentences.
   a. Jane obtained satisfaction from the responsibilities she has in her new job.
   b. My cousin remembered everything that happens on her trip to Paris.
   c. The report on the new project is being completed. It is up-to-date and all changes had been added.
   d. The attorney concludes that the defendent was likely to embezzle again because he gained a lot of pleasure from deceiving any company that trusted him with huge sums of money.
   e. In any crisis, Laura is able to remain calm and never got upset.

7. Locate and correct the misplaced words in the sentences that follow.
   a. When inflated with enough hot air ten people can be carried by the balloon.
   b. Jack was mopping the deck of his boat with Hugo.

    c. Charles Evans has decided to retire from public life after more than thirty years to everyone's regret.

    d. Joe took his dog to a groomer that needed his nails clipped.

    e. This article has a lot of information for people arranged by towns.

8. Combine each of the following ideas into one sentence.

    a. The best way to greater command of the English language. Reading will help you gain a wider control of the English vocabulary.

    b. Our company has one aim. Our company provides people with superior financial advice.

    c. Joe Stile traded stocks and bonds for twenty years. When Joe traded stocks and bonds he worked for one company. The brokerage house he worked for is in New York.

    d. The function of the agency is to obtain jobs for retired executives. The agency deals primarily with retired banking and advertising executives looking for some kind of challenging position.

    e. Sharon walked to the Circle Theatre from her office. She works five blocks away from the theatre. Her job is in television programming. She works for ABC.

## Report Project

Begin the first draft of your report, bearing in mind the principles and techniques discussed in this chapter.

# CHAPTER 8

# Using Illustrations in the Report

**THE NEED FOR ILLUSTRATIONS**

The adage about one picture being worth a thousand words can apply tenfold to the value of illustrations in a business report. Aside from adding significantly to a report's visual appeal, good illustrations support written discussion of major issues and help draw the reader's attention to important details and facts. As with every aspect of a business report, illustrations require careful planning, and are used *selectively* at only those times when they can truly enhance or clarify a textual discussion. Only then can they contribute most effectively to the reader's understanding of complex data. In these cases they can save both writer and reader time and effort.

In no instance should an illustration totally replace the written word in a business report. Rather, two choices are available to the writer. Their use depends on the nature and purpose of a report, as well as on its audience. Illustrations can be used to support the text in longer formal reports. Or the *text* can supplement or explain the illustrations in somewhat shorter *summary* or *executive* reports. The summary report offers a more concise format, in which major ideas and details are emphasized for those individuals who are too busy to read all the details or who are uninterested in every specific aspect of the report. Here, illustrations visually represent major facts

**137**

and observations, and the text serves to comment on or to explain the graphic information.

Some organizations might have both versions of a report prepared for different readers (for executives, technicians, and the general public) or purposes (decision-making, or future reference). For both formats, the illustrations included are drawn from similar basic categories: tables and figures.

**TYPES OF ILLUSTRATIONS**

Illustrations generally fall into two categories: *tables* and *figures*. Tables present quantitative and numerical data in a series of rows and columns. Figures include charts, graphs, drawings, photographs, maps, and pictograms that are used to indicate relationships, values and trends. Both tables and figures can be used to do the following:

- Depict complex data and details that are difficult to describe.
- Display concise views and relationships between ideas and physical properties.
- Provide visual depiction of abstract concepts.

The basic qualities of effective illustrations are

- Simplicity.
- Clarity.
- Relevance.

Examples of several basic types of illustrations used in reports, along with general advice for their construction, can be found on the pages that follow.

**PLACEMENT OF ILLUSTRATIONS IN THE REPORT**

Illustrations should be placed where they can be of most use to the reader. Sometimes an illustration can be incorporated in the text; on other occasions it can appear on a separate page either directly opposite or following the discussion relating to it. If the illustrations are used primarily for reference rather than for clarification, they may be included in an appendix to the report. No matter where they are positioned, however, no illustration should distract the reader from the discussion at hand due to premature placement. Illustrations should not appear two or more pages ahead of the appropriate textual reference, or the reader will become confused about their function and subsequently be distracted from the text. Too many illustrations can overwhelm the reader as well, so the need to be selective is strong. The writer should bear in mind that while one picture may be worth a thousand words, no amount of illustrations can ever totally replace the written word.

## IDENTIFY THE ILLUSTRATIONS

All illustrations in the report are identified by titles or headings, and by either numbers or letters to indicate the order of placement. It is common practice to distinguish tables from all other figures (graphs, charts, drawings, etc.) when referring to illustrations. Titles for tables are usually placed above and are numbered with Roman or Arabic numerals, while titles for figures are placed below and noted with Arabic numerals (see Figure 8–1).

For the reader's convenience, list the illustrations on a separate page titled *Table of Illustrations* or *Illustrations*. For specific details concerning its format, see pages 102–103 of Chapter 6.

## COMPUTER GRAPHICS

One practical advantage of modern technology for the report writer is the capability of specially programmed computers to design graphics and charts (see Figure 8–2). Many computers are equipped to draw and print line graphs, tables, pie charts, bar graphs, maps, flow and organizational charts, and drawings. They can do so at incredible speeds, due to the introduction of new software (programs) in recent years. While the writer must provide the computer with all the necessary data, the machine will do the work of composing the illustration and properly incorporating the pertinent data. As more organizations add the latest technological equipment to their offices, the report writer should have little difficulty gaining access to a computer capable of designing many of these graphics.

## TABLES

Tables are used to compare information visually and to indicate the relationship between various data. Tabular information often allows the reader to grasp complex relationships more easily and concisely.

**Table 1**

| Various Savings Media | | | | | | | | | |
| --- | --- | --- | --- | --- | --- | --- | --- | --- | --- |
| Year End | Commercial Banks | | Savings & Loan Associations | | Mutual Savings Banks | | Credit Unions | | Total Billion Dollars |
| | Billion Dollars | % of Total | Billion Dollars | % of Total | Billion Dollars | % of Total | Billion Dollars | % of Total | |
| 1980 | 753 | 51 | 511 | 35 | 151 | 10 | 84 | 4 | 1,479 |
| 1979 | 653 | 49 | 470 | 35 | 144 | 11 | 58 | 5 | 1,323 |
| 1978 | 612 | 49 | 432 | 35 | 141 | 12 | 53 | 4 | 1,238 |
| 1977 | 551 | 49 | 387 | 35 | 134 | 12 | 47 | 4 | 1,119 |
| 1978 | 489 | 50 | 384 | 34 | 123 | 12 | 29 | 4 | 985 |
| 1975 | 448 | 51 | 288 | 33 | 110 | 18 | 33 | 4 | 375 |
| 1974 | 418 | 52 | 243 | 31 | 39 | 18 | 23 | 4 | 737 |
| 1973 | 385 | 51 | 227 | 32 | 63 | 18 | 25 | 4 | 712 |
| 1972 | 314 | 50 | 207 | 33 | 92 | 14 | 22 | 3 | 384 |
| 1971 | 292 | 50 | 174 | 32 | 81 | 15 | 18 | 3 | 548 |

*Source:* Federal Home Loan Bank Board

(a)

WORLDWIDE FILM RENTALS — *NINE U.S. COMPANIES
(In Millions of Dollars — at Year End)

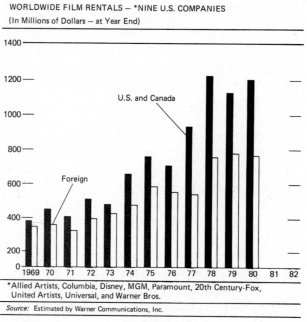

*Allied Artists, Columbia, Disney, MGM, Paramount, 20th Century-Fox, United Artists, Universal, and Warner Bros.

*Source:* Estimated by Warner Communications, Inc.

Figure 2

(b)

*FIGURE 8–1. Illustrations should be identified as (a) tables or (b) figures.* [Adapted with permission from *(a) Industry Surveys,* a publication of Standard & Poor's Corporation (April 1982, vol. 1, p. B15); *(b) Industry Surveys* (April 1982, vol. 1, p. L30).]

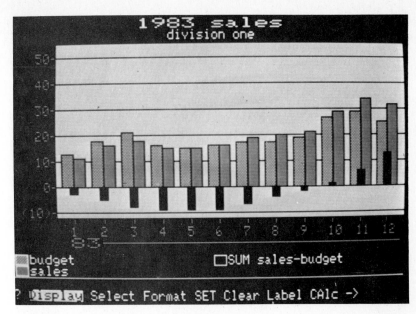

*FIGURE 8–2.    A computer graphic illustrating the budget and sales of
a company.* [Courtesy Cullinet Software, Westwood, Mass.]

Such data are conveyed through the use of rows and columns arranged according to any number of factors: time, cost, size, quality, and so on.

Tables contain titles and subheadings that are boxed by horizontal lines separating the title from the body of data, the various subheadings from one another, and the entire table from the text that follows. Units of measurement and other comparative data are distinguished by vertical lines, thus forming columns. The information related should be sufficiently spaced to avoid congestion and possible confusion. Footnotes or prefatory comments are used to explain symbols, to reveal sources of information, to point out trends, and to note exceptions. Footnotes can be denoted by a number, letter, or by symbol such as an asterisk (*). In general, tables should be

- Simply and clearly worded.
- Relevant to the report.
- Either boxed or properly margined to be distinguished from the text.

**TABLE I.** *United States Population Projections**

|  | 1981 | | 1985 | | 1990 | |
| --- | --- | --- | --- | --- | --- | --- |
| Age Group | Number (Thou.) | % of Total | Number (Thou.) | % of Total | Number (Thou.) | % of Total |
| Under 5 yrs. | 16,620 | 7.4 | 18,803 | 8.1 | 19,437 | 8.0 |
| 5 to 17 yrs. | 45,021 | 20.0 | 43,490 | 18.7 | 45,339 | 18.6 |
| 18 to 24 yrs. | 29,512 | 13.2 | 27,853 | 12.0 | 25,148 | 10.3 |
| 25 to 29 yrs. | 19,324 | 8.6 | 20,581 | 8.8 | 20,169 | 8.4 |
| 30 to 34 yrs. | 18,138 | 8.1 | 19,278 | 8.3 | 20,917 | 8.6 |
| 35 to 39 yrs. | 14,290 | 6.4 | 17,274 | 7.4 | 19,261 | 7.9 |
| 40 to 54 yrs. | 34,524 | 15.4 | 36,559 | 15.7 | 42,642 | 17.5 |
| 55 to 64 yrs. | 21,413 | 9.6 | 21,737 | 9.3 | 20,776 | 8.5 |
| 65 Yrs. & over | 25,368 | 11.3 | 27,305 | 11.7 | 29,824 | 12.2 |
| All Ages | 224,212 | 100.0 | 232,880 | 100.0 | 243,513 | 100.0 |

* Includes Armed Forces abroad.
*Source:* Department of Commerce, Population Series P-25, as of July 1.

- Numbered, titled, and correctly keyed to the text.
- Contain titles or captions for all columns and rows bearing information.

Table I measures population projections in the United States according to age group over a ten-year period. Note that the yearly columns are subdivided into both the numbers in thousands and the percentage of total population each age group represents.

**SIMPLE BAR CHARTS**

Bar charts or graphs measure data either horizontally or vertically against criteria that can denote value, quality, time, quantity, magnitude, or any other variable. Usually the units of measurement begin at point zero at the left margin for horizontal bars, and at the bottom for vertical ones. The bars must be the same width and of equal distance apart. All bar charts must contain a title as well as indentifying captions or labels for each bar. The chart shown in Figure 8–3 indicates the number of households in the United States, in terms of millions (horizontally), and according to annual income (vertically).

HOUSEHOLDS BY INCOME CLASS — U.S.(1980)
(In Millions)

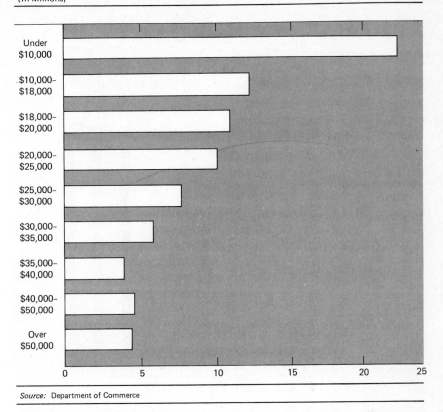

*Source:* Department of Commerce

*FIGURE 8–3.   Bar chart that measures data both horizontally and vertically.* [Adapted with permission from *Industry Surveys,* a publication of Standard & Poor's Corporation (April 1982, vol. 1, p. L14).]

## MULTIPLE BAR CHARTS

Multiple bar charts are similar to simple bar charts. They differ in that they compare two or more variables rather than one. The numerous bars can be distinguished by shading, hatching, or color to avoid confusing the reader.

In Figure 8–4, two bars (one light, the other dark) are used to measure motion picture box office trends over a ten year period. The light bar designates the number of admissions. The dark one denotes actual box office receipts in terms of millions of dollars. The years spanning 1970–1981 are listed horizontally so that the reader can

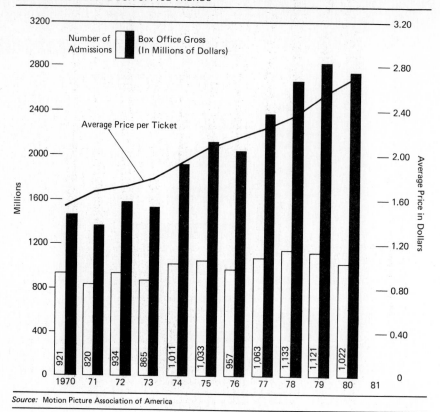

U.S. MOTION PICTURE BOX OFFICE TRENDS

*Source:* Motion Picture Association of America

FIGURE 8–4.   *Multiple bar chart.* [Adapted with permission from *Industry Surveys,* a publication of Standard & Poor's Corporation (April 1982, vol. 1, p. L31).]

compare the average price of a ticket with the number of admissions and box office receipts on a yearly basis.

Figure 8–5 depicts the number of homes reached by various broadcasting systems in 1982 and makes predictions for 1990.

**SUBDIVIDED BAR CHARTS**   Subdivided bar charts present comparisons of data within individual bars. Either varying degrees of shading or hatching can distinguish the data each bar is measuring. In Figure 8–6, note how a bank's as-

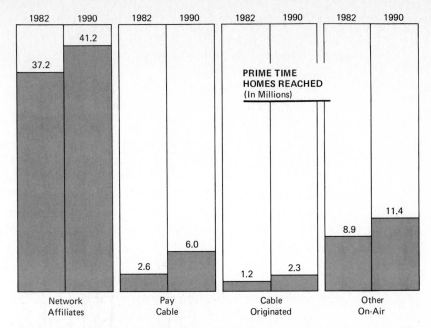

FIGURE 8–5. Multiple bar chart. [Adapted with permission from CBS, Inc., 1982 Annual Report, p. 15.]

ASSETS OF SAVINGS & LOAN ASSOCIATIONS
(In Billions of Dollars)

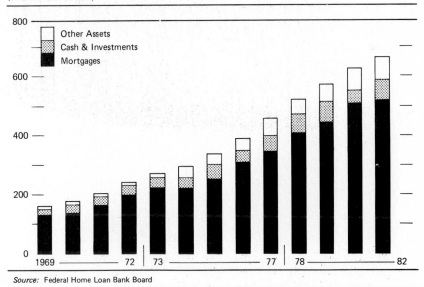

FIGURE 8–6. Subdivided bar chart. [Adapted with permission from Industry Surveys, a publication of Standard & Poor's Corporation (October 1982, vol. 1, p. B27).]

sets are divided into cash, mortgages, and other forms of investment on a quarterly annual basis.

**LINE CHARTS**     Line charts or graphs can measure change and growth, can indicate the relationship or compare two or more kinds of data. Line charts can also reveal trends, cycles, movements, or simply point out the importance of various data. The data is plotted as a continuous line on a grid. (See Figure 8–7).

Grids are composed of a horizontal axis (line), usually referred to as the *X axis*, which plots time, and a vertical or *Y axis*, which plots

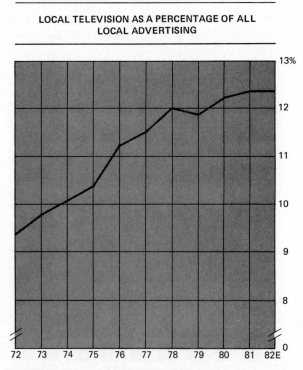

**LOCAL TELEVISION AS A PERCENTAGE OF ALL LOCAL ADVERTISING**

*Source:* McCann-Erickson Inc. and CBS Economic Analysis.

*FIGURE 8–7. Line chart.* [Adapted with permission from CBS, Inc., *1982 Annual Report,* p. 18.]

values. By plotting the point(s) that meet at right angles along the horizontal and vertical axes, the relationship between the data being measured is revealed.

***Dual Line Charts*** Sometimes two or more lines are used to measure or indicate various data (See Figure 8–8). Each line must be distinguished by a separate label. In Figure 8–8*a*, one solid line represents the various money market funds, the broken line denotes thrift units (banks), and both are compared for changes in assets.

In devising a line chart, it is essential to keep the following guidelines in mind:

1. Divide the horizontal and vertical axes into equal parts or units.
2. Note the zero (0°) point at the lower left corner of the chart.
3. Time is usually plotted horizontally; values, vertically.
4. Progressions in amount or quantity are listed on the vertical axis, beginning at the bottom and moving upward.
5. Progressions in time move from left to right on the horizontal axis.
6. Any wording or captions should be printed horizontally.
7. All line charts should bear titles and be appropriately numbered.

**PIE CHARTS** Pie charts measure and compare information by segmenting it into "slices" that are labeled and that represent a percentage of the whole. When preparing a pie chart, begin dividing the pie at the top (twelve o'clock position) and move clockwise, progressing from the largest portions to the smallest (see Figure 8–9).

**PICTOGRAMS** Like bar charts, pictograms measure information. Yet pictograms are more dramatic visually, because the pictures are usually indicative of the special product, material, or concept under discussion.

The pictogram illustrated in Figure 8–10 depicts the relationship between workers and the baby-boom years in the United States. It does this through varying the size and color of baby blocks.

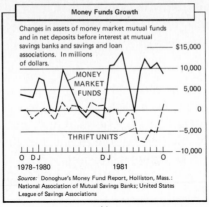

Money Funds Growth

Changes in assets of money market mutual funds
and in net deposits before interest at mutual
savings banks and savings and loan
associations. In millions
of dollars.

$15,000
10,000
5,000
0
−5,000
−10,000

MONEY
MARKET
FUNDS

THRIFT UNITS

O D J      D J      O
1978–1980   1981

Source: Donoghue's Money Fund Report, Holliston, Mass.:
National Association of Mutual Savings Banks; United States
League of Savings Associations

(a)

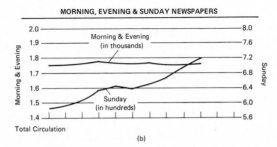

MORNING, EVENING & SUNDAY NEWSPAPERS

2.0                                  8.0
1.9    Morning & Evening            7.6
       (in thousands)
1.8                                  7.2
1.7                                  6.8
1.6                                  6.4
1.5    Sunday                        6.0
       (in hundreds)
1.4                                  5.6

Morning & Evening

Sunday

Total Circulation

(b)

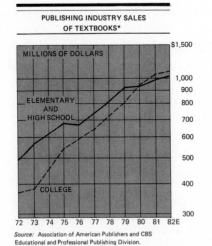

PUBLISHING INDUSTRY SALES
OF TEXTBOOKS*

$1,500

MILLIONS OF DOLLARS

1,000
900
800
700
600
500
400
300

ELEMENTARY
AND
HIGH SCHOOL

COLLEGE

72 73 74 75 76 77 78 79 80 81 82E

Source: Association of American Publishers and CBS
Educational and Professional Publishing Division.

*Includes domestic and export sales.

(c)

FIGURE 8–8. Dual line charts.
[Adapted with permission from (a)
The New York Times, January 10,
1982, p. 64; (b) Industry Surveys, a
publication of Standard & Poor's
Corporation (October 1982, vol. 1, p.
C69); (c) CBS, Inc., 1982 Annual Re-
port, p. 34.]

**American Agricultural Exports**

In billions of dollars. In the crop year ended Oct. 1, 1981, farm exports reached $43.8 billion, or 18.7 percent of total exports of $233.7 billion. Shaded area shows grain and feed exports, which totaled $21.9 billion.

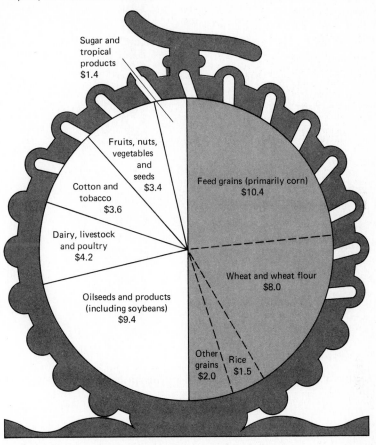

Sugar and tropical products $1.4

Fruits, nuts, vegetables and seeds $3.4

Cotton and tobacco $3.6

Dairy, livestock and poultry $4.2

Oilseeds and products (including soybeans) $9.4

Feed grains (primarily corn) $10.4

Wheat and wheat flour $8.0

Other grains $2.0

Rice $1.5

*Source:* Agriculture and Commerce Department

*FIGURE 8–9. Pie chart depicting various American agricultural exports during 1981.* [Adapted with permission from *The New York Times*, January 10, 1982.]

**ORGANIZATIONAL CHARTS**

Organizational charts reveal the hierarchical structure of a system in descending order of importance and function. To construct such a chart, begin at the top. Next, label and enclose in boxes (connected by horizontal and vertical lines) the descending and lateral levels

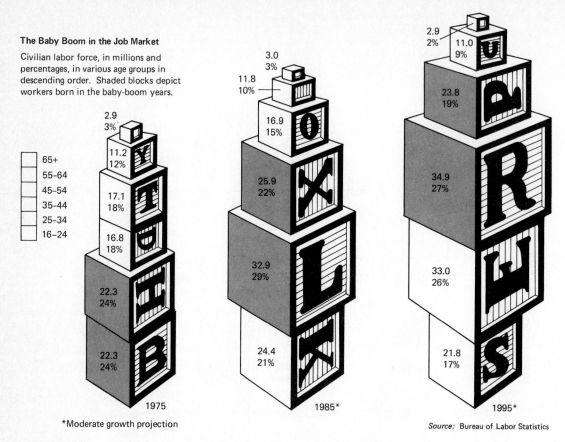

**The Baby Boom in the Job Market**

Civilian labor force, in millions and percentages, in various age groups in descending order. Shaded blocks depict workers born in the baby-boom years.

*Moderate growth projection

*Source:* Bureau of Labor Statistics

*FIGURE 8–10. Pictogram.* [Adapted with permission from *The New York Times,* January 10, 1982, p. 18.]

(subdivisions) of authority and responsibility. The lettering in each box should be printed horizontally and simply. (See Figure 8–11.)

**FLOW CHARTS**   Flow charts indicate the sequence of a process or activity from start to conclusion. As with other kinds of illustrations, flow charts include titles and numbers. To devise such a chart, begin the sequence at the left hand margin, using arrows to indicate the flow direction. All stages of the sequential flow must be noted and indicated by pictures, symbols, or boxes. (See Figure 8–12.)

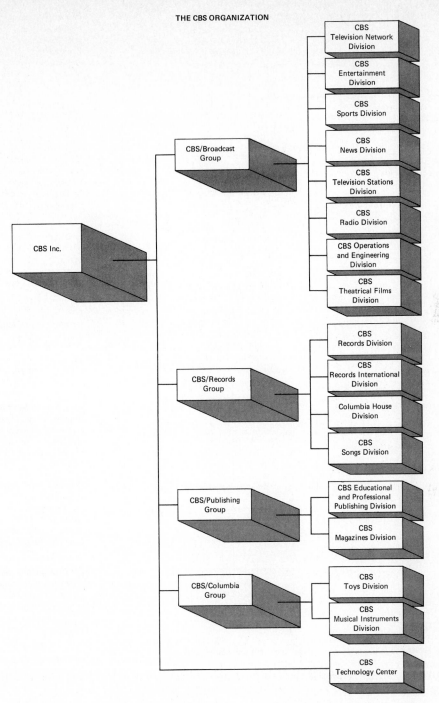

*FIGURE 8–11. Organizational chart.* [Adapted with permission from CBS, Inc., *1983 Annual Report*, p. 8.]

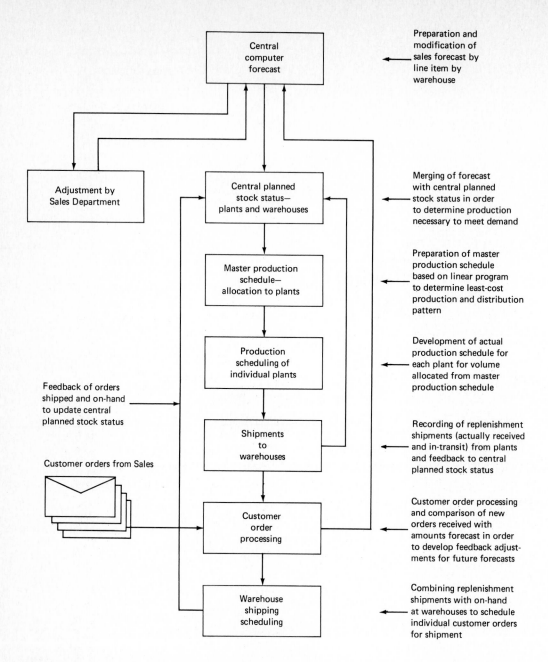

Figure 1. Schematic example of computerized central stock control plan.

FIGURE 8–12. *Flow chart.* [Adapted with permission from Victor P. Buell, *Handbook of Modern Marketing* (New York: McGraw-Hill, 1970), p. 4.65).]

**DRAWINGS**  Use drawings to present details and relationships that are difficult to describe or to portray in a graph. As with tables, charts, and other figures, drawings especially should be relatively simple and easy to understand. Many organizations maintain a graphics arts department whose staff can create particular art work according to the report writer's needs. Professional illustrators can also be engaged for a fee. There is no need for the writer to feel personally responsible for executing drawings, although it is a good idea to work closely with the illustrator to insure correct design.

**MAPS**  Maps indicate either geographical or informational features of a particular location or terrain. In preparing maps, all the boundaries should be clearly indicated. Areas that need to be highlighted can be shaded, hatched, or variously colored. A scale should be included to indicate proportions in terms of miles or feet. Above all else, avoid providing unnecessary details and information that will only clutter the map.

**SUMMARY**

1. All information conveyed through an illustration should be expressed as simply and clearly as possible. Avoid unnecessary pictorial embellishment and excessive detail.
2. Illustrations should be placed close to the relevant textual reference, never long before or after.
3. All illustrations must include titles or captions and be numbered consecutively.
4. A key or legend must be provided for symbols, abbreviations, and acronyms; a scale should indicate proportions or dimensions.
5. A proper visual frame should be provided by properly utilizing the surrounding negative (blank) space to highlight the illustration.
6. In instances where many illustrations are required, it is essential to prepare a Table of Illustrations or List of Figures to indicate placement in the text.

***CHAPTER***   *Questions*
***REVIEW***

1. Discuss the role of illustrations in a business report.

2. List three qualities of effective illustrations.

3. Describe the ways an illustration can be placed in a report.

4. Define the following illustrations and note their functions:
   a. Table.
   b. Line chart.
   c. Bar chart.
   d. Pie chart.
   e. Flow chart.
   f. Organizational chart.
   g. Pictogram.

*Exercises*

1. Determine the type of illustration that best visualizes the following data:
   a. A comparison of money market funds with U.S. treasury bills.
   b. Allocation of state dollars for one year.
   c. Comparison and list of the ten largest corporations' profits for the last three years.
   d. Sales figures of different products manufactured by the same company.
   e. Population growth in Arizona, Texas, Nevada, New Mexico, Utah, and California in the last ten years.
   f. Cost over thirty years between mortgage rates of 12 percent and 16 percent for homes priced at $65,000, $100,000, and $250,000. Assume the owner's downpayment ranges between one third and one fourth of the total price.
   g. Comparison of any professional sports team's performance over five seasons.
   h. Advertising revenues of CBS, NBC and ABC for the last year.

2. Devise an administrative organizational chart representing your college or company.

3. From any newspaper, magazine, journal, or report, collect one example of a *table, bar chart, line graph, pie chart,* and *pictogram.* Discuss the effectiveness of each illustration.

### Report Project

1. Wherever appropriate, prepare illustrations for the report you are presently writing.

2. If you have access to the proper equipment, provide a series of computer graphics to support the text of your report.

# CHAPTER 9

# The Final Draft: Revising the Report

**THE NEED FOR REVISION**

The first draft of a report may be compared to a rough diamond that must be polished to reveal its sparkling beauty. In the same way, the writer reviews and revises his or her work to emphasize those qualities essential to successful written communication: clarity and exactness.

The revision process requires even extra stamina and discipline, because of the tendency to resist a further struggle with conveying and refining thoughts on paper after the time and effort spent on the rough draft. The writer becomes like the exhausted runner who must run hardest in the last mile, or the tired boxer who rises when the bell sounds one last round.

Accordingly, allow some time to pass between the first and later drafts of the report. This will contribute to achieving objectivity. Distance and objectivity go hand in hand, so take a break by doing some other work such as going for a walk, ordering lunch, telephoning a friend. Whether ten minutes or several days pass before the writer attempts to revise a report, the breathing space will increase the chances for a more fruitful revision, and the result will ultimately be a more readable report.

**157**

***Revise to Improve Content and Structure***   In general, when revising a rough draft, note the content (what has been stated) and the structure (how it has been stated). Attempt to eliminate or correct flaws in either aspect by considering these questions:

1. Have I considered my purpose?
2. Have I considered my readers?
3. Is the subject and focus of my report clearly stated at the outset?
4. Does the opening sentence or paragraph clearly indicate the report's purpose?
5. Have I included all essential details and examples to support my findings?
6. Have I presented my ideas fully and in order of importance?
7. Are there any confusing statements that might be misunderstood or misinterpreted by the reader?
8. Is there unnecessary jargon or unfamiliar terms that may prove confusing to the reader?
9. Are conclusions and recommendations worded clearly and emphatically?
10. Have I checked carefully for correct spelling, punctuation, grammar, and tone of voice?

## METHODS FOR REVISION

Here are some time-saving techniques for revising initial writing:

1. *Neatly cross out* words, phrases, and sentences that are wordy, irrelevant to the subject matter, or that inhibit the flow and development of ideas.

> Market research ~~company~~ studies suggest ~~that~~ the best ~~and most suitable~~ time to introduce the new~~ly created and certainly highly exciting~~ sun-tan lotion is ~~late in the spring towards~~ the end of May.

The revised sentence now reads as follows:

> Market research studies suggest the best time to introduce the new sun-tan lotion is the end of May.

2. *Insert new material or changes* by writing or typing the material above the old lines and placing a caret (∧) directly beneath the line to indicate exact placement.

in several cities
The new product has been tested ˄ and proven popular around the country.

The revised sentence now reads as follows:

The new product has been tested in several cities and proven popular around the country.

3. *Indicate new paragraphs* by placing the symbol ⁋ before the first sentence.

Our bank's attempt to increase its presence in international banking has been very successful. Last June, we bought five European and Latin American operations of a Swiss-based banking firm for $450 million in cash and securities. ⁋ This purchase provided us with an overseas network to expand our trading and investment banking activities in London, Paris, Milan, Buenos Aires, and Rio de Janeiro.

The revised passage now reads as follows:

Our bank's attempt to increase its presence in international banking has been very successful. Last June, we bought five European and Latin American operations of a Swiss-based banking firm for $450 million in cash and securities.

This purchase provided us with an overseas network to expand our trading and investment banking activities in London, Paris, Milan, Buenos Aires, and Rio de Janeiro.

4. *Transfer material from one area to another* by encircling it and then drawing a line with an arrow toward the new location in the passage.

Last June, we bought five European and Latin American operations of a Swiss-based banking firm for $450 million in cash and securities. Our bank's attempt to increase its presence in international banking has been very successful.

This purchase provided us with an overseas network to expand our trading and investment banking activities in London, Paris, Milan, Buenos Aires, and Rio de Janeiro.

**Revise the Beginning**   The logical place to begin revising the rough draft is in the opening statement, whether it is expressed in sentence or paragraph form. In stating the subject and purpose of the report, the beginning should do so clearly, directly, and in such a way as to arouse the reader's

interest. Here are some helpful methods for writing effective beginning statements:

**1. Begin with a Direct Statement of Fact.**    In the rough draft, the
opening statement may have been loosely or awkwardly expressed,
and may not have highlighted the purpose and focus of the report.
Beginning with a direct statement of fact allows the writer to concentrate on the report's principal concern in a sort of no-frills way.
It also quickly establishes the scope of the report for the reader.

> From 1980 through 1984, the Human Resources and Training Division
> of the Interborough Electric and Gas Company conducted seventy-five sem-
> inars in management development which have been evaluated for effective-
> ness and quality.

**2. Begin with a Statement of Opinion.**    Stating an opinion at the
outset is another way of informing the reader of the report's direction and subject matter. Rather than beginning with a statement of
fact that allows the reader to reach his or her own conclusions and
judgments, this approach requires ample justification and support
in the discussion that it introduces. At the outset, the writer's position is clear to the reader. This method is illustrated by the following
example:

> The management development seminars conducted by the Human Re-
> sources and Training Division of the Interborough Electric & Gas Company
> from 1980 through 1984 have proven highly successful.

**3. Begin with an Anecdote.**    Entertaining anecdotes arouse the
reader's interest and at the same time state the purpose and focus
of the report. Their use, of course, depends on the topic as well as
the audience. For example:

> Last Friday at the luncheon to celebrate Jim Peterkin's promotion to sen-
> ior vice-president, he surprised everyone by modestly announcing that his
> recent success might not have materialized had he not taken one of the
> management development seminars offered by our training division.
> This report describes the nature of the courses offered between 1980 and
> 1984, and evaluates their effectiveness in terms of improving job perfor-
> mance among the many participants.

**Revise the Body of Discussion**    The body of the report requires the greatest effort and time, as it is usually the longest section. The success of this section depends upon the degree to which the sentences and paragraphs contain details that clearly support, develop, and elaborate on the topic or opening statement.

Each sentence must contribute to the development of the discussion. Irrelevant ideas and data must be eliminated to avoid interrupting the reader's flow of thought. The reader expects and is justified in demanding that the writer not waste otherwise valuable time by adding sentences that merely take up space. All ideas should be logically presented and developed, without digression and unnecessary repetition. Revision will become much easier and less chaotic if the writer follows these guidelines. In time, and with a great deal of practice, the writer will draw upon these principles from instinct rather than from conscious effort.

**Revise the Conclusion**    Conclusions should leave a lasting impression on the reader. Therefore, the writer must work for a strong ending, one that neither lacks clarity and force nor that introduces a new topic unexpectedly. Most endings or conclusions will either offer a variety of the following approaches or a mixture of all four:

**1. Restate the Topic Statement.**    Restating the topic sentence in a conclusion reinforces the report's central purpose in the reader's mind. In effect, the message travels full circle, though this time it is introduced by one of the various concluding transitional words or phrases, such as *therefore, finally, so, thus, in conclusion, as a result,* and so on. For example:

> In all, seventy-five seminars were conducted by the Human Resources and Training Division in order to improve and develop management effectiveness between 1980 and 1984.

**2. Summarize Main Ideas and Findings.**    Very often summarizing the main ideas and findings provides the reader with an overview of the report's major points, ideas, or findings. This is apparent in the following example:

> As a result of enrolling in the various seminars offered by the Human Resources and Training Division between 1980 and 1984 to improve manage-

ment effectiveness, most participants displayed greater ability to handle crisis situations in their departments, gained increased confidence in personal judgment, and were more readily able to arrive at complex or difficult decisions amidst daily responsibilities.

**3.  *Draw from Evidence Previously Stated.***    At times, the writer will need to incorporate conclusions drawn from data observations previously stated in the report. What the writer does, in effect, is wait until the very end to "pull all the strings together," in order to provide the report with a climax. This conclusion should be logically or intellectually satisfying to the reader, as is true in the following case:

> In conclusion, based on the positive effects on the majority of participants who enrolled in one or more of the management development seminars offered by the Human Resources and Training Division between 1980 and 1984, this program can indeed be judged worthwhile and highly successful in meeting our corporate training goals.

**4.  *Urge Action.***    Urging action in a conclusion can be a most effective persuasive device. If the writer has presented and developed the report's central points and ideas through ample details and evidence, the reader will find it difficult to refute the climactic call for action. For example:

> Therefore, in view of the positive effects in terms of productivity, improvement and growth on those employees who participated in the series of management development seminars presented by the Human Resources and Training Division between 1980 and 1984, I strongly recommend that this program be continued for another three years.

***Revise the Words***    Just as a machine fails to function when a part is defective, so too does unclear and confusing writing cause the communication process to break down. It is like having to replace the worn machine part with a new one, for during the revision stage the writer replaces a vague, unfamilar, or imprecise word with a more concise and exact one.

All too often, however, people believe that the secret to effective writing rests solely in the ability to draw upon a vast vocabulary of fancy words and complex expressions. They fail to see that there is no point in substituting a difficult word for a simpler one merely to impress the reader. The road to effective writing, for some, is paved with spending many hours poring over dictionaries and preparing endless lists of words to memorize. While this is one method for building a vocabulary, a far more effective approach exists in underlining unknown words in newspaper and magazine articles, books, memos, letters, and reports, or in recording unfamiliar words and expressions overheard during a conversation, while listening to a speech, or even on the train home. The point is that people learn best about what they are most interested in knowing. Just as awareness of content and structure and the basic principles of composition can improve the quality of writing, so can knowledge of different words that convey similar meanings (synonyms) be an indispensable source of strength during the revision phase.

It is a good idea, then, for the writer to become familiar with either Roget's *Thesaurus* or any standard, recent dictionary of *synonyms*. These can be consulted when the writer is searching for the right word to ensure greater clarity. The following entry contains many words expressing similar meanings or variations of one idea:

*Humorist*- n. wit, punster, joker, jester, buffoon, mime, clown, gag-man, harlequin, charlatan, banterer.

**DICTION**  Diction refers to the style of writing determined by a writer's choice of words and phrases. Depending on the words selected, the writing can seem eloquent, formal, serious, humorous, informal, friendly, harsh, and even poetic. In speech, informal words and colloquial expressions are preferred. The following is an example of colloquial diction:

Our clients are talking about throwing more money into the cable TV ads.

For informal memos and letters, this style of writing is acceptable. Yet the same sentence may seem out of place in a formal status report prepared for a corporate chairperson. In such a case, the writer might choose a more standard format, as is true of the following sentence:

Our clients are planning to increase their budgets for advertising on cable television stations.

In preparing a business report, the writer draws upon experience, judgment, and common sense to create a diction that is appropriate to its topic and audience.

**SLANG AND REGIONALISMS**  Most report writers avoid slang and regionalisms because both are exclusive forms of expression that will be unfamiliar to those readers outside a particular circle, profession, group, or community. Regional expressions relate to specific geographic locations. Although they are often colorful, these terms will confuse readers outside the region. For instance, someone unfamiliar with the geographic reference of *bean-eater* (residents of Boston traditionally fond of baked beans) would take the word at its literal rather than geographic meaning. Or take the word *gig* used in the South to denote a child's toy but which is defined among jazz aficionados as a party or performance.

1. Johnny has a new *gig*. (toy)
2. Johnny went to a *gig* last night. (party)
3. Johnny's band is playing a *gig* at the Blue Note. (session)

**CONCRETENESS**  Some words are *abstract*, or general, vague and often inexact terms; others are *concrete*, or specific. In business report writing, as in any other, the writer should give preference to concrete words and phrases. This practice helps to avoid confusion or misunderstanding. Most readers will have little doubt about the precise meaning of the following sentence:

Our *marketing* consultant suggested a new *direct mail* campaign.

This next sentence, however, leaves a lot of room for imagination:

Some expert suggested a new campaign.

Hence, the obvious advantage of using concrete words is that they promote clarity and precision.

**JARGON**  Jargon is technical vocabulary or professional slang that is familiar to those who use it but confusing or unknown to others. For instance, there is legal jargon and there is business jargon. Additionally, those in medicine, academia, engineering, government, and the military all know and use specialized terms and expressions daily. However, jargon obscures and confuses effective writing when it is used excessively or without regard for the reader's background and level of understanding.

Imagine the average person attempting to understand the following excerpt from a financial statement:

Aggregate annual maturities of long-term debt during the five years after 1980 are as follows:

When we eliminate the jargon, the statement reads:

The amount of long-term debt that becomes due during each of the next five years is:

There is quite a difference between the two sentences. If the report writer knows that most readers share a common background and expertise, he or she can expect them to understand the jargon in the report. If the writer is uncertain of the reader's ability to understand specialized or technical language, it is best to define the term by using parentheses:

Our bank's amount of *demand deposits* (checking accounts) has increased significantly this year.

Give an example:

The photographic industry manufactures equipment and *sensitized materials*. The sensitized materials include photographic film, paper, plates, and chemicals.

Build an explanation into the sentence:

There is continual speculation that changes will occur in the Federal Reserve banks' *discount rate,* or interest rate charged on secured borrowings by member banks.

**"BIZBUZZ"**   William Safire once began an article on business jargon:

Nobody can apply for a job these days—or interface with a personnel recruiter in the hopes of impacting on his bottom line—without a degree in "bizbuzz," the jargon that prioritizes the career path of the rising young ballpark figurer. (*The New York Times,* September 19, 1982, p. 10)

Mr. Safire then listed and described a variety of "bizbuzz" words and expressions that have replaced simpler and clearer ones to such an extent that anyone unfamiliar with them would feel uncomfortable and baffled. The problem with "bizbuzz" is similar to using slang; each tends to be exclusive. Meaning is restricted to members only, and anyone outside the group will become easily frustrated and confused in deciphering the true meaning behind facade. As Safire further pointed out, many of the words which comprise "bizbuzz" are either grammatically incorrect (*finalize* is not a verb) or improperly used (*hands-on* originally meant "vocational" and now means "practical").

Jargon, whether technical, medical, legal, business, academic, or otherwise, will continue to be used by too many people. Yet any writer who wants to communicate clearly to his or her readers should use less jargon and more familiar words. The following is a list of common "bizbuzz" words and phrases:

Impact (often improperly used as a verb).
Interface (originally meant the joining point between two pieces).
Bottom line responsibility (*bottom line* originally denoted earnings).
Ballpark figure (rough estimate).
Back-of-the-envelope sum (a figure easily arrived at).
Bailout (used in place of *rescue*).
Belly up (used in place of *bankrupt*).
Hands-on (whose hands?).
Careerwise (an example, as well as those which follow, of the tendency to "marry" or combine words which were never meant for each other).
Industry-wide.
Smartwise.
Personnel-wide.
Labor-intensive.
Profit-intensive.
Assets-intensive.
Technology-intensive.
Manager style.

**CLICHÉS**    Clichés are overworked and overly familiar expressions that can diminish a report's effectiveness and originality. Although there is nothing intrinsically wrong with these often colorful phrases, the writer should avoid using clichés (or at best use them selectively). The following list includes some commonly used clichés:

After all is said and done
All work and no play
Better late than never
Too funny for words
Cold as ice
Green with envy
On the ball
Slowly but surely
By leaps and bounds
Last but not least
At this point in time
This day and age
Busy as a bee

**REDUNDANT TERMS**

Redundant terms are often referred to as *roundabout* expressions, because their meanings are repetitive and seemingly go in circles. Some examples are

| Redundancy | Meaning |
|---|---|
| universal the world over | universal |
| round in shape | round |
| true fact | true |
| large in size | large |
| absolutely nothing | nothing |
| total of five | five |
| throughout the whole | throughout |
| fewer in number | fewer |
| circle around | circle |
| advance warning | warning |
| but nevertheless | use either one |
| combine together | combine |
| green in color | green |
| advance planning | planning |

**ACTIVE VS. PASSIVE VOICE**   In addition to checking verbs for correct spelling and tense, the writer should prefer active to passive voice when he or she creates direct and forceful sentences. *Active voice* verbs place the emphasis on the subject:

> Joe took the test.

In *passive voice*, the subject is acted upon:

> The test was taken by Joe.

Notice how the active voice sentence is more vigorous and shorter than the passive construction. It has more life, and can subsequently best hold the reader's attention and interest. Here are some additional examples:

> *Passive:*   Your letter of the fifth *has been received,* and the order *will be shipped* immediately.
> *Active:*    *We have received* your letter and *will ship* your order immediately.

At the same time, *passive voice* has its uses, particularly when the writer wants to place the emphasis on an activity rather than on the actor:

> A decision has been reached concerning the proposal.

The passive voice is also acceptable when a process is described:

> The compound is then added to the mixture.

It is useful as well when the subject is unknown or should not be disclosed:

> The accounts-receivable book has been lost.

**VERBAL EXPRESSIONS**   Verbal expressions often consist of too many verbs to express an action or state of being. These excessively worded constructions rely on verbs such as *make, have, give,* and *be* (is, will). For instance, the following sentence contains too many verbs:

> The payroll office *has a need* for new equipment.

It can be revised to this:

The payroll office *needs* new equipment.

Additional examples:

The book *will be of use* to her in her business.
She can *use* this book in her business.

The manager *will have a talk* with the sales staff.
The manager *will talk* with the sales staff.

The writer can avoid writing verbal expressions by concentrating on the key verbs rather than on auxiliary or helping ones.

## REVISE THE SENTENCES

The ability to improve and clarify awkward, confusing, and wordy sentences during the revision stage depends on the ability to identify imprecise and unfamiliar words. The writer must also have an awareness of the relationships between the ideas.

For instance, sometimes ideas are *coordinate*, or equal in value or importance. The best way to join such ideas and to indicate their relationship is by connecting them with such conjunctions as *and, or, but, nor*, and phrases such as *either . . . or* and *neither . . . nor*. This will result in greater economy and clarity, as is indicated by these examples:

Ideas Before Coordination
1. Management desires greater understanding with labor. Labor also feels the need to understand management better.
2. Tony Powell is a fine candidate for the new sales director position. Equally promising, however, is Janet Kingsley. Either one would do a very good job.

Ideas After Coordination
1. Management *and* labor desire greater understanding of each other.
2. *Either* Tony Powell *or* Janet Kingsley would do a fine job as the new sales director.

At other times, ideas may be subordinate to each other. That is, one idea may be more important than the other, or may be dependent on another for expressing its meaning accurately. For example, in the statement

The accountant was late, and the boss wasn't in a good mood.

the relationship between both ideas (the accountant who was late and the boss's mood) is not clear. Did one cause the other? Or are these ideas totally unrelated? By subordinating one idea to the other, the cause-and-effect relationship becomes clear. This is because one part of the sentence becomes dependent on the other in conveying the true meaning:

Because the accountant was late, the boss wasn't in a good mood.

Words that often introduce dependent ideas include the following:

| | |
|---|---|
| after | though |
| although | unless |
| as | until |
| because | when |
| before | whenever |
| if | whether |
| since | while |

These words are helpful when subordinating ideas in sentences to distinguish primary from secondary emphasis, indicate the main thought among minor ones, and avoid awkward, choppy, or unclear sentences. Notice how connecting words and subordination contribute to clarifying the meaning of the following sentence:

*Before:*    Jack felt anxious after the interview. He knew he had a good chance of getting the job.

*After:*    *Even though* Jack felt anxious after the interview, he knew he had a good chance of getting the job.

When presenting ideas in a series, place the most important item last, to underscore its prominence in the reader's mind:

Mr. Burden listed three factors that had led to his success: luck, skill, and plain hard work.

Another helpful device in revising sentences involves *parallelism*. This concept is defined as the consistent grammatical expression of two or more coordinated ideas in a single sentence. When the words and phrases are parallel, they are balanced, so that the nouns, verbs, and other parts of grammar mirror one another, and result in a smooth flow of ideas. Here are some examples:

Nonparallel
1. Good writing involves being *clear* and *precision.* (Adjective and noun)
2. Jake has many hobbies. He *likes to build* model airplanes. *Racing* vintage sports cars is another pastime. The *collecting* of rare books *has been pursued* for the pleasure it offers him. (various verb tenses)
3. Mr. Marks likes to walk through Central Park every morning for the fresh *air* and *feeling to get some exercise* before going to his office. (noun and phrase)

Parallel
1. Good writing involves *clarity* and *precision.* (Two nouns)
2. Jake has many hobbies. These include *building* model airplanes, *racing* vintage sports cars, and *collecting* rare books. (consistent verb tense)
3. Mr. Marks likes to walk through Central Park every morning for the fresh *air* and *exercise* before going to his office. (two nouns)

At other times, *appositives* (words and expressions that either refer to or elaborate upon an item previously named), help to achieve tighter sentence structure. Notice how an appositive phrase can transform a series of loosely connected sentences into a tightly constructed one:

*Before:*   Mary Brown is an experienced public speaker. She will address the next annual convention of women executives. This will be held in Salt Lake City next summer.

*After:*   Debbie Schotz, *an experienced public speaker,* will address the next annual convention of women executives, *which* will be held in Salt Lake City next summer.

***Vary Sentences***   Monotonous sentences can lull the reader to sleep as fast as can wordy and confusing ones. To prevent this from happening, the writer should vary the sentences in terms of structure, length, and content. Simple sentences can be mixed with compound and complex sentences. At times, straightforward declarative statements can be offset by sentences that begin with dependent phrases and by others that are connected by commas, conjunctions, and semicolons. In some sentences, the ideas can be coordinated; in others subordinated. Statements of fact can comprise some sentences and opinions. A mixture of both will form others. The following are examples of the various ways in which an idea can be expressed:

Simple Statement (one independent idea)
Larry ordered a brandy and soda at the Ritz.

Compound Statement (two independent ideas joined by a
    conjunction)
Larry ordered a brandy and soda at the Ritz, and he listened to a jazz trio
for an hour.

Complex Statement (one independent and at least one dependent
    idea)
Even though he had little money left, Larry ordered a brandy and soda at
the Ritz.

Compound-Complex Statement (at least one dependent and two
    independent ideas)
Larry ordered a brandy and soda at the Ritz, and even though he had little
money left, he listened to a jazz trio for an hour.

*Revise According
to Specific Needs
and Style*

No standard approach exists to revising a report. Aside from reviewing it in terms of content and structure, every writer revises according to his or her needs and particular style. For some, a report is
never finished. One person can revise quickly; another needs three
days. The truth is that there is no such thing as a perfect report. The
practical writer will regard revising a report as a series of steps rather
than as a solitary procedure. The sole criteria for revision should be
that the final version of the report represents the writer's best work.
But follow one note of caution: over-revision leads less often to a
perfect report than to a disorganized one. Careful revision, along with
common sense, will produce coherent as well as well-written reports.

Remember that the following characteristics of a poorly written
report should be corrected when revising for content and structure:

- Too many specialized or unfamiliar words.
- Excessively long sentences and paragraphs.
- Little or no variety in sentence length.
- Confusing phrases and expressions.
- Redundant terms.
- Clichés.
- Slang and unnecessary technical jargon.
- Overuse of the passive voice.

- Lack of organization.
- Errors in spelling, punctuation, and grammar.

**SUBMIT A PROFESSIONAL MANUSCRIPT OF THE POLISHED REPORT**

The final or polished draft of the report should be prepared according to traditional guidelines or an organization's standard format. Even if the finished product is a printer's responsibility, the writer should submit a professionally prepared manuscript. Here are some basic guidelines:

1. Use good quality 8½″ × 11″ white bond paper. Unless asked to do so, avoid using brightly colored or fancy paper.
2. Leave margins of 1¼″ at the top and left-hand side; 1″ to 1½″ at the bottom and right-hand side of each page. If the report is to be bound, leave an additional ¼″ to ½″ at the left-hand margin to allow for binding.
3. Indent the first word of the first line of each paragraph five spaces.
4. Type the text of the report double-spaced. Use single-spacing for long passages quoted or paraphrased from secondary sources.
5. Capitalize the first word and key words in the title, *except* for articles (a, an, the), prepositions (in, of, from, etc.), and conjunctions (and, or, but, nor, etc.).
6. Center or type in line with the left-hand margin, titles, headings, and captions. For emphasis, titles may be underlined or typed in upper case letters. Place no punctuation after titles and headings.
7. Number all pages except front matter (preface, table of contents, title page) in Arabic numerals, beginning with page 1 on the first page of the report's text. Page numbers can either be centered at the bottom of the page (double- or triple-spaced beneath the last line of text) or in the upper right-hand margin two spaces above the top line of the text.

**CHAPTER REVIEW**

*Questions*

1. What aspects of a business report should the writer focus on during revision?

2. List the various methods for revising an earlier draft of a report.

3. Describe the ways a report's beginning might be improved.

4. How can a report's conclusion be revised for greater effectiveness?

5. Define *jargon* and *bizbuzz*. When might the use of each be appropriate in a report? When not?

6. Give five recent examples of jargon and bizbuzz from your own reading or experiences.

7. List three other obstacles to effective writing.

8. Distinguish between active and passive voice.

9. How can a writer vary sentence structure for greater interest and clarity?

10. Discuss the difference between coordinate and subordinate relationship of ideas.

## *Exercises*

1. Simplify the redundant expressions in the following sentences.
   a. The appeal of the movie is universal the world over because it contains a lot of true facts about space travel.
   b. The board chairman's new airplane was blue and silver in color and large in size.
   c. The front office will be combined together with the entrance foyer and green carpeting will be used throughout the whole room.
   d. Attendance for the conference has been fewer in number but nevertheless everyone is having a good time.
   e. The taxi had to circle around the block twice because Carl forgot the address.

2. Change the passive to active voice in these sentences.
   a. It has been observed by the chief engineer that too much time is being spent by laborers on construction of the bridge's tower.
   b. Reference is made to your letter of date June 24, 1984.
   c. This document was prepared by Mr. Wilson Townley at the request of Mr. Philip Dickens.

d. It has been found by the federal auditor to have been an oversight made by your accountant.

e. Your recommendations will thoroughly be reviewed by the board of directors and all comments will be submitted by them to you by September 1.

3. Eliminate unnecessary verbal expressions here.
   a. The manager has made a complete analysis of the incident.
   b. Jane O'Malley has made the suggestion that lunch hours be expanded to two hours.
   c. The specialist from the chemical division achieved the investigation of the water and made the conclusion that it was safe to drink.
   d. Dave decided to consider the shift in population if he wanted to achieve an accurate study.
   e. The waitress will have a talk with the night manager about working overtime.

4. Revise the following vague, inexact, and otherwise confusing sentences.
   a. I believe something has just occurred which may be concernable.
   b. Enclosed for your use are the following stuffs.
   c. It is requested that you analysis the impact of such an exposure to your company.
   d. To apply the document to our worldwide locations there, it should be as general and specific as possible for its acceptance.
   e. Quality candidates were sourced from both inside and outside XYZ to backfill.
   f. Your memo illustrates graphically why this problem has not been resolved over two years—the tendency to side-step the issue continues full bore.
   g. An urgent answer is required.
   h. Notify development manager whenever a program or project is superannuated.
   i. You now have the subject Corporate Procedures which supercede and override any previous procedures/instructions in your possession to the exclusive extent of any conflicting statements.

j. It was proposed to establish standards and procedures for ensuing homogeneity and synchronocity of data.

k. In this strategy-oriented environment, it is vital to trim down complex open-ended problems to key issues, thus forestalling an anticipated ad-hoc judgmental scenario at this point in time.

l. I postulate the ball into your court and assume you will address my concerns ASAP adequately sizing the what have you we'll need to wrangle some sense out of this. Let's stop waffling and drive a peg through the head of this knotty issue.

m. You must solution the problem by May 28.

n. A presentation is a string text form of a single instance of two entities in a participating relationship and any associated categorizations that makes that instance of the presentation unique.

o. It is agreed that the need for common interbusiness unit communication methodology will be accomplished by adopting a standard interface approach between the existing demand and supply systems.

5. Revise this passage containing a number of fancy, vague, and inexact expressions.

   This office is gratified to know that the allocation process has been accelerated somewhat and hopes that additional measures can be undertaken further to expedite this process. A procedure which might be initiated with a view to improving the classification problem would be to establish a practice whereby the analysts of the Civil Service Commission, prior to classifying a position at a grade lower than that recommended, would personally survey the position and afford the operating bureau an opportunity to discuss the proposed action with the Commission. If this were followed, misunderstandings surrounding the nature of duties involved in positions would be clarified and the institution of reconsideration and appeals processes might be precluded. Frequently the time lapse between the submission of the initial class sheets to the Civil Service Commission and the time the Commission has prepared to make final allocation has resulted in the development and crystallization of additional plans involving new responsibilities for the unit. A further investigation by the Commission analysts with the operating bureau might adduce more recent information which would affect classification of the positions. With respect to this problem it is anticipated that the imminent conferences with the Civil Service Commission will contribute to a better understanding.

## *Report Project*

1. Revise your report according to the guidelines outlined in this chapter.

2. Rewrite either the entire report or appropriate sections that are in need of substantial revision.

3. Proofread the entire report for both content and structure. Use the checklist provided on page 158.

# CHAPTER 10

# Writing an Abstract
# of the Report

**FUNCTION OF AN ABSTRACT**
An abstract summarizes and describes the major ideas in a report. Though an abstract is optional for short reports, it is essential for highly detailed, long ones. The benefit of an abstract is that it gives the busy reader the opportunity to review key points, findings, and conclusions amidst the ever-increasing daily flow of information generated through memos, letters, newspaper and magazine articles, and meetings.

**FORM AND CONTENT**
The abstract should occupy a separate page or pages. Usually an abstract represents 10 percent of the report's length. The information should be significant, yet it should be presented concisely and clearly. In short, an abstract is a precise mini-report. Repetition and abbreviations are to be avoided, and jargon must be kept to a minimum.

The abstract should not contain information that is not discussed in the report. This fault can occur if a writer constructs an abstract upon completing a report, and then revises the report by adding, deleting or altering information. The abstract must be revised to reflect those changes.

The ideal time to compose an abstract is after the report has been revised for content. An abstract should be placed before the entire body or text of the report, but it must not be confused with nor used instead of an introduction.

## COMPOSING AN ABSTRACT

On the surface, writing an abstract can appear deceptively simple. As a result, important details might be excluded, or the writer might list the facts in a series of awkward or incomplete sentences for the sake of brevity. When composing an abstract, use the following guidelines to produce an abstract that is complete and flows as smoothly as the text of the report.

- *Read* the entire report to determine the scope and point of view.
- *Underline* important sentences and phrases in each paragraph and section. Avoid including minor points or ideas.
- *Write* the underlined sentences in the order in which they appear.
- *Condense* ideas by eliminating unnecessary words and phrases, and by combining ideas from two or three sentences into one. Do not include anecdotes, illustrations or any other material that will encourage digression from the main ideas.
- *Organize* the material so that it flows smoothly. Use transitional words to link the ideas and show relationships. While an abstract should be concise, the sentences should not be incomplete; nor should they resemble the wording in a telegram.
- *Consider* the readers' needs when writing the abstract. Ask these questions: "What does my reader want to know about my report's subject?" "What are the report's key ideas?"
- *Review* the abstract for completeness. *Revise* it for clarity.

The following passage defines "business cycles." It is immediately followed by an abstract of its key ideas.

Business Cycles *

Business cycles are best defined as fluctuations in the general level of economic activity, or more specifically, in the levels of employment, production, and prices. The figures on the following pages show fluctuations in wholesale prices in four Western industrialized countries from 1790 to 1940.

* Excerpted from *Encyclopaedia Britannica*, p. 536.

Though some regularities in price movements are apparent, it is possible to ask whether the movements are regular enough to be called cycles.

The word cycle derives from the Greek word for circle. An object moving around a circle returns to its starting point; a wave motion, with upward and downward curves, may also be considered a cycle. The various movements characteristic of economic activity are not always as regular as waves, and for this reason some prefer to call them fluctuations.

There are many types of economic fluctuations. Because of the complexity of economic phenomena, it may be that there are as many types of fluctuations or cycles as economic variables. There are daily cycles in commuter traffic or the consumption of electricity, to cite only two examples. Almost every aspect of economic life displays seasonal variations: sales of coal or ice, deposits in savings banks, monetary circulation, agricultural production, purchases of clothing, travel, and so on. As one lengthens the span of observation, one finds new kinds of fluctuations such as the hog cycle and the wheat cycle, the inventory cycle, and the construction cycle. Finally, there are movements of general economic activity that extend over periods of years.

Business Cycles (abstract)

Business cycles are defined as fluctuations in general levels of economic activity: in employment, production, and prices. Because economic activity is not always as regular as a "wave" in movement, cycles may be referred to as fluctuations. There are as many types of fluctuations or cycles as economic variables; among these are daily and seasonal cycles in the use of electricity, savings bank deposits, agricultural production, and clothing purchases. By lengthening the observation span, one can find new kinds of fluctuations, including inventory or construction cycles. Some movements of general economic activity extend over periods of years.

## *CHAPTER REVIEW* *Questions*

1. Define an abstract.

2. What is the function of an abstract?

3. Who will most likely read an abstract of a business report?

4. How is the length of an abstract determined?

5. List the steps a writer follows when preparing an abstract.

## Exercises

1. Underline the key ideas in the following report.*

### Book Publishing: Sales Gains Moderating

Total book sales for 1981 could approximate $7.7 billion, an increase of 9.4% from the $7.04 billion estimated for 1980 by the Association of American Publishers (AAP). The 1980 tally is 11.2% above 1979's total of $6.33 billion. While virtually all segments of the book publishing industry are believed to have registered sales gains in 1981, price increases were probably the prime propellant behind the advances, since unit volume was up only about 1%. Assuming an improving economic climate, additional sales gains are expected for 1982.

According to AAP estimates, sales increases by major categories in 1980 were as follows: trade books, 17.0%; religious books, 19.0%; professional, 12.9%; book clubs, 7.3%; mail-order publications, 16.7%; mass-market paperbacks, 8.3%; university press publications, 18.7%; elementary and high school texts, 1.1%; college textbooks, 15.4%; standardized tests, 9.1%; subscription reference texts, 0.3%; and audio-visual materials, 13.9%.

The number of books published in the U.S. during 1981 declined 11.6% to 37,425 titles, from 42,377 in the previous year, according to *Bowker's Weekly Report.* Of the total number of books published in all subject categories during 1981, 30,808 were new titles, and 6,617 were new editions, including revisions, new treatments, reprints, etc. Hardcover titles accounted for 72.4% of the books published in 1981, down slightly from 73.7% in 1980. U.S.-published books that were imported totaled 3,830 titles in 1981, versus 5,390 in 1980.

### Education the Largest Segment

Sales of learning materials, as estimated by the AAP, amounted to $2.13 billion in 1980, compared with $1.96 billion in the prior year. The 1980 total broke down as follows: college textbooks, $952.7 million (44.8% of the total); elementary textbooks, $596.2 million (28.0%); high school textbooks, $344.1 million (16.2%); audio-visual and related media, $166.7 million (7.8%); and standardized tests, $67.2 million (3.2%). While textbooks and standardized tests accounted for 30% of total estimated book sales in 1980, this figure is substantially understated because it does not include other types of books that have educational uses.

Reflecting unfavorable trends in student enrollments, the student population, and birth rates, sales growth of textbooks for elementary and sec-

* From Standard and Poor's *Industry Survey,* October 1982, pp. C73–C76. Reprinted with permission.

ondary schools (el-hi) has not kept pace with that of many other segments of the book publishing industry. From 1972 through 1980, for example, sales of el-hi textbooks rose 89%, while trade, religious, and mass-market paperback books experienced gains of 186%, 199%, and 161%, respectively. Over that same period, gains recorded by the other segments of the educational market were: college textbooks, 154%; standardized tests, 154%; and audio-visual materials, 44%.

*Textbook Development Is Costly*

The development of el-hi instructional materials is a complex, time-consuming, and expensive procedure. Major instructional programs usually consist of a series of basic textbooks, as well as correlated materials in a variety of other formats. A new program in a basic subject area can require a prepublication investment of at least five years and expenditures approaching several million dollars.

Because of the hefty capital outlays necessary to publish a textbook series, as well as the difficulties involved in gaining educator acceptance, entry into the field is difficult. These constraints on new competition, however, allow the industry some degree of stability. The large capital demands favor concentration of the business among the larger publishers.

Since el-hi instructional programs are tailored to meet grade-level requirements in specific subject areas, they tend to be organized in series. College textbooks, however, are not similarly organized. College texts are written primarily by college and university faculty members, and the investment required for their development is lower. A trend that is expected to benefit publishers of educational materials is the "return to the basics"; at the el-hi level, the movement is back to reading, writing, and arithmetic, while college-level courses are more structured, with greater dependence placed on textbooks.

El-hi textbooks are sold to school systems, usually on a contract basis, with the majority of deliveries made in the first few years. Books are sold through either the "open territory" or "state adoption" methods. Under the open territory method, both the choice and the purchase of textbooks are made entirely by local school districts. Under the latter method, the state approves several acceptable texts, with the local districts then determining which books on the approved list will be purchased. While about half of the states maintain some form of approved lists, considerably less than half of the pupil population falls under the state adoption procedure.

College textbooks are sold directly to the student, primarily through school or private book stores. Since this type of selling involves considerably fewer books than does the sale of an el-hi textbook to an entire school district, college texts typically carry a higher price tag. There is also an active used-book market in college texts, which reduces sales of new books within two or three years of publication.

Used books account for approximately 20% of all college bookstore sales. However, when sales by private bookstores and transactions between individuals are included in the tally, the aggregate market for used textbooks is probably much larger. As tuition costs climb, students increasingly look to the purchase of used books to save money, with the result that secondhand books have been garnering an increasing share of the college textbook market in recent years. With prices generally 25% below those of new books, the demand for used college texts exceeds the supply.

*School Enrollment Declining*

According to projections by the Department of Education, student enrollment for the 1981–82 school year will total approximately 56.6 million, 1.8% below the 57.7 million of the preceding year. Elementary and secondary school enrollment is expected to total 44.9 million students (versus 46.1 million in 1980–81). Of this total, the elementary grades (kindergarten through grade eight) will account for 30.6 million (31.2 million), and high school (grades nine through 12) 14.3 million (14.9 million). College and postsecondary enrollment is estimated at 11.7 million (a gain of about 79,000 students).

Elementary school enrollments have been declining since 1969, as earlier fall-offs in the birth rate have led to a decrease in the five- to 13-year-old population. However, this trend is expected to be reversed in the mid-1980s, as recent increases in the birth rate result in a larger number of individuals in this age group. High school enrollments, which have been declining since 1976, are expected to drop further during the balance of the decade as a result of continued reductions in the 14- to 17-year-old population. Another decline in college enrollment is expected in the 1982–83 school year, a trend that is likely to continue throughout the 1980s.

While these demographics will result in a shrinking customer base for several years, the declining enrollments and the accompanying reduction in demand for classrooms and teachers should make a larger portion of the educational dollar available for books and other learning materials. Supporting this contention is the fact that outlays for classroom materials have traditionally accounted for less than 1% of educational spending.

For the 1981–82 school year, the National Center for Educational Statistics (NCES) estimates that spending for education will total $198 billion, versus $181 billion in 1980–81. Of the total, elementary and secondary schools should spend $127 billion, while outlays by public and private colleges and universities are estimated at $71 billion. Public institutions are expected to spend $161 billion, while expenditures by private institutions are estimated at $37 billion. Funding sources for these expenditures are estimated by the NCES as follows: $20 billion (10% of the total) from the federal government; $77 billion (39%) from state governments; $50 billion (26%) from local governments; and $51 billion (26%) from private sources (fees, tuition, endowment incomes, gifts, etc.).

*Breakdown of Book Sales by Type*

*Trade books* are marketed to consumers, principally through bookstores, and to libraries. While the trade segment encompasses primarily hardcover books, the percentage of paperback books has been rising. Trade books include both adult and juvenile titles, ranging from fiction to many nonfiction subjects.

During 1980 (latest available), total trade book sales rose 17.0% to $1.27 billion (18.0% of the overall book market, as estimated by the AAP). The various subsectors making up the trade segment recorded the following increases: adult hardbound, 14.4% to $695.9 million; adult paperbound, 24.5% to $364.6 million; juvenile hardbound, 11.2% to $168.5 million; and juvenile paperbound, 26.4% to $42.3 million.

*Religious books* consist primarily of Bibles and prayer books, as well as other works, such as theological treatises. While these books are distributed mainly through specialized bookstores, some titles related to wider subject areas may be sold elsewhere as trade or textbooks. In 1980, sales of religious books reached an estimated $351.4 million (5.0% of total book sales), up 19.0%, year to year.

*Professional books* are divided into medical, technical, scientific, business, and other categories. These books are directed specifically at persons in related occupations. Although professional books may be used in educational programs, this is a secondary market. Sales of professional books in 1980 rose 12.9%, year to year, to $999.1 million, or 14.2% of total book industry sales. By segments, technical/scientific books climbed 11.2% to $334.8 million, business and other professional books advanced 14.7% to $424.4 million, and sales of medical books were up 12.1% to $239.9 million.

*Book clubs* are simply channels of distribution for books published by others. However, some clubs do arrange for the printing of their own editions for distribution to members. Books clubs are divided into consumer, or general-interest, clubs and special-interest clubs. In 1980, book club sales increased 7.3% to $538.3 million and accounted for 7.6% of total sales.

*Mail-order publications* are titles created specifically to be marketed by direct mail to the consumer. These books may be either one-time offerings, or part of a continuing series on a particular subject. Unlike book clubs, there is no commitment to purchase a minimum number. The market for these books expanded 16.7%, year to year, to $566.9 million in 1980 and accounted for 8.1% of all book sales.

*Mass-market paperbacks,* either original titles or reprints of titles originally published in hardcover, are sold primarily through newsstands, drugstores, chain retail stores, and general and paperback bookstores. Besides utilizing a different method of distribution than trade paperbacks, mass-market paperbacks are usually printed on less costly paper, have flashier covers, and normally measure $4\frac{1}{4} \times 7$ inches.

Sales of mass-market paperbacks amounted to $653.3 million in 1980, 8.3% above those of a year earlier, and represented a 9.3% share of the total book market. A problem for mass-market paperback publishers is the waste arising from unsold copies. According to the AAP, returns in 1980 for a representative group of rack-size paperback book publishers averaged 34.4% of gross dollar sales and 37.1% of unit sales.

*University press publications* originate as nonprofit adjuncts to universities, museums, or research institutions. Titles are similar in subject matter and distribution to trade or professional books, but they tend to concentrate on scholarly or regional topics. This market expanded 18.7%, year to year, in 1980 and represented 1.1% of total book sales.

*Educational publications and materials* account for a good chunk of the book publishing industry. Sales of elementary and secondary school texts climbed 1.1% to $940.3 million (13.4% of the total) in 1980, while college textbooks advanced 15.4% to $952.7 million (13.5%). Standardized tests, which are used to provide general measures of intelligence, aptitude, ability, and achievement, accounted for sales of $67.2 million in 1980 (1.0%). 9.1% above those of a year earlier. Sales of audio-visual products (2.4%) rose 13.9% to $166.7 million, from $146.3 million in 1979.

*Subscription reference books* primarily comprise sets of encyclopedias sold through the mail, door to door, and to libraries. Dictionaries, atlases, and other publications are also included in this category, which totaled $384.7 million (5.5%) in 1980, up a slight 0.3% from 1979.

2. Organize the ideas in a logical order.

3. Write an abstract of the report.

4. Visit your library. Select and write an abstract of a business article from a newspaper, magazine, or journal.

## *Report Project*

Write an abstract of your report according to the method outlined on p. 180.

# CHAPTER 11

# Oral Reports

*Speak briefly and to the point.*
—*Cato*

**ORAL VS. WRITTEN REPORTS**

At first glance, the most noticeable difference between an oral and written report is in the manner of presentation, namely the use of the spoken word (sound) as opposed to the printed one (symbol) to convey an idea. As a result, the subtle distinctions between the two modes of reporting may not be immediately apparent. Both methods provide information in the form of facts, opinions, judgments, numerical data, conclusions, and recommendations. Both require similar tasks during preparation: (1) the purpose and scope of the report must be identified; (2) the audience must be analyzed; (3) a plan must be devised to investigate and develop the presentation of key ideas and major points; (4) illustrations and other visual aids may be employed to aid the reader's or listener's understanding; and (6) the tone and approach can be either formal or informal, depending on the occasion, nature, and scope of the topic.

On closer examination, however, it becomes apparent that there are advantages and differences unique to both oral and written reports. As a tangible document, composed of so many pages and various tables, graphs, charts, and other illustrations, the written report somehow conveys a concreteness and permanence that underscores its importance. Even though the reader may scan the report at a leisurely pace, the reading process requires active participation on his or her part. This often leads to the reader's feeling of involvement with the topic. Also, the written report can be read in part or in its entirety. Certain passages can be marked and highlighted, commented upon in the margin, or read again at another time.

The oral report, by contrast, offers the speaker the opportunity verbally to emphasize major points through vocal tone, inflection, volume, and well-timed pauses. The oral reporter can offer explanations and otherwise clarify any confusion and misunderstanding that may arise in the listener's mind during the question-and-answer period that often follows the presentation. At the same time, the oral report allows the speaker to address many "readers" at once, thus conveying important ideas to a large percentage of the audience for whom the report was designed to reach. Also, an oral report conveys a sense of certainty that key ideas have indeed been transmitted to a particular audience. There is less fear or doubt that the report has been given attention.

Oral reporting permits greater flexibility in terms of grammatical correctness, usage, and punctuation. Of course, oral reports cannot blatantly violate the rules of standard English usage and principles of composition. Rather, the speaker, through interjected phrases and words and through facial and bodily expressions, gains a certain leverage not easily undertaken in a written report. A written report insists on a tighter structure and economy of expression.

Finally, though a writing style can convey a distinct personality on paper, the very physical presence of a speaker can reinforce an audience's view of his or her friendliness, intelligence, sincerity, and competence. The speaker can quite possibly influence the listener's positive and negative reaction to the content.

Unless someone is specifically requested to present a report in writing or orally, he or she can choose which mode is best to effectively convey essential information. Should the oral format be selected, there are a number of points that should be considered to insure the success of the presentation.

**PLAN THE PRESENTATION**

Like a written report, an oral presentation requires careful planning. Important factors to consider include the scope, purpose, and focus of the report, as well as questions regarding the organization and development of major ideas and findings. The fact that information will be orally expressed lends an added perspective to the presentation. To be truly effective, a middle ground must be sought somewhere between thorough expression of ideas and conciseness. This combination can be achieved if the speaker does the following:

- Avoids discussing difficult and complex ideas and principles in excessive detail.
- Limits the use of facts and numerical data to supporting key ideas and findings.
- Presents the most important points at the beginning or end.
- Summarizes main ideas in the concluding remarks.
- Uses an informal, conversational style of speech.

Even though the report may first be written out, the bulk of the findings can be adjusted to fulfill the twin demands of an oral presentation—maintaining the interest of an audience and keeping within a limited time span.

**CONSIDER THE SETTING AND THE AUDIENCE**

Unless the setting and the audience are carefully considered, the chances of sustaining the listener's attention are indeed slim. The setting or location where the report is to be delivered is a crucial factor in determining the best presentation. Will the report be addressed to a small group in a conference room? Or will the audience number many hundreds assembled in a large lecture hall or auditorium? Does the room have a great many windows that might offer distractions to the listener? Is the room illuminated merely by glaring light bulbs or soft overhead lamps? Are there paintings, murals, signs, or other illustrations on the walls that might distract the audience from what is being said? If possible, then, the speaker should visit the room and walk around it, considering these and other questions in order to decide where best to place the lectern for maximum effect and visibility.

The need to analyze a report's audience is no less important for an oral presentation than it is for a written one. The same questions must be posed in terms of the listeners' background, interest in the report's topic, and ability to comprehend any complex or possibly unfamiliar material. The speaker must try to identify the audience clearly in order to hold its attention. He or she must decide if the presentation should be informal or formal. Should the speech include a number of entertaining anecdotes, or should it be limited strictly to factual findings? Should the speaker perhaps allow for a question-and-answer period directly following the discussion? Ignoring one's audience will almost certainly invite indifference in return. This is true no matter how dynamic the speaker, or how interesting the topic.

**DETERMINE THE LENGTH OF THE REPORT**

When listeners begin to shift nervously or uncomfortably in their seats after fifteen minutes, or begin to look for something to read, or stare at the ceiling, there is one reason for those telltale signs of lack of interest and boredom. The speaker is taking too much time getting to the point. Often this has to do with excessively worded sentences or an uninteresting delivery style. For the most part, however, the speaker has mistakenly assumed the audience shares his or her interest and enthusiasm for the topic to such an extent that economy and precision of expression could be forgotten. For this reason, it is essential to assume the listener's chair and ask these questions:

1. How would I like this topic presented? Formally or informally?
2. What would make me interested in following each word of the presentation: Suspense? A dynamic speaking style? Topical relevance?
3. What can be done to enhance or highlight certain aspects of the topic under discussion? Films? Slides? Drawings? Anecdotes?
4. Given the subject matter, at what point in the presentation might my mind begin to wander? After twenty minutes? In the middle? During the slide show?
5. Which points are most important to the listener? Are they clearly related and illustrated by ample examples and details?
6. Am I getting too much—or not enough—information?

Answering these questions will help the speaker determine not only an appropriate method for presenting the information but also a means of determining the length of the report. A sense of timing is indispensable to the public speaker and more than welcomed by an audience.

**PREPARE AN OUTLINE**

For many speakers, the greatest fear is that at some crucial point in the discussion their minds will suddenly go blank, and they will embarrassingly stutter and stumble from one incohesive thought to another until memory suddenly puts them on the right track again. The mere anticipation of such an occurrence can lead to unnecessary mental and emotional anxiety.

At the same time, the very awareness of this dreaded possibility works to offset the actual loss of memory. A number of steps can be taken to diminish the likelihood of forgetting important ideas. For one, long sentences should be reduced to key phrases that contain enough information to serve as "touchstones" to memory. For instance, observe the following sentences:

> The School of Business Education serves approximately 1,500 students, of which 60% are undergraduate and 40% graduate students, with a full time faculty of 30.

This statement can be reduced to:

> School of Business Education, 1,500 students.
> 60 percent undergraduate, 40 percent graduate.
> 30 full time faculty.

On a larger scale, an outline of the complete report can be constructed from noting key phrases, passages, or numerical data either on 3″ x 5″ index cards, which should be numbered, or on sheets in a loose-leaf binder. The various topics can be developed through the use of one or more of the same thought patterns that a report writer would use: *problem–solution*, *cause–effect*, *definition–example*, *comparison–contrast*, and *order of importance* or *chronology*. These relationships can be indicated on the note cards that can be rearranged according to the speaker's needs prior to the presentation.

In this way, the speaker has available a general outline of the entire report, as well as a list of key points and details that can be elaborated upon during the presentation according to the audience's response and apparent interest. A speaker therefore can feel a lot less pressure to remember and deliver each bit of information. An outline ensures greater flexibility in delivering the presentation. Assuredly, an outline can serve as a memory booster at a time when every bit of reassurance is welcome.

**CONSIDER USING VISUAL AIDS**

Just as a written report contains illustrations, graphs, tables, and other graphic aids that may be necessary to clarify vital points, so too can an oral report be supported by films, slides, charts, models, and chalkboards.

Because we live in an audio-visual age, and more people watch the evening news on television than read a book or newspaper, the public speaker should wisely use available audio-video technology to enhance the presentation. At the same time, the use of video-casette recorders, closed circuit television, tape recorders, and other visual-aid devices must be selective and tempered by good judgment and taste to avoid the danger of opting for sensationalism rather than informative substance.

As a general rule, visual aids should lend either credence, clarity, or support to a discussion. Once the oral report is judged suitable or in need of illustrations, the following guidelines should be observed:

1. Limit the amount of information each visual aid provides.
2. When using chalkboards, charts, and overhead transparencies, write ideas in the form of phrases or telex language rather than in long sentences or paragraphs. When possible, *print* rather than write the information.
3. Be certain the room or lecture hall is conducive to visual-aid equipment. Check to see if the equipment is available for the day of the presentation.
4. Set up the visual apparatus where everyone can easily view it.
5. If the equipment appears complicated or difficult to use, request a technician's assistance.
6. Decide the appropriate size of a screen for films and slides. Base the decision on the room size and number of expected listeners.
7. Place information on charts and chalkboards *before* the presentation.
8. Use printed handouts for large audiences. Remember that these can also prove distracting, so use them with discretion and only when absolutely necessary for clarification or illustration of key ideas.

9. Rehearse in advance the moments when visual aids will be used. Note their occurrence on notecards in red pen or other form of highlighting.
10. Address comments always to the audience, not toward the visual aid. Be careful not to block anyone's view through bodily movement.

Once the oral report has been carefully planned in terms of content, setting, audience analysis, preparation of an outline, and possible use of visual aids, the next step is to consider the best means of actually delivering the presentation.

**PRESENTING THE ORAL REPORT**

Most people who deliver oral reports are not professional speakers. For the most part, they are average individuals who have varying degrees of experience in public speaking. Yet with patience, practice, and a sincere belief that what they have to say is important, these people can project a confident, appealing and well-informed image. Some speakers are naturally shy, while others are more outgoing; some like to share their thoughts openly, while others are more reclusive and private; some welcome a challenge and the opportunity to expand their skills, while others tremble at the idea of attempting something new.

Speaking in front of a group of any size can intimidate anyone who has rarely publicly expressed his or her thoughts. Stage fright and nervousness can afflict the seasoned as well as novice public speaker. Even so great and experienced an actor as Laurence Olivier recently testified in his autobiography to having suffered stage fright even after many years of performing in the theater.

Some public speakers have a natural charisma and appealing style. Most others have to work very hard and long to perfect what is often referred to as "platform communication skills." Although few individuals ever deliver a speech with the vitality and eloquence of Winston Churchill or John F. Kennedy, there are a number of steps the average person can follow to deliver a winning report.

*Be Prepared*

Being prepared in terms of subject knowledge, audience needs, and presentation will generate confidence in the least of self-assured speakers. The speaker's awareness of what has to be said in what manner to a specific audience is the key to capturing and holding the most reluctant listener's interest. By focusing on the report's major ideas, and by highlighting and commenting on those details that clearly lend support to any findings and conclusions, the speaker indicates both a sense of having done homework and a sincere regard for the audience's time and patience. If an audience decides that a speaker has not adequately prepared for the presentation, or that the content of the talk is unimportant or irrelevant to particular interests and needs, he or she might as well step down from the podium. Careful preparation will not go unrewarded; nor will it go unnoticed, because the listener will return in kind the same respect and consideration that led the speaker to construct a thoroughly informative report.

## Rehearse the Presentation

Just as professional stage actors rehearse long and hard before opening night, the public speaker must also practice his or her presentation. There is no set time for rehearsing a speech. One, two, or ten hours may be adequate for some presentations; others may require two or three weeks. At best, the time should be broken into segments that can be repeated at various intervals—perhaps every two days—with a final practice session just before the actual delivery. Keep in mind that the rehearsals should occur neither a month before nor solely the night before the presentation.

For the speaker, the great comfort of rehearsing an oral report is that it causes, familiarity with the actual presentation of ideas. To reinforce this awareness, the speaker might note major points either alphabetically or numerically. He or she should also develop cues for visual aids. Items that require dramatic emphasis should be underlined in red or preceded by an asterisk (*). One direct by-product of rehearsing is decreased nervousness and anxiety and increased facility in delivering the presentation. For these reasons alone, the importance of rehearsal should not be taken lightly. The very quality of the writer's oral presentation can be increased immeasurably by practice.

## Dress Neatly and Appropriately

Few speakers would address an audience in their underwear or in formal evening dress accompanied by sneakers. The speaker's clothing should reflect both good taste and be appropriate for the occasion. No one can dictate taste and fashion to another. Taste, like style, evolves from someone's personality and judgment. What one person prefers in clothes is often disdained by another. Although various professions almost stereotypically insist on regimental dress codes (gray and blue pin-stripe suits for bankers; gold chains for Hollywood producers) there should be some expression of individuality in the way a speaker dresses.

Just as charm and wit cannot be taught, good taste and common sense must emanate from within. If a man strolls on stage before a convention or meeting of his company's stockholders wearing orange pants decorated with blue and gold fish, it would be very difficult for anyone in that audience to pay more attention to what he is saying than to his trousers. This speaker has made the fatal mistake of calling more attention to himself than to his presentation. Perhaps a simple blue suit, white shirt, and attractive but not outlandish tie would be more suitable for the occasion. At the same time, someone addressing a group of executives at a Florida poolside luncheon would best avoid wearing a tuxedo and black patent leather shoes if the chances are that everyone else will be dressed casually. In the end, there is no standard way to dress for success during an oral presentation. There can, however, be disastrous consequences for anyone who fails to give the subject serious thought or who ignores it entirely.

## *Be Aware of Body Language*

Body language, or nonverbal communication, involves facial expressions, gestures, and other bodily movements that can transmit unconscious signals, messages, or feelings. It can be interpreted in a positive or negative way by other people. For example, a clenched fish can indicate anger or nervousness; hands folded and placed on top of someone's head can indicate boredom or impatience. The public speaker must be aware of his or her body language to avoid misunderstanding on the part of the listener. Distracting physical movements can undercut the effectiveness of a speech.

A good speaker is careful not to speak too loudly, to overgesticulate by flailing the arms wildly, or to pound a lectern incessantly. Also distracting are excessive grinning (which may result from nervousness or an attempt to appear relaxed) and frowning (perhaps the result of an attempt to project a serious image). The best image, of course, is the one that feels most natural. If someone is reserved by nature, he or she should not try to seem overly friendly and outgoing. By the same token, a pleasant individual should make every use of his or her enjoyment of people. No speaker should give any indication of straining to be what he or she is not.

Above all else, the speaker should assume a relaxed yet erect posture. He or she should stand comfortably and naturally to have a positive effect on the listener. An unnaturally stiff and awkward posture will generate a negative response.

**Speak Clearly**    Mumbling words, and speaking in a very low tone of voice or in a monotone tend to tranquilize rather than stimulate the listener. At all times, the speaker should enunciate every word and phrase in as natural a voice as possible. Difficult words should be pronounced correctly. Fill-in words such as "uh," "like," and "you know" must be avoided. Nor should the words be uttered too fast or too slowly.

In emphasizing important ideas and passages, the voice tone can be raised slightly, then followed by a pause, which in turn is followed by repeating the idea or point. All speakers, perhaps, would do well to bear in mind Hamlet's advice on public speaking and acting:

> Speak the speech, I pray you, as I pronounced it to you, trippingly [naturally] on the tongue; but if you mouth it, as many players do, I had as lief [just as soon] the town-crier spoke my lines. Nor do not saw the air too much with your hand, thus; but use all gently: for in the very torrent, tempest, and—as I may say—whirlwind of passion, you must acquire and beget a temperence [moderation] that may give it smoothness.
> —*Hamlet III, ii, 1–8*

Anyone who can combine a pleasant tone of voice with a well-balanced modulation of pitch, clarity of enunciation, and natural expression will undoubtedly deliver a convincing, appealing, and effective oral presentation.

**Establish Eye**    People tend to place greater trust and confidence in someone who
**Contact**    can establish direct eye contact (not to be confused with staring) during a conversation or while delivering a speech. There is often a great resistance to those who continually cast their eyes downward or sideways, and this kind of eye behavior will never engender trust from an audience. The best approach, perhaps, is either to glance at

various individuals in the audience from time to time, being careful not to focus on anyone too long, or to fix an eye on an object, an area, or some point in the rear or nearby distance. Whatever the choice of method, the speaker's credibility with an audience will be greatly heightened. This can lead to enthusiasm rather than resistance to the ideas presented.

## *Don't Just Read the Report*

A speaker who merely reads a report for more than a few minutes is certain to lose the audience's attention. One reason for this is probably related to the similarity between an oral presentation and a conversation. In both cases the speaker should convey a sense of animation, interest, enthusiasm, and participation. Not many people enjoy a one-sided discussion with another person. So too does an audience, whether large or small, want to feel that a speaker is talking *to* rather than *at* them. Reading a report, unfortunately, robs the speaker of the lively give-and-take the same information might generate in a conversation or meeting.

Therefore, the means of delivering the information should vary. At some moments, the speaker can glance at the note cards or paper that outline key points in their order of presentation. At other times, some information can be relayed from memory or in an ad-lib manner. Perhaps the talk can be sprinkled with interesting facts or anecdotes, not merely to distract or entertain, but to invest it with a liveliness and momentum that is graceful from beginning to end. What is a speech, after all, but a conversation with a number of people who are in need of or who are interested in the tale the speaker has to tell? An oral report should never be confused with a lecture.

## OPENING THE PRESENTATION

There is no guaranteed way of attracting an audience's attention during the opening moments of an oral presentation. However, if listeners are not "hooked" in the midst of the opening remarks, there is little chance they will come around and be aroused during the middle or at the end of the discussion. The initial minutes of an oral report thus are important in terms of generating the audience's curiosity and underscoring the importance of the topic. There are, however, a number of proven techniques the speaker can use to get an audience involved at the beginning. Here are some suggestions:

**1. Offer Interesting Facts.**   Sometimes unusual or controversial bits of information can get the listener to listen. Yet no speaker need rely on sensational gimmicks to attract an audience's attention. The information might concern an unusual fact that may not be widely known or has yet to be publicly disclosed. For example:

> It is hard to believe that despite the enormous educational opportunities in the United States there are over 25 million functionally illiterate Americans.

**2. Involve the Listener.**   All successful sales people know they must first succeed in getting a potential customer's attention before writing an order. This fact is no less important for the public speaker, who must involve the listener or else face an indifferent, and perhaps bored, audience. One method is to state something of importance to the listener. For example:

> What can we do about this problem that is certain to undermine our political and economic stability and growth in the coming decade?

**3. Use a Suitable Quotation.**   Here the speaker must be careful to select quotations that are relevant to the development of the topic. These should be neither too long nor complex. They should instead be precise and colorful touchstones for launching a discussion. Note the following quotations:

> "There is only one thing in the world worse than being talked about, and that is not being talked about."
> —*Oscar Wilde*, Picture of Dorian Gray

> "There was things which he stretched, but mainly he told the truth."
> —*Mark Twain*, The Adventures of Huckleberry Finn

Each quotation would provide an excellent introduction to reports on advertising. The first might introduce a discussion of the relationship between advertising and sales; the second might precede a study of truth in advertising. The combination of wit and wisdom provides the speaker with an entertaining yet relevant and thought-provoking basis for further discussion.

**4. Relate an Anecdote.**   The speaker can tell an amusing story or relate an interesting anecdote. All anecdotes should be relevant to the topic and serve as a suitable lead-in to the body of the discussion. Also, they should not be very long; nor should they be one-line jokes containing a punchline designed to get a laugh and little else. In selecting an anecdote, the speaker must exercise good taste and discretion lest any member of the audience take exception to any implied sarcasm or criticism behind the story, whether real or imagined. Here is one way someone might introduce a report on functional illiteracy in the United States:

> The other day I was absolutely astounded when the computerized cash register at my local supermarket broke down, and the cashier was unable to manually add up the prices of a gallon of milk, a dozen eggs, a box of dog biscuits, and a loaf of bread. Almost ten minutes must have gone by before she reached a total figure. Another five minutes must have passed as she subtracted the price from a twenty-dollar bill, and another few minutes passed before she gathered the correct change.
>
> My experience is not unique. Quite a number of people have told me similar stories involving someone's inability to fill out a job application, understand simple instruction, or read a bus schedule. I was not all that surprised, then, to learn that more than twenty-five million native-born Americans are functionally illiterate. After looking into this phenomenon, I'd like to share my findings with you today in discussing the state of basic skills in the U.S. work force.

**5.  *Provide Background Information.***   Background information provides a smooth introduction to an oral report, and gives the listener a frame of reference for judging and evaluating the report's central concerns. Very often this information can include definitions of terms that will be repeated throughout the report. It can also state the purpose of the report, any factors that may have limited its success such as time, or the unavailability of data, and any other insights which may help the listener fully appreciate the findings.

The amount of details should be kept to a minimum, to avoid distracting the listener from the main thrust of the presentation. The purpose should be to orient the audience toward the report's focus and scope rather than merely to overwhelm with endless facts and figures. Here is a successful statement:

> Last year 35 percent of the corporations surveyed for this report repeated basic high school training for their employees. One major communications firm spends $6 million dollars a year to train 14,000 employees in basic reading, writing, and math skills.
>
> This report will examine the causes for this crisis in basic skills among the American work force, and offer some possible solutions to this problem.

The factual background data here clearly allows the speaker to effect a smooth transition to the body of the report. It offers disturbing examples of the problem the major discussion will address as well as a framework to judge its importance.

**SUSTAINING THE LISTENER'S INTEREST**

Once the presentation is underway, the speaker must sustain the listener's interest by offering additional details and thoughts that both stimulate attention and develop the major premise. Digression and unnecessary repetition will only impede the forward momentum established by a good beginning. Therefore, the oral reporter must take care to construct a well-organized presentation plan that will convey the main ideas in a concise yet thorough manner.

**CONCLUDING THE PRESENTATION**

While the opening remarks of the presentation must attract the audience's attention, and the body of the discussion must sustain it, the conclusion is equally important in making a lasting impression and reinforcing key points and findings. The ending is an apt time to offer conclusions and recommendations or to urge action of some kind. As with a written report, no new information should be offered that has not been previously discussed. When the presentation is finished, a simple ''Thank you'' is the best postscript.

**CHAPTER REVIEW**

*Questions*

1. Note the factors that can contribute to an oral report's success.

2. List the characteristics unique to oral reporting.

3. What factors should the speaker consider about the report's audience and setting?

4. Discuss the value and use of visual aids.

5. How can a speaker achieve maximum effect with visual aids?

6. List the steps a speaker can take to insure the success of an oral report.

7. Discuss the role of voice and diction in relation to body language.

8. Comment on the importance of appropriate dress and appearance.

9. List three ways to open a speech effectively.

10. Summarize the qualities of a lively, informative oral report.

## Exercises

1. Discuss the similarities and differences between a written and oral report.

2. Describe a time or occasion when a speaker's manner and physical appearance influenced your response to a speech or lecture.

3. Construct an outline for a five–ten minute oral report in which you do the following:
   a. Discuss a matter of interest concerning a social, political, business, or academic topic.
   b. Argue for or against a controversial issue on campus or for a specific profession or industry.
   c. Describe a favorite hobby or pastime.

4. Evaluate a speech or talk delivered by a prominant individual on television, or a class lecture by a professor, or speech presented by someone to a convention or gathering you once attended. Use the guidelines discussed in this chapter as criteria for judgment.

5. If the equipment is available, tape-record or videotape an oral presentation that can be evaluated by you yourself, by a classmate, or by a class at large.

## Report Project

Transform your report into an oral presentation, bearing in mind the needs of the audience, appropriate tone, amount of details, and possible visual aids.

# CHAPTER 12

# English Usage Handbook (Including Exercises)

**SUBJECT AND VERB AGREEMENT**

A subject and verb must agree in number and person.

|  | Singular | Plural |
|---|---|---|
| First person: | I walk | we walk |
| Second person: | you walk | you walk |
| Third person: | he walks |  |
|  | she walks | they walk |
|  | it walks |  |

Most writers have little problem with typical sentences that have clearly either a singular or plural subject.

> He works every day.
> The boys are going fishing today.
> Bob and Jane have moved to New York.

Some subjects, however, can pose a problem for the writer.

***Collective Words.*** Collective words refer to a group of people or things. They take *singular* form when members act as a unit.

> The school *board* is visiting the new district.

They take plural form when members act individually:

The *jury* <u>are taking</u> their seats.

The following list includes some collective words:

| | |
|---|---|
| assembly | department |
| association | faculty |
| audience | family |
| board | firm |
| cabinet | group |
| class | jury |
| commission | majority |
| committee | minority |
| company | number |
| corporation | orchestra |
| council | public |
| crowd | staff |

The following collective words are singular, though they appear plural in form:

news
apparatus
summons

They are used as in the next example:

The evening *news is* entertaining.

These collective words are plural:

assets
earnings
odds
premises
savings
wages
winnings

For example:

The *odds are* in his favor.


**Indefinite Pronouns.**   Indefinite pronouns require singular verbs. Study the following list:

anybody
anyone
any one
anything
each
either
every
everyone
everybody
everything
neither

Here is an example:

*Everyone has* arrived for the party.

When two singular subjects are joined by *or, either . . . or,* or *neither . . . nor,* the verb is singular:

*Either* Jack *or* Mary *is* going to win the prize.

In the case of two plural subjects joined by *or, either . . . or, neither . . . nor,* the verb is plural:

*Neither* the boys *nor* their fathers *are* expected today.

If the subject includes a singular and plural noun, the verb agrees with the nearer word:

*Either* the Prime Minister *or* her *assistants are* arriving this morning.

**Words that Measure.** Words that denote measurement require a singular verb:

*Fifty dollars is* the average price of dinner at that restaurant.

However, when the items being measured are viewed individually, use a plural verb:

*Fifty dollars are* in that jar on the counter.

When fractions and expressions that denote measurement are followed by a prepositional phrase, the object of the phrase determines the number of the verb:

*Three-fourths* of the report *is* completed.
*Three-fourths* of the reports *are* completed.

The term "the number" is singular; "a number" is plural:

*The number* of birds on the lawn *is* surprising.

*A number* of stockholders *are* happy today.

**Titles and Names.** Titles of books, articles, reports, plays, art, and subjects or topics ending in *s* are singular:

*Stock Reports is* a helpful magazine.

Interpersonal Communications *is* a new course.

Mathematics *is* difficult for many people.

**VERB FORMS** With few exceptions, the irregular verbs in Table 12–1 change their spelling to form the past tense.

*Irregular Verbs*

**TABLE 12–1.** *Principal Parts of Troublesome Verbs*

| Present Infinitive or Present Tense | Past Tense | Part Participle |
|---|---|---|
| arise | arose | arisen |
| awake | awoke, awaked | awaked |
| be (am, are, is) | was | been |
| bear (carry) | bore | borne |
| bear (give birth to) | bore | borne, born |
| begin | began | begun |
| bid (command) | bade | bidden |
| bid (offer to pay) | bid | bid |
| bite | bit | bitten |
| blow | blew | blown |
| break | broke | broken |
| burst | burst | burst |
| buy | bought | bought |
| catch | caught | caught |
| choose | chose | chosen |
| come | came | come |
| creep | crept | crept |
| dive | dived, dove | dived |
| do | did | done |
| drag | dragged | dragged |
| dream | dreamed, dreamt | dreamed, dreamt |
| draw | drew | drawn |
| dwell | dwelt | dwelt |

**TABLE 12–1.** **(continued).**

| Present Infinitive or Present Tense | Past Tense | Part Participle |
|---|---|---|
| drink | drank | drunk |
| drive | drove | driven |
| eat | ate | eaten |
| fall | fell | fallen |
| flee | fled | fled |
| fling | flung | flung |
| fly | flew | flown |
| forget | forgot | forgotten, forget |
| freeze | froze | frozen |
| get | got | got, gotten |
| give | gave | given |
| go | went | gone |
| grow | grew | grown |
| hang (suspend) | hung | hung |
| hang (execute) | hanged | hanged |
| hide | hid | hidden |
| know | knew | known |
| lay (place) | laid | laid |
| lead | led | led |
| lend | lent | lent |
| lie (recline) | lay | lain |
| lie (falsify) | lied | lied |
| light | lighted, lit | lighted, lit |
| lose | lost | lost |
| mean | meant | meant |
| meet | met | met |
| pay | paid | paid |
| prove | proved | proved, proven |
| raise | raised | raised |
| read | read | read |
| rid | rid | rid |
| ride | rode | ridden |
| ring | rang | rung |
| rise | rose | risen |
| run | ran | run |
| say | said | said |
| see | saw | seen |
| seek | sought | sought |
| set | set | set |
| shake | shook | shaken |
| shed | shed | shed |
| shine (beam) | shone | shone |
| shine (polish) | shined | shined |

*TABLE 12–1. (continued).*

| Present Infinitive or Present Tense | Past Tense | Part Participle |
| --- | --- | --- |
| show | showed | shown, showed |
| sing | sang | sung |
| singe | singed | singed |
| sink | sank, sunk | sunk, sunken |
| sit | sat | sat |
| slide | slid | slid |
| speak | spoke | spoken |
| spring | sprang, sprung | sprung |
| steal | stole | stolen |
| sting | stung | stung |
| strive | strove, strived | striven, strived |
| swear | swore | sworn |
| swim | swam | swum |
| swing | swung | swung |
| take | took | taken |
| teach | taught | taught |
| tear | tore | torn |
| tell | told | told |
| throw | threw | thrown |
| wake | waked, woke | waked, woken |
| wear | wore | worn |
| weave | wove | woven |
| wring | wrung | wrung |
| write | wrote | written |

## Exercises

*Select the correct verb in each of the following sentences.*

1. The committee (has, have) met all week and (is, are) now concluding its investigation.

2. Neither the clock nor the table (is, are) going to be replaced.

3. The number of auto accidents in this city (is, are) incredibly high.

4. The public (has, have) the right to know every aspect of the issue.

5. The profits from last quarter (was, were) tremendous.

6. One of the secretaries (was, were) ill yesterday.

7. A box of flowers (is, are) on the hall table.

8. Bob's folder on the new housing plans (is, are) on his desk.

9. Physics (was, were) an interesting subject.

10. *Art News* (contain, contains) a fascinating article on rare illuminated manuscripts.

**PRONOUN USAGE**

Personal pronouns can sometimes trouble the writer who does not regard their role as being subjective, objective, or possessive. Compare the following statements:

*Subjective:*  *My wife and I* (we) are going to Scotland in May.
*Objective:*  Harvey gave *Joan and me* (us) a beautiful present.
*Possessive:*  That car is *ours*.

Note that an apostrophe is never placed after a possessive pronoun.

**Pronoun Agreement**

Personal pronouns (see Table 12–2), whether singular or plural, must always agree with their antecedents (the word to which the pronoun refers). For instance:

The *mechanic* fixed *his* friend's car at no charge.

*Diane* is happy with *her* new haircut.

The *students* were very anxious to see *their* grades.

*TABLE 12–2.  Personal Pronouns*

|  | Nominative | | Objective | | Possessive | |
|---|---|---|---|---|---|---|
|  | *Singular* | *Plural* | *Singular* | *Plural* | *Singular* | *Plural* |
| First | I | We | Me | Us | My<br>Mine | Our<br>Ours |
| Second | You | You | You | You | Your<br>Yours | Your<br>Yours |
| Third | He<br>She<br>It | They | Him<br>Her<br>It | Them | His<br>Her<br>Hers<br>Its | Their<br>Theirs |

Some common problem areas concern indefinite pronouns, collective nouns, compound antecedents, and comparative and incomplete clauses.

**Indefinite Pronouns.**    Indefinite pronouns (each, everyone, someone, etc.) are often confusing because they can be singular or plural. Here is a list of rules:

1. *Always singular:* each, someone, either, neither, somebody, nobody, everybody, anyone, nothing
   a. Everyone must choose his or her own career.
2. *Always plural:* both, few, many, several
   a. Both houses are a bargain.
3. *Singular or plural:* some, any, none, all, most
   a. None of the reports are ready.
   b. Some of the equipment is ready.

**Collective Nouns.**    Collective nouns can be either singular or plural depending on whether or not the members of the unit are considered as one group or individually. Compare the following:

*Each person:*    The *jury* presented *their* findings.
*One unit:*    The *jury* presented *its* findings.

**Compound Antecedents.**    Compound antecedents with *or, nor, either* . . . *or, neither* . . . *nor,* and *not only* . . . *but also* are followed by pronouns that agree with the nearest antecedent. For example:

*Neither* Jim nor the *boys* are sailing *their* boat today.
*Neither* the boys nor *Jim* is sailing *his* boat today.

**Comparative and Incomplete Clauses.**    Comparative and incomplete clauses use a pronoun in the same manner as if the idea of the clause were fully expressed:

He is younger than I. (am)
The chancellor felt that no one could do as well as she. (could do)

## Exercises

*Select the correct pronoun.*

1. Frank is as tall as (he, him).

2. Harry plays tennis better than (they, them).

3. This message is for Terry and (I, me).

4. Everybody but (she, her) went to the ballgame.

5. James and (he, him) offered to help Susan move her furniture.

6. My friend says she knew Larry long before (they, them).

7. The company received permission from the federal authorities to publish (its, their) findings.

8. Advertising affects the consumer because (he, she, they) often associate a product with a particular life style.

9. Mr. Scott will transmit the messages to (we, us).

10. That brownstone is older than (they, them).

## SENTENCE ERRORS

The three principal areas of sentence errors concern fragments, comma splices, and run-on constructions.

*Fragment sentences* occur when the writer omits a subject or verb, or mistakes a phrase for a complete sentence.

| | |
|---|---|
| a. *Missing Subject:* | Went to his summer house. |
| *Correction:* | Mark went to his summer house. |
| b. *Missing Verb:* | Fine as an idea. |
| *Correction:* | It is fine as an idea. |
| c. *Phrase:* | When he was in Chicago. |
| *Correction:* | Bill had many sales meetings when he was in Chicago. |

*Comma splices* occur when two independent sentences are joined by a comma rather than a period or semicolon.

Mr. Smith is attending a conference the morning, in the afternoon he is flying to San Francisco.

The corrected sentence reads:

Mr. Smith is attending a conference this morning. In the afternoon he is flying to San Francisco.

or

Mr. Smith is attending a conference this morning; this afternoon he is flying to San Francisco.

*Run-on* sentences are the result of no punctuation:

The company's policy concerning promotion was reviewed yesterday the committee feels that it should be revised the result will be improved employee morale.

The corrected sentence reads:

The company's policy concerning promotion was reviewed yesterday. The committee feels that it should be revised. The result will be improved employee morale.


## Exercises

*Correct the following sentences that contain errors in structure (fragment, comma splice, run-on).*

1. How long, have you been waiting to see Mr. Thompson?

2. Representatives from every industry. Including government experts, are attending the conference.

3. Marie types so well. Been promoted to supervisor of the typing pool.

4. High on the list of our goals.

5. There are many people who believe that luck plays a great part in achieving success there are others who feel that only hard work and perseverance will help someone reach the top and still others who think it's best to be the boss' son or daughter.

6. You will find that this lamp is as good as any other. When repaired properly.

7. The report that Ron wrote is exceptional, he will certainly win a great deal of praise from everyone who reads it.

8. Do not confuse length with depth in a report one thing has little to do with the other.

9. Wouldn't it be great to see Greta again? After all those years.

10. There are some great restaurants in Florence and Venice those cities have such a wealth of art also and the people are charming they seem to like tourists.

## PUNCTUATION REVIEW

*Comma.* A comma should be used in the following instances:

1. To separate items in a series:

Helen likes tennis, riding, golf, and badminton.

2. After long introductory phrases and clauses:

When he was a national sales manager, Phil had the chance to travel a great deal.

3. To set off interruptive or parenthetical phrases or clauses:

My brother, a graduate of Harvard, has been promoted to senior vice-president at NBC.

4. To indicate a pause:

Last night I read your report, which was excellent.

5. To separate two independent sentences connected by *and, or, but, for, nor, so,* or *yet:*

Bob Williams is a very capable young man, and everyone expects he will go very far in the business world.

6. After *yes* and *no:*

Yes, the company won the perfume account.

7. After words of address:

Mrs. Johnson, that was an excellent presentation.

8. To set off dates and places:

On May 27, 1972, _____
In Salem, Massachusetts, _____

9. To introduce quotations:

According to Charles Carr, "Profits are up for new model cars this quarter."

10. To set off titles and degrees:

Matthew Paulson, Ph.D.
Richard Brown, Jr., has succeeded his father as chairperson.

### Exercises

*Place the commas correctly in the following sentences.*

1. The chairperson spoke on the many problems faced by managers of corporations and his comments generated a lively discussion afterwards.

2. After his trip to Colorado Mr. Zeluck is traveling to California Oregon Washington and Detroit Michigan.

3. When she was at the beach the other day Jackie met an old friend from her high school days.

4. A great deal of preparation is necessary although this is an easy assignment.

5. Maureen and Janet anxious to go sailing leave their jobs early every Friday during the summer.

6. Bruce wants to attend Princeton but his parents insist he enroll at Stanford.

7. While my sister is completing her masters program she works part time for an attorney.

8. Lenny is taking cooking lessons because he wants to impress his girlfriend Pat a gourmet chef.

9. The Blue Star a fine French cafe has closed for the summer.

10. Even though everyone said he would never do it Johnny won the prize for dancing.

***Semicolon.*** A semicolon should be used in the following instances.
1. To join two separate sentences:

My car is considered a classic; it is over forty years old.

2. To connect two independent sentences joined by a conjunctive adverb *(however, moreover, nevertheless, therefore, consequently, finally, also, then, thus, indeed, instead, accordingly, otherwise, meanwhile, still, furthermore):*

My girlfriend works in her father's office; moreover, she just received a promotion.

3. To separate items in a series that contain commas:

The following people have consented to furnish letters of reference: Mr. James Morgan, supervisor, Harris Paper Company; Mrs. Lucille Holmes, vice-president, Winston and Partners; Ms. Roberta Jones, owner and president, Jones and Doyle, Inc.

***Colon.*** A colon should be used in the following instances.
1. To introduce lists or series:

Here are the stocks that have provided the highest returns:

2. To indicate emphasis:

These are the qualities of good writing: clarity and precision.

***Question Mark.*** Use a question mark to distinguish between a direct question and one that is indirect or paraphrased:

*Direct:*  Carol asked her boss, "When can I have my desk installed?"
*Indirect:*  Carol asked her boss when she might have her desk installed.

***Dash.*** Use the dash selectively, since it can substitute for a comma, semicolon, or colon:

Everyone—including Jack—attended the retirement party.

*Apostrophe.* The apostrophe is used in the following ways.
1. To indicate possession:

Karen's house . . .
The firm's new offices . . .

Note that most nouns add an *s* to show that they are plural. In the cases of plural nouns, simply add an apostrophe.

The boys' toys . . .
The cars' engines . . .

When a word ends in *s* or *z*, add only an apostrophe to indicate possession.

Lois' boat. . . .

2. To form contractions:

*is not* becomes *isn't*
*cannot* becomes *can't*
*I will* becomes *I'll*

3. To form the plural of letters, numbers, symbols used as words:

*b*'s
7's

Note that one does *not* use an apostrophe after a possessive pronoun:

yours, theirs, ours

### Exercises

*Correctly place either a semicolon, colon, apostrophe or dash in the sentences that follow.*

1. The two new salesmen attracted a great deal of business therefore each received a generous bonus at Christmas.

2. Fred and Ethel car broke down again.

3. My brother an excellent sportsman has entered the tennis tournament.

4. These daily exercises are time-consuming however I enjoy them.

5. Mike arrived at noon subsequently he was an hour early for his interview.

6. The girls hat blew out the window.

7. Joe is everyones best friend.

8. These men are among the winners Al Dickson, Lonny Moore, Gene O'Hara and Frankie Forwood.

9. My opinion nevertheless is that you should invest in those stocks and bonds.

10. Lois new boat can sleep eight people.

**CAPITALIZATION**   *Proper Nouns.*   Capitalize names of persons, places, and things that have a proper meaning:

James Sloan
Madison Avenue
Paris
Princeton University

Do *not* capitalize common nouns that hold general meaning:

street
college
town
avenue

Capitalize proper names of organizations:

United States Senate
Department of Commerce
New York State Highway Commission

Capitalize countries, regions, calendar divisions, holidays, and historic events:

France
the Midwest
the North Atlantic
January
War of 1812
Christmas

*Note:* Do *not* capitalize the names of the seasons (spring, summer fall, winter).

Capitalize titles following names:

Thomas Jefferson, President of the United States
Cyril Jackson, Director of Internal Affairs

Capitalize (and italicize) titles of publications:

*The New York Times*
*Newsweek*
*Business Week*

### Exercises

*Capitalize these sentences correctly.*

1. The mayor spoke on fifth avenue, broadway and other streets.

2. Charlie is a member of the elk's club.

3. My brother is president of the local mental health organization.

4. Don's new assistant is from the midwest.

5. By next spring, our sales will be up again.

6. Everyone enjoyed the film version of the maltese falcon.

7. Most freshman have to take two semesters of college english.

8. Broadway and 42nd street is known as times square.

9. George Washington high school is two blocks away from saint mary's school for girls.

10. The thames and seine rivers are among the most famous in the world.

**OFTEN CONFUSED WORDS**  Among writers, two troublesome areas often concern (1) the correct use of prepositions with preceding words and (2) the confusion of similar sounding words. Tables 12–3 and 12–4 illustrate the correct use of selected words.

**TABLE 12–3.  Correct Use of Prepositions**

*Prepositions Combined with Other Words*

| | | |
|---|---|---|
| *accompanied* | | |
| by | a person | |
| with | a thing | |
| *account* | | |
| for | an action | |
| to | a person | |
| *adapt* | | |
| from | to be patterned after | |
| *agree* | | |
| in | to be alike | |
| on | to be in accord | |
| to | consent | |
| with | to concur | |
| *angry* | | |
| with | a person | |
| at or about | a situation | |
| *capacity* | | |
| for | ability | |
| of | content or space | |
| *compare* | | |
| to | to liken | |
| with | to show resemblance or difference | |
| *confer* | | |
| about | to talk about something | |
| upon | bestow | |
| *correspond* | | |
| to | agree with | |
| with | communicate by writing | |
| *differ* | | |
| from | to be different from something else | |
| in | disagreement | |
| with | disagreement with a person | |
| *different* | | |
| from (never *than* or *to*) | | |
| *disappointed* | | |
| by or in | someone | |
| with | something | |
| *speak* | | |
| to | a listener | |
| with | an exchange of ideas | |

*TABLE 12—4.  Similar Words*

| Word | Definition |
|------|------------|
| absorption | a taking up—engrossment |
| adsorption | adhesion of gas or liquid to the surface of a solid |
| adapt | to adjust |
| adept | skilled |
| adopt | to take for one's own |
| adverse | opposing, unfavorable |
| averse to | disinclined toward |
| advice | recommendation |
| advise | to counsel |
| agenda | a list of things to be done |
| addenda | things to be added |
| aid | to help |
| aide | a confidential assistant |
| allusion | reference to |
| illusion | visual deception |
| delusion | a false idea |
| aloud | audibly |
| allowed | permitted |
| already | previously |
| all ready | all in readiness |
| alternate | a substitute |
| alternative | a choice between two |
| altogether | entirely |
| all together | in one group |
| ante | before |
| anti | against |
| anyway | in any event |
| any way | in any one way |
| appraise | to estimate the value of |
| apprise | to inform |
| assent | consent |
| ascent | a rise |
| accent | a stress |
| awhile | for a while |
| a while | if "for" is used, *a while* should be two words |

**TABLE 12–4.** *(continued)*

| Word | Definition |
| --- | --- |
| beside | by the side of |
| besides | moreover |
| born | brought into life |
| borne | endured, carried |
| capital | chief |
| capitol | official building in Washington, D.C. |
| casual | incidental, unimportant |
| causal | pertaining to a cause |
| coarse | unrefined |
| course | a passage |
| condemn | to pronounce opinion against |
| contemn | to despise |
| confidant | one to whom secrets are entrusted |
| confident | possessed of self-assurance |
| contemptible | deserving contempt |
| contemptuous | expressing contempt |
| continuation | pertains to length |
| continuance | pertains to time |
| council | an assembly for legislative purposes |
| counsel | advise, one who is consulted for advice (an attorney) |
| consul | a commercial representative of a foreign country |
| credible | believable |
| credulous | prone to believe on slight evidence |
| creditable | deserving esteem, praiseworthy |
| credit | to give credit for |
| accredit | to attribute |
| descent | respectable, proper |
| descent | downward progress |
| dissent | disagreement |
| decree | a decision or order |
| degree | a step or point in a series |
| definite | clear |
| definitive | final, conclusive |
| depository | the place where something is deposited |
| depositary | the person with whom something is deposited |

### TABLE 12–4. (continued)

| Word | Definition |
|---|---|
| deprecate | to express earnest disapproval of |
| depreciate | to decrease in value |
| desecrate | to profane |
| device (noun) | a contrivance |
| devise (verb) | to contrive |
| disburse | to pay out |
| disperse | to scatter |
| disinterested | impartial |
| uninterested | not interested |
| disprove | to prove to be false |
| disapprove | not to approve of |
| eldest | pertains to age of persons in one family |
| oldest | age of other persons and things |
| eligible | qualified |
| legible | plain, easy to read |
| illegible | impossible to read |
| envelop (verb) | to wrap around |
| envelope (noun) | a cover or wrapper |
| exceed | to surpass, go beyond |
| accede | to assent or yield to |
| except | to leave out |
| accept | to receive with approval |
| expeditious | quick, speedy |
| expedient | personally advantageous |
| extant | still existing |
| extinct | no longer existing |
| extent | measure, length, degree |
| facetious | causing frivolous laughter |
| factitious | artificial |
| fictitious | not real |
| factious | caused by a faction or party strife |
| farther | pertaining to actual distance |
| further | additional |
| forbear | to refrain from |
| forebear | an ancestor |

**TABLE 12–4.** *(continued)*

| Word | Definition |
|------|-----------|
| formerly | previously |
| formally | in a dignified manner |
| | |
| forward | eager, bold |
| froward | willful |
| | |
| full | abundant |
| fulsome | coarse |
| | |
| genius | inspired talent |
| genus | a classification of species |
| | |
| homogenous | alike in structure because of common origin |
| homogeneous | composed of like parts |
| | |
| human | pertaining to man |
| humane | compassionate, merciful |
| | |
| hypercritical | overcritical |
| hypocritical | deceitful |
| | |
| illicit | unlawful |
| elicit | to draw out |
| | |
| immerge | to plunge under |
| emerge | to rise out of |
| | |
| imminent | threatening to happen at once |
| immanent | inherent, indwelling |
| eminent | distinguished |
| emanate | to originate or start from |
| | |
| imply | to suggest indirectly |
| infer | to gather or deduce from |
| | |
| incredible | unbelievable |
| incredulous | unbelieving |
| | |
| indiscreet | unwise |
| indiscrete | compact, made up of similar elements |
| | |
| inept | awkward, foolish |
| inapt | unfitted, unqualified (sometimes spelled unapt) |
| | |
| insight | mental vision |
| incite | to arouse to action |
| | |
| insure | to guarantee against financial loss |
| ensure | to make sure or certain |

*TABLE 12–4.*   *(continued)*

| Word | Definition |
|------|-----------|
| intelligent | possessed of intelligence |
| intelligible | understandable |
| its | possessive of it (no apostrophe) |
| it's | it is or it has |
| judicial | pertaining to a judge |
| judicious | showing sound judgment |
| liable | responsible |
| libel | written, published defamation |
| meritorious | deserving of praise |
| meretricious | tawdry |
| meticulous | careful |
| moral | pertaining to right conduct |
| morale | state of mind, spirit or feeling |
| peremptory | absolute, decisive |
| preemptive | having the right of preference |
| perpetrate | to carry through, to be guilty of |
| perpetuate | to make lasting |
| personal | individual, private |
| personnel | persons engaged in a certain service |
| perspective | mental view in correct proportion |
| prospective | expected, anticipated |
| practical | efficient |
| practicable | capable of being efficiently used |
| precede | to go before |
| proceed | to advance |
| precedence | priority |
| precedents | established rules |
| predicate | to assert |
| predict | to foretell |
| prescribe | to designate |
| proscribe | to outlaw, prohibit |
| preview | a view in advance of public showing |
| purview | the range, scope, limits of |

*TABLE 12–4.    (continued)*

| Word | Definition |
| --- | --- |
| principal | chief, main |
| principle | (noun only) rule |
| proceeding | moving forward |
| preceding | going before |
| recourse | a resorting to for assistance |
| resource | that supply to which one turns for support |
| respectfully | with respect |
| respectively | each to each in order designated |
| shone | emitted light |
| shown | displayed |
| sometime | at an indefinite time |
| some time | a period of time |
| sometimes | now and then |
| spacious | large |
| specious | apparently but deceptively right |
| specialty | a distinctive thing |
| speciality | a distinctive quality |
| stationary | not movable |
| stationery | writing paper |
| statue | a carved likeness |
| statute | an enacted law |
| stature | height, elevation attained |
| subtile | delicate |
| subtle | sly, clever |
| suspect | to imagine, mistrust |
| expect | to count upon |
| suppose | to think, believe, conclude |
| sustenance | that which sustains life |
| subsistence | maintenance, livelihood |
| tantamount | equivalent |
| paramount | the highest; chief |
| taught | instructed |
| taut | tense, tight |

*TABLE 12–4.* *(continued)*

| Word | Definition |
|------|------------|
| team | two or more |
| teem | to abound or swarm (with) |
| temerity | rashness, reckless boldness |
| timidity | shyness |
| tenant | a lessee |
| tenet | a principle or belief held to be true |
| terminal | the end |
| terminus | the boundary or goal |
| their | a pronoun |
| there | in that place |
| they're | they are |
| through | from beginning to end |
| thru | |
| threw | did throw |
| thorough | fully or completely done |
| to | a preposition |
| too | also |
| two | a couple |
| typical | conforming to the type |
| atypical | not of the typical kind, irregular |
| unabridged | entire, in full |
| abridged | shortened |
| expurgated | cleared of objectionable things |
| undo | to unfasten |
| undue | not due |
| undoubtedly | without a doubt |
| indubitably | with too much evidence to doubt |
| unquestioned | has not been questioned |
| unquestionable | cannot fairly be questioned |
| unconscionable | without conscience, unjust |
| usable | workable |
| useful | helpful |
| use | act of employing or putting into service |
| usage | customary way of doing |
| veracious | truthful |
| voracious | greedy |

**TABLE 12–4.** *(continued)*

| Word | Definition |
| --- | --- |
| vindictive | revengeful |
| vindicative | tending to justify or clear a suspicion |
| vocation | a regular occupation |
| avocation | an occupation for amusement, a hobby |
| waver | to fluctuate |
| waiver | (law) a relinquishment |
| whose | a possessive pronoun |
| who's | who is or has |
| your | belonging to you |
| you're | you are |
| yore | time gone by |

# APPENDIX *A*

# Report Writing Assignments

The following report assignments are designed to provide practice in writing realistic reports for such areas as general business, accounting and finance, management, marketing, and economics.

## General Report Writing Exercises

Plan carefully before writing a report on any of these topics and situations. Be sure to limit the topic after analyzing the report's purpose and probable readers. Consider the need for research and whether the tone should be informal or formal. Include necessary components. Prepare a work schedule and set a completion date.

1. Inspect a public facility or building and report on its physical characteristics, personnel, and quality of service. Some choices might include the following:

   - Bank.
   - Supermarket.
   - Restaurant.
   - Clothing store.
   - Sporting goods shop.
   - Gas station.
   - Shoe Store.
   - Audio-visual center.

2. Conduct a feasibility study for a branch location of any of the following businesses:

   - Department store.
   - Bank.
   - Hardware store.
   - Investment house.
   - Rare book shop.
   - Stereo and record center.

   Be certain to consider these factors in your report: *location, local population, competition, rent, public transportation, taxes, highway access.*

3. Compare your company's product or service with a leading competitor in terms of *quality, price, availability, service or repair contracts,* and *durability.*

4. Compose a status report on worker productivity at your plant in the light of mass layoffs and wage freezes.

5. Evaluate five newly hired salespeople in terms of the following criteria: sales figures generated by each, and customer acceptance or rejection of recently developed products each has introduced to old and new clients.

6. Your firm is considering moving to another city or state. Your assignment is to analyze three possible choices and to select one on the basis of *cost of living, housing, taxes,* and *worker availability.*

7. Your firm has entrusted you with $3,500,000 for investment in a number of public stocks and bonds. Select five–ten and justify your recommendations. Create a chart indicating how many shares of each stock or bond should be acquired.

8. Compare the advantages and disadvantages of leasing vs. buying office space, cars and trucks, and office and plant equipment.

9. Evaluate the business outlook for the next year for any of these industries:

   - Housing.
   - Steel.
   - Lumber.
   - Paper products.
   - Electronic components.
   - Airlines.
   - Mass entertainment (film, television, concerts).

10. Write a *memo report* for one of the following purposes:
    a. To your supervisor outlining a specific office problem.
    b. To a colleague notifying him or her that action must be taken immediately on a particular issue.
    c. To full-time employees indicating changes in company benefits.
    d. To all staff members announcing the results of a committee study of employee productivity.
    e. To all sales people indicating changes in shipping and billing procedures.

11. Three years ago your company considered investing in a new technology industry (microcomputers, video cassette recorders,

cable television, satellite communications, etc.) but decided against it. However, in light of the growing success of these industries, they now appear attractive areas of investment.

Write a report on any one of these industries (or a comparable one of your own choice) describing growth over the years and the possible advantages and disadvantages offered to investors.

12. Write a recommendation report suggesting ways of improving college library services.

13. You have been asked to research various restaurants for a fare-well dinner honoring the firm's retiring chairman. In an informal report, list and evaluate three choices in terms of location, size, quality of food and service, atmosphere, clientele, and local reputation. Be certain to list the reasons for your final recommendation of one of the three restaurants.

14. Your college is interested in offering students a medical insurance package providing coverage for hospital and physician fees. As a member of a joint staff-student committee, investigate at least two medical insurance plans in terms of cost and coverage. Prepare a feasibility study concerning the likelihood of success for this program if offered next semester.

15. Mr. Olsen, the sales manager for your company, has complained often about the disorderly manner in which his sales staff file monthly reports. He asks you to develop a standardized format for the recording of necessary data. You are to include the number of calls each sales person makes, names of possible clients, follow-up calls and visits, actual sales figures, and comments.

16. Prepare a feasibility report concerning the need for and possible site for new dormitories.

17. Select a course and instructor and compose a descriptive report of the following:

- Course content.
- The instructor's teaching methods.
- Assignments.
- Examinations.
- Textbooks.
- Recommendation to other students.

18. Write a report in which you evaluate three employees for promotion to manager. Consider such factors as:

    - Experience.
    - Education.
    - Potential for growth.
    - Work habits.
    - Capacity for responsibility.
    - Ability to work with people.
    - Maturity of judgment.
    - Personal appearance.
    - Ability to make decisions.
    - Ability to supervise others.
    - Verbal and written communication skills.

19. In a brief report, compare the advantages and disadvantages of owning a car and motorcycle. Then recommend a particular brand and model, along with reasons for your choice.

20. Report on the feasibility of establishing a credit union for students on campus. Consider such factors as collateral, rate of interest on loans, payment plans, and collection procedures. The loans can range from $50 to $2,500.

21. Write a procedural report that outlines steps for:

    - Improving student tuition-reimbursement system.
    - Traffic flow in and around the campus.
    - Registration for classes.
    - Graduation ceremonies.

22. Compare two graduate schools you are considering attending. In a letter report to your parents, discuss your preference for one of the schools, neither one of which is known to them.

23. Select a product or service. Suggest ways for improving its market and sales.

24. A college committee has been formed to suggest ways of improving its sports programs. Discuss your ideas of this matter in a letter report to the committee chairperson, Dr. William Sharp.

25. In a brief report, analyze your college's counseling program, considering its ability to meet students' needs and its overall quality.

26. Compose a letter report, for a consumer magazine, on the best time to buy a new car.

27. As a member of the graduation committee at your college, you must investigate and suggest names of celebrated individuals likely to be successful speakers at the June ceremonies. List the names according to order of preference, noting backgrounds, reasons for attracting students' attention, and availability. The maximum speaker allowance is $3,500.

28. Compare student housing on- and off-campus in a brief report.

29. Report on job possibilities in any of these fields:

   • Engineering.
   • Marketing.
   • Banking.
   • Accounting.
   • Economics.
   • Advertising.
   • Public relations.

   Include starting salary scale and likely responsibilities for someone who lacks experience.

30. Write a status report on the automobile and housing markets from data appearing in the latest *Standard and Poor's Industry Survey*, *The Wall Street Journal*, *Business Week*, *Forbes*, *Fortune*, *The New York Times* or *U.S. News & World Report*. Use at least one source of information.

31. A large corporation has donated $50,000 to your college endowment fund. Report on various investment options (stocks, bonds, money market funds, C.D.'s, and U.S. Savings Bonds) likely to offer safety and growth.

32. Discuss rewards and pitfalls for women executives in the 1980s.

33. Outline the problems and suggest solutions regarding water pollution caused by industry.

34. Analyze the future sales potential of home video equipment.

35. Your supervisor has asked you to prepare a report on the functions and efficiency of two branch offices the company is considering closing.

36. Your town supervisor has asked you to help write a report concerning the feasibility of constructing a new airport to accomodate small private and business aircraft. The site would be near a string of private homes surrounded by vacant land.

37. Five ways to improve local bus and train service.

38. A report recommending a colleague for promotion to vice-president.

39. Investigate a problem of personal, local, national, or professional concern.

40. Conduct a market survey of a product or service of particular interest to you.

41. Report on various ways of investing $250,000 your aunt has just won in a state lottery.

## Accounting and Finance Report Exercises

1. Submit a report to a large corporation suggesting comparative methods of inventory control of their apparel products.

2. Choose two recent accounting theories and procedures; compare them to two traditional ones.

3. In a letter report, advise the *XYZ* Company of recent tax changes.

4. Analyze the reasons for cash flow problems that exist in a medium-sized company. Suggest a plan to remedy the situation.

5. In a letter report, suggest ways of modernizing procedures within an accounting department that has long resisted innovation.

6. Prepare a comparative study for your firm to lease or buy office equipment.

7. Discuss the advantages of incorporating for two partners in a fast-growing designer handbag company.

8. Study and recommend a means to finance a new research and development center for a small but growing computer manufacturer.

9. Analyze two companies that manufacture the same product in terms of sales, operating costs, and net income for the current fiscal year.

10. Devise a report suggesting a method of improving the operating income of a company whose accounting records show a high marginal income ratio and production below maximum capacity.

11. Compile a departmental monthly report on employee idleness (due to recent slowdown in sales and an unexpected delay in receiving raw materials). Classify each department and supply information concerning standard vs. active productive hours and hourly rates of pay.

12. Prepare an advisory report for a budget committee seeking ways to cut costs for a large restaurant chain operation.

13. Prepare a feasibility report for a new product for a large manufacturing firm. Since 75 percent of 1984 production capacity was utilized, management believes idle manpower could be directed to producing the new product. Market research predicts that 25,000 units at $45 each could be sold in 1985. The cost of producing the new item is estimated at $8.50, which includes materials, labor, selling expenses, plant overhead, advertising, and promotion costs.

14. Devise a cost-of-production report for any industry.

15. Create a standardized cash-flow analysis report to be issued on a monthly and quarterly basis.

16. In a letter report, suggest an expansion plan for a small brokerage house in Chicago.

17. Write an advisory report for Company A, which is planning to acquire Company B. List assets, liabilities, operating costs, and net income of Company B. Based on this data, advise for or against acquisition.

18. Report on the need to divest certain assets for a large company. Cite all reasons.

19. Discuss various tax shelters for someone earning over $150,000 yearly.

20. Write a financial summary report for any company, taking into account such factors as

- Sales (units).
- Gross sales in dollars.
- Net sales in dollars.
- Production costs.
- Gross profit.
- Advertising fees.
- Research and development costs.
- Interest on long term obligations.
- Taxes.
- Rate of return on assets.
- Net income.

## Management Report Exercises

1. Report on the relevancy of your college business education courses to probable everyday management problems occurring at work.

2. In a letter report to a business magazine, discuss three management theories and their practical applications.

3. Develop two business administration courses needed for students in the 1980's. Include course rationale, goals and content.

4. Devise an employee evaluation system for a large corporation.

5. Prepare a report outlining ways of attracting liberal arts majors to a Wall Street investment firm. Justify your goals and hiring strategy.

6. Report on how a lunchtime "life enrichment" program devised to expand employees' interests and knowledge beyond the range of the company's concerns will increase productivity. The program would consist of speakers and films on such topics as stress, marriage, politics, art, literature, and mental and physical well-being.

7. Write a memo report in which you suggest a weekly exercise program for upper-level management. Discuss location of facilities and specific activities.

8. Report on the changing status of women in any industry.

9. Develop a report that outlines a fringe benefits plan for lower and middle management.

10. Evaluate the use of robots in a specific industry or job in terms of productivity and profits.

11. In a letter report, compare your college's business degree program offered in the evening with one offered by a nearby college.

12. Prepare a report elaborating on a way to restructure managerial hierarchy in your organization.

13. Design an expansion plan for branch operations in your firm.

14. In a memo report, outline aspects of an employee grievance system to be instituted by your firm next spring.

15. Develop a five year strategic management plan for a medium sized company. Consider such factors as

    - Mission or goals.
    - Company philosophy.
    - Short- and long-range objectives.
    - Policies.
    - Financial situation.
    - Product or service.
    - Competition.
    - Markets.

16. Analyze any company or product in terms of

    - History or background.
    - Product or service.
    - Sales.
    - Profits.
    - Manpower.
    - Competition.
    - Future growth.

17. Write a management planning report designed to improve internal coordination of daily activities and internal communications.

18. Prepare a report outlining retraining procedures for employees

whose jobs are being replaced by modern technology or are being eliminated because of decreased production.

19. Prepare a performance report on each member of your department for the director of human resources of your company.

20. For the director of training, prepare a report suggesting a series of seminars designed to improve management skills.

## *Marketing Report Exercises*

1. Report on the marketing possibilities offered by local cable television stations.

2. Design a promotion campaign for someone opening a home video sales center. Note all aspects of the promotion in a letter report to the client.

3. Outline a number of successful marketing procedures in a memo report to new staff members.

4. Devise a marketing strategy for a computer that writes reports.

5. Write a customer-analysis report for a motion picture company seeking to market their classic film library on video cassettes and discs.

6. Conduct a market survey of competitors catering to college students in terms of the following:

   - Market share.
   - Product quality.
   - Price.
   - Sales.
   - Gross profits.

   Select any product or service.

7. Report on any company's particular strengths and weaknesses in attempting to cash in on the growing home entertainment market.

8. Write a report that identifies and explains reasons for any prod-

uct or service becoming obsolete in the 1980's. Suggest a substitute that will have appeal and high sales potential.

9. Report on two markets most or least vulnerable to technological innovation.

10. In a letter report, recommend a new product line for any industry.

11. In a memo report, outline new markets for any product or service.

12. Survey and compare information retrieval systems for a medium-sized business library. In a report, recommend one system best suited for marketing to such libraries across the country.

13. Survey and analyze customer attitudes toward any product or service.

14. Write a report that discusses consumer trends in purchasing home video equipment and games.

15. Construct a questionnaire designed to measure office productivity.

16. Prepare a report that contains plans for measuring the effectiveness of television and radio advertising campaigns.

17. Prepare a feasibility study concerning marketing products to foreign countries.

18. Discuss the benefits of a direct mail marketing campaign.

19. Analyze two advertising campaigns selling competitive soft drinks.

20. Write a marketing strategy report for an American car company seeking outlets in Japan.

## Economics Report Exercises

1. In a brief report, discuss the changes in community revenue effected by a new tax plan that favors a particular income group (low, middle, or upper).

2. Select three industries and prepare a report on how changes in

supply and demand have altered the fiscal health of each for better or worse.

3. Analyze in a report any current government fiscal policy, be it on a city, state, or federal level. Comment on its benefits and drawbacks.

4. Select five products or services. In a forecast report, predict their future rate of growth, based on changing household consumption and needs.

5. In a letter report, suggest any steps or procedures the Federal Reserve System might take to increase the supply of money so banks can make greater numbers of loans and foreign investments.

6. Report on how three goods or services can be reduced in output in order to free government resources for investment in other areas.

7. Survey national income distribution and suggest methods for more equitable future distribution.

8. Discuss any trends or apparent changes in the Gross National Product in light of recent economic conditions in any of these areas:

   - Consumption.
   - Gross private domestic investment.
   - Government purchases of goods and services.
   - Net exports.

9. Prepare a report that analyzes how recent economic factors have influenced the price mechanism in any three of these areas:

   - Cars.
   - New homes.
   - Steel production.
   - Food.
   - Motion picture production.
   - Computer technology.
   - Hotel and restaurant services.
   - Travel and leisure.
   - Sporting equipment.

10. Write a report that discusses a production possibilities curve for five commodities.

11. For the same product under two different economic conditions, construct a demand schedule and include it in a brief letter report.

12. Write a memo report in which you compare consumer price indexes for the last five years and offer reasons for variance.

13. Discuss the external and private costs of an undertaking (labor, materials, equipment, tax incentives, etc.) by a large private corporation for inner-city housing facilities.

14. Comment on how production factors such as labor, capital, natural resources, and so on, have altered in the last twenty years for any industry.

# APPENDIX *B*

# Sample Reports

The business reports that follow are examples of actual report formats and writing styles employed by several business firms. The reports have been selected to serve as guides to the various forms of business writing.

# MEMO REPORT

## IRVING
## SMITH
## KOGAN
AND COMPANY, INC.
220 East 42nd STREET
NEW YORK, N.Y. 10017

Client:        Sherry Institute of Spain        Date:    June 30, 1984

Subject:     Sherry presentation to           Place:   New York, New York
             women executives

Present:     For agency: Daniel Langdon
             For presentation: Barbara Gee

Distribution:    F. Garcia-Delgado, J. L. Breton, R. Aguilar,
A. Llanos, L. Carderera, M. Rubio, L. Guerra, B. Abbott,
B. Rosenblatt, J. Dubois, M. Domecq, J. Umbach, M. Franklin,
H. Kahn, J. Poust, D. Milligan, S. Ringe, R. J. Pellaton,
N. J. Cooper, L. B. Fox, D. Langdon, M. Guiliano, I. S. Kogan

---

Agency has agreed to participate in a series of six lecture/
fashion shows for women executives in Boston.  These events
are being hosted by Bonwit Teller department store in Boston
and will begin in mid-September.  Approximately 160 women are
expected to attend each session at which a minimum of two
styles of Sherry will be served.  In addition, literature will
be distributed and an agency representative will be on hand
to answer questions.  Agency to follow.

#        #        #

SI-1653
SI-1654
SI-1655
SI-1656
SI-1657
SI-1658

lf

A memo report prepared by Irving Smith Kogan of New York for
the Sherry Institute of Spain. Reprinted with permission.

# LETTER REPORT

## MORGAN LE FAY
### Limited Editions

TEL. 201-567-5780

346 AUDUBON ROAD, ENGLEWOOD, NEW JERSEY 07631

August 17, 1983

Kate Smallwood
California Mart
110 East 9th Street
Los Angeles, California 90079

Dear Kate:

Here is an inventory of our fall handbags currently in stock, as of August 15:

|        | Style 260 | Style 270 | Style 255 |
|--------|-----------|-----------|-----------|
| Black  | 16        | 4         | 6         |
| Wine   | 11        | 6         | 2         |
| Taupe  | 18        | 14        | NA        |
| Gray   | 10        | 3         | 5         |
| Plum   | 12        | 9         | NA        |

Please call if I can be of further assistance. I'll send a new list next week.

Best regards,

*Renee P. Iacone*

Renee P. Iacone

A letter report prepared by Morgan Le Fay of Englewood, N.J. Reprinted with permission.

# LETTER REPORT

THE
JANEWAY
LETTER

Vol. 26 No. 1481                                    August 9, 1983

## SHOCKS AND SURPRISES AHEAD FOR THE MARKETS

*Focus on Interest Rates: Is This a Peak or a Pause?*

*JANEWAY JUDGMENT:* Rates are going higher, despite the growing perception that higher rates will slow down the economy. Rallies in the credit markets will be technical flurries and speculative traps.

*The Strength of the Dollar:* It's here to stay for a while. The technical reason for this dollar rally is the one that's always the most influential. It's the buildup of a big short interest, invited by the prevalent market perception that the dollar was overpriced and overdue to come down a peg. The fundamental reason, for once, happened to reinforce the technical reason. The entire foreign banking system—central banks and commercial banks alike—is making money hand over fist riding the dollar up as if it were a hot stock. It's the only winner they have this year. More than 95 percent of the assets of the German Bundesbank are represented by its holding of paper dollars. The foreign banking system is relying on the daily markup in its dollar positions to offset its lost income in delinquent interest and its overdue write-offs on bad loans. On top of this, the 1983 improvement in the US economy has not benefited from any lift in exports. Quite the contrary: It has subsidized a surge in US imports that, while marginal in GNP terms, represents a sheik's ransom to the various economies selling goods and services in America. Thanks to the bull market in the dollar, the countries selling goods and services for dollars are finding themselves able to increase their take-home pay in the universal currency they all want, while marking down selling prices in their local currencies. Too many dollar users who are not US nationals are making too much money out of the "overpriced level" of the dollar to provide an incentive for its rise to be reversed. Washington's ill-fated intervention aimed at pricing the dollar back down was too little and too late. It merely ensured a new run of strength for the dollar, accentuated by panicky short-covering.

*The Weakness of Currencies and Commodities:* The dollar and US interest rates are spiraling upward together. Their rise is having a magnetic effect on money all around the world, drawing it to New York. It's little wonder, therefore, that demand for commodities from outside the US is on the wane. Now that the improvement inside the US has culminated in this upward spiral of dollar exchange rates and US interest rates, hopes of recovery following around the world are being abandoned. Contrary to experience and theory, the weakness of foreign currencies against the dollar is not stimulating foreign economies. In fact, neither experience of past cyclical upturns nor theories regarding them are helpful or relevant in today's entirely new international situation, dominated as it is by the US government's runaway borrowing needs and its relentless upward pressure on interest rates. Forecasts based on the upsets of the 1970s, when dollar weakness went with overseas economic strength, are misleading. Gold ran wild on price inflation and interest rates were no obstacle. Today, by contrast, the fiscal crisis is far enough advanced to blow the ceiling off US interest rates and to put a ceiling on world economic activity. But it is not yet far enough advanced to blow the ceiling off gold.

*Conclusion:* Sell any bonds or notes held, and don't take any speculative bait advertising them as cheap because they're down. This goes double for US tax-exempt bonds. Those free from any credit risk are still subject to market risk, which outweighs any hope of market gain from lower yields. Respect the strength of the dollar as a portent of higher interest rates. Avoid speculation on commodities for the same reason.

# PROGRESS REPORT

# IRVING SMITH KOGAN

AND COMPANY, INC.
220 EAST 42nd STREET
NEW YORK, N.Y. 10017
PHONE: (212) 907-9380

THE SHERRY INSTITUTE OF SPAIN

Progress Report

February 1983

**PUBLIC RELATIONS COUNSELING AND SERVICE**

A progress report prepared by Irving Smith Kogan of New York
for the Sherry Institute of Spain. The text has been reprinted with
permission.

Projects Completed - February 28

MAGAZINE - Liquor Store Magazine, a trade publication
edited by Peter Wulff, requested that the agency provide
information on its materials and services as a resource
for retailers.  This information has been sent and is
scheduled to appear in the publication's April issue
(SI-1561).

TELEVISION - Agency was informed by Prof. DeMar, of
Brooklyn College, that a half-hour segment on Sherry
taped by a representative of Sherry Institute was re-
broadcast on cable television -- Channel 25 -- on
February 14 at 4:30 PM.  This program is one of a 13-
week series on Wines of the World originally prepared for
educational (public service) television stations (SI-1553).

MAGAZINE - Agency was contacted by Stanley Dry, who has
prepared an article for the April edition of Boston
magazine (circulation 110,000) on Sherry.  Mr. Dry had a
number of questions on production methods and was also
seeking some up-to-date statistical information.  This
journalist was among the party who attended the 1982
Vendimia (SI-1549).

MAGAZINE - Agency was contacted by wine writer, Eunice
Fried, who is preparing an article on Sherry and the
Sherry-producing region for Travel Life magazine, a Time/
Life Publication in Canada.  Ms. Fried was given statistical data, information on this year's Vendimia and a
listing of bodegas which offer tours (SI-1534).  Agency
representative had previously met with Georgina Cannon,
publisher of Travel Life.  Agency provided her with
background information and original photographs of the
area (SI-1533).  This article is tentatively scheduled for
publication this spring.

TRADE - Agency has responded to a request from Henry Soble

Projects Completed                                           Page 2

of the Wine Press in Brookline, Massachusetts, for a variety
of materials. He was sent copies of the Service Guide for
staff training and other literature for in-store promotion
(SI-1531).

TRADE - Agency has fulfilled requests for the Sherry
Service Guide from the following restaurateurs:  John
Swierk of Ponderosa Steak House in Woonsocket, Rhode
Island (SI-1530); William Nelson of Weld Inn in Weld,
Maryland (SI-1529); Michael Hill of the Silverscope Cafe
in Amherst, Massachusetts (SI-1528); John Demarkis of JP's
Harborside in Manchester, Massachusetts (SI-1527); and,
Harry Alexion of Alexion's Famille Restaurant in
Pawtucket, Rhode Island (SI-1526).

TRADE - Agency has sent to Steve Cignetti materials to be
used at Bargain Spot Liquors for in-store promotion.  This
retailer has locations in Medford and Somerville, Massachusetts (SI-1525).

TRADE - Agency has responded to requests for members of the
trade for generic materials to be used for staff training
and in-store promotion.  These requests were made by:
Adele Rex, London Wine Company in Brookline, Massachusetts
(SI-1524); Tom Karlson, East Bethel Liquor Supply Company
in Cedar, Minnesota (SI-1523); J. Simmons, Key West Food
Emporium in Key West, Florida (SI-1522); Eamon Von Pramba,
Sales Division of the Pennsylvania State Liquor Control
Board in Quakertown, Pennsylvania (SI-1521); Union Square
Beverage Corp. in Sommerville, Massachusetts (SI-1520);
Sheffield Liquors in Boston, Massachusetts (SI-1519); and
Sr. Gonzalez, Acapulco Restaurant in Boston, Massachusetts
(SI-1518).

WINE COURSE - Agency has provided materials and information
to Robert Lewis, an Associate Professor at the University
of Massachusetts, Amherst.  He had requested these for his
introductory wine course which has an enrollment of 50
students (SI-1517).

Projects Completed                                    Page 3


WINE COURSE - Agency has forwarded information and literature on Sherry to Dr. Paul Martin (Chevalier de Tastevin)
for an adult wine appreciation course he teaches in
Worcester, Massachusetts.  Thirty persons are enrolled in
the course and one session will be devoted to Sherry
(SI-1516).

TRADE - The following members of the trade have received
copies of the Sherry Service Guide:  B. P. Allen, Bosque
Notre Restaurant; Paradise, California (SI-1515); P.
Feskan, Ralbys Restaurant, Vallejo, California (SI-1514);
D. R. Cook, LaCosta Hotel, Carlsbad, California (SI-1513);
J. A. Schmidt, Rocking Horse Foods, Missoula, Montana
(SI-1512); G. MacDonald, Hudson Bay Resort, Bayview,
Indiana (SI-1511); R. Lee, Northeast Gallery Garden
Restaurant, Seattle, Washington (SI-1510); E. Schreiner,
Señor Gato Restaurant, Portland, Oregon (SI-1509); P.
Champion, Host International Hotel, Seattle, Washington
(SI-1508); and L. A. Rinaldis, Versailles Restaurant,
Lake Havasuc, Arizona (SI-1507).


Projects Pending - February 28

WINE COURSE - Agency has received a request for Sherry
literature from wine writer and educator Patrick Fegan of
Chicago, Illinois.  These will be used in an upcoming wine
appreciation course in which some 20 people are enrolled.
Agency will follow (SI-1584).

TRADE - Agency has been in contact with John Boonshaft of
the Marriott Corporation hotel chain.  Mr. Boonshaft is
seeking material and information on Sherry for a training
manual he is putting together for employees of Marriott.
This hotel chain has more than 100 specialty restaurants
whose staffs will receive the manual.  Agency will follow
(SI-1583).

Projects Pending                                          Page 4

ADMINISTRATION - At the request of the Literary Affairs Committee of the Vintage Festival, agency will distribute information on the International Jerez Prize. This annual competition is open to journalists who have published a generic story on Sherry during the past year. Agency will follow (SI-1582).

MAGAZINE - Agency has agreed to prepare an article for the Massachusetts Beverage Journal on the trade luncheon recently held in Boston. The article will be accompanied by photography commissioned by agency. Publisher of the Journal, Maury Shugrue, plans on running the story in the magazine's April issue. Agency to follow (SI-1581).

ADMINISTRATION - The Commercial Office of Spain in Montreal, Canada has contacted agency with a request for literature on Sherry from Spain. Sr. Bozancus has asked for copies of Noble Wine, Gracious Hospitality and the Sherry Service Guide. Agency to follow (SI-1580).

WINE COURSE - Agency has been contacted by Frederick Brodzinski of Ramapo College of New Jersey (Mahwah, New Jersey) with a request for literature and a copy of the Sherry film. These are to be used as part of his course, "Understanding and Enjoying Wine" which has an enrollment of 25 students. Agency to follow (SI-1579).

TRADE - Agency has received requests from a number of retailers for literature to be used for in-store promotion of Sherry. These requests came from: James Vos of the Liquor Shoppe in St. Cloud, Minnesota (SI-1576); Eugene Ore of Ham Lake Liquors in Cedar, Minnesota (SI-1577); and Cecelia Gilchrist of Shell City Liquors in Miami, Florida (SI-1578). Agency will follow.

WINE COURSE - Agency has received requests for Sherry materials to be used in wine courses from the following: Kevin Zraly, wine consultant to the Inhilco hotel chain,

Projects Pending                                           Page 5

for a course given to consumers in which 250 people are
enrolled (SI-1575), and Bruce Pelzer, whose course at
Northeastern University (Boston, Massachusetts) has an
enrollment of 50 students (SI-1574).  Agency to follow.

TRADE - Agency has received requests for generic litera-
ture from the following retailers:  Frances Curran of PX
Liquor Store in St. Cloud, Minnesota (SI-1573), and
Pierre Vinet of Regent Liquor in Madison, Wisconsin
(SI-1572).  Agency will follow.

SEMINAR - Paul Hammer, wine manager for McKesson Wine &
Spirits (a Boston area distributor), has contacted agency
requesting assistance for a Sherry seminar in which his
firm is participating.  This event is being held as a
fundraiser and agency has agreed to provide generic
literature, posters and a copy of the Sherry film.
Agency to follow (SI-1571).

SEMINAR/TASTING - On March 9, agency representative will
give a Sherry presentation to new students of the International Bartending School in New York City.  Emphasis will
be placed on proper serving, glassware and storage.
Literature will be distributed, the film shown and a
modest sampling of wine (supplied by the school) will be
tasted.  Agency to follow (SI-1570).

WINE COURSE - Agency has received a request for Sherry
education materials including Gracious Hospitality, the
pocket guide and a set of wine educator slides, from Dr.
Pacilio.  These will be used as part of an introductory
course on wine which he is giving at the Wine Academy in
Atlanta, Georgia.  Agency will follow (SI-1569).

PROMOTION - National Public Radio, a non-profit
nationally syndicated radio show, will be doing a series
on Andrés Segovia this spring when the Maestro comes to
the U.S. for a concert tour.  NPR is planning a reception

Projects Pending                                           Page 6

for 150 persons at the Spanish Institute's building on
Park Avenue in Manhattan and asked the Sherry Institute of
Spain to donate a modest quantity of Sherry (3-4 cases)
for this event.  Agency will follow (SI-1568).

WINE COURSE - Joseph Formica, a member of the Society of
Wine Educators, has requested that the agency provide him
with educational materials.  These will be used by Mr.
Formica in conjunction with a wine appreciation course he
gives at Virginia Commonwealth University (Richmond,
Virginia).  Thirty students are enrolled in the course.
Agency to follow (SI-1567).

SEMINAR/TASTING - Agency has received a request for
materials and assistance from Mr. Vessel of the Kansas
City, Kansas, chapter of Les Amis du Vin.  This chapter of
the wine appreciation group is holding a Sherry tasting
featuring the four basic styles of varying producers at
which 50 persons are expected to attend.  Agency will
follow (SI-1566).

WINE COURSES - Agency has received requests for literature
and copies of the Sherry film from the following wine
educators to be used in conjunction with their courses:
Dr. Harm de Blij for a Geography of Viticulture course at
the University of Miami (Coral Gables, Florida) in which
60 students are enrolled (SI-1565); Mark Brahmstedt for a
consumer course in Burlington, Vermont (SI-1564); and
Richard Naylor for a wine appreciation course in York,
Pennsylvania (SI-1563).  Agency to follow.

MAGAZINE - Agency has received a request for materials and
background information from Mrs. Carol Doolittle, editor
of the American Wine Society Journal.  This publication is
a quarterly sent to the Society's 2,500 members.  Agency
will follow (SI-1562).

TRADE - Agency has received a request for literature and

Projects Pending                                        Page 7

posters from Mr. Paul Marks of Northside Liquors in
Ithaca, New York.  These will be used for in-store promotion and agency will follow (SI-1560).

WINE COURSE - Agency has received a request for educational materials from Professor Christian of Cornell
University's School of Hotel Administration.  This
semester some 400 students are enrolled in Christian's
wine courses.  Agency will follow (SI-1559).

ADMINISTRATION - Chairman Brian Abbott, has called a full
meeting of the Sherry Committee for March 21, 1983.
Preliminary agenda items are:  review of advertising and
public relations programs for 1982; report and discussion
of trade promotion plans reviewed at special Sherry
Committee meeting in Boston on January 27, 1983; and,
consideration of future plans for Oscar de la Renta TV
commercial.  Agency has been asked to report on the first
two items and recap market research on TV commercial for
the third agenda point.  Agency will follow (SI-1558).

TRADE - Agency has received requests for its Service Guide
from the following members of the trade:  W. Crosta of
Daggatts at Tolovana in Manzanita, Oregon (SI-1557);
M. Belcher of De Marcos Restaurant in Artesia, California
(SI-1556); and L. Rosenbloom of All American Restaurant in
Los Angeles, California (SI-1555).  Agency will follow.

MAGAZINE - Agency was contacted by Susan Carlton, of
"Off-Hours," a leisure magazine (circulation 100,000)
edited for physicians.  Publication is preparing a feature
article on fortified wines for its March issue and Ms.
Carlton requested information and assistance with four-
color photographs to illustrate the text.  Agency has
arranged to meet with magazine's art director, Joan
Simpson, and will follow (SI-1554).

WINE COURSE - Agency was contacted by wine educator Henry

Projects Pending                                          Page 8

Parkinson, who requested educational materials (film,
booklets, brochures) for his April classes.  The Sherry
session will be conducted on April 8 (SI-1553).  A
similar request came from Ron Kapon, who conducts wine
courses and seminars given at the Long Island Academy of
Marketing.  These will be used in his Spring classes
(SI-1552).  Agency to follow.

TRADE - Agency has received a request for copies of the
Service Guide from M. Scott, owner of Philadelphia West
restaurant in North Hollywood, California.  Agency to
follow (SI-1550).

TRADE - Continuing the second half of its promotional
efforts in Boston, agency is developing another issue of
the Sherry newsletter.  As with the previous edition, it
is designed to provide information on Sherry and give news
on various activities in the Boston market.  It will be
sent to some 3,600 restaurants, hotels and bars in the
greater Boston area; additional copies will be distributed
in bulk to Boston distributors and importers' regional
sales managers.  Agency will follow (SI-1548).

TRADE - Agency has received requests for copies of its
Sherry Service Guide from Monroe Furst, an assistant
manager at the Hotel Pierre in New York City (SI-1547)
and S. Huey, chef at the Red Lion Inn in San Martin,
California (SI-1544).  Agency will follow.

BOOK - Agency was contacted by writer, Carolyn Heard, who
is currently working on a travel/phrase book for Simon &
Schuster.  A portion of the section on Spain will deal
with local food and wine and Ms. Heard has asked for
information on these topics.  Agency will follow (SI-1543).

WINE COURSE - Agency has been contacted by wine educator
and consultant, Peter Kroon, who has requested materials
and assistance for a forthcoming Sherry tasting he is

Projects Pending                                    Page 9

giving as part of a wine appreciation course in Amherst,
Massachusetts.  Some 50 to 75 persons are expected to
attend and agency will follow (SI-1542).

TRADE - Agency has been asked to provide educational
materials for in-store promotions by Christine Thomas of
Circle Liquor Store in Somers Point, New Jersey (SI-1541)
and Joan Bernard of Jobi Liquors in Boston, Massachusetts
(SI-1539).  Victor Hamer, food and beverage manager of the
Sheraton Bal Harbor Hotel (Bal Harbor, Florida) also
requested materials to be used for distribution to patrons
and for staff training (SI-1538).  Agency to follow.

TRADE - Agency has received requests for the Sherry Service
Guide from the following members of the trade:  T. A.
Morris, chef for Wilsons Restaurant in Paso Robles,
California (SI-1537); G. D. Matthias of Simms Landing
Restaurant in Golden, Colorado (SI-1536); and, J. L.
Williams, manager of the Hyatt Regency Waikiki Hotel in
Honolulu, Hawaii (SI-1535).  Agency will follow.

SEMINAR/TASTING - Agency has agreed to give a Sherry presentation for members of Boston's Premier Wine Club.
Originally scheduled for January 4, this event has been
postponed.  Agency will follow (SI-1459).

TRADE - Agency met with Kathleen Talbert, training
director for Hilton Hotels International, who was
assembling material on Sherry for a training manual to be
used by food and beverage managers of some 90 international
hotels in the chain.  The manual will consist of 49 frames
of microfilm (7 rows of 7 frames each) plus a printed
brochure.  Agency furnished Ms. Talbert with Sherry color
slides, literature, lecture notes, transparencies, flow
charts, etc.  She reviewed these materials and subsequently
contacted agency with several technical questions.  A
draft of the manual has been submitted and agency is
currently reviewing the material.  Agency has also offered

Projects Pending                                   Page 10

to supply the Sherry Service Guide in quantity (about
5000 may be needed) as a leave-behind for those taking the
course.  Agency will follow (SI-1454).

CONSUMER CONTEST - Agency again met with representatives
of Iberia Airlines to discuss a cooperative effort for a
consumer contest in Boston.  Iberia is about to formally
announce the inauguration of direct flights from that
city.  It is envisioned that this contest would take
place in the Fall and Iberia would provide free transportation as part of the top prize.  In return for their
participation, Iberia would be given promotional consideration when publicizing and/or advertising the contest.
Agency will follow (SI-1337).


                    #        #        #

# PROCEDURAL REPORT

SETTING GOALS:  A GUIDE FOR MANAGERS

INTRODUCTION

In a recent survey (June 1984) conducted among managers, a majority (93 percent) expressed concern about the difficulties of setting, measuring, and achieving goals related to both personal and corporate performance. In response to this need, senior management sought the advice of several experts and consultants in the field. The following suggestions highlight their major points and comments about how managers can best set and meet goals as individuals and as members of a larger corporate entity.

SELECTING THE RIGHT GOALS

Just as an organization must carefully select the goals most beneficial to yearly health and growth, so too must its managers focus their energies on goals most suited to their particular needs and special skills. By focusing their efforts and resources on selected rather than on numerous goals, managers can increase the chances of significant success. On a larger scale, these efforts can affect and enhance corporate vitality and stability.

The most pressing question, of course, is "How do I know what the best goals are?" One solution involves preparing a list of alternative goals, and then asking the following questions:

- What do I want/need to accomplish in the next six to twelve months?
- Which goals warrant priority? Why?

- 2 -

- Which goals would senior management like to see me accomplish?

- How do the goals affect my staff, their priorities, and an ongoing workload?

- What do I do best?  Where are my skills most forceful and productive?

- What are my weaker areas?

- How will these goals contribute to my department or to the organization at large?

- Do I have a plan?

- Do my goals duplicate or conflict with the goals of others or with corporate policy?

- Are my goals realistic?

- Can I set a tentative completion date?

- How can I evaluate the long range effects of my activities?

## PREPARING A PLAN

Once the goals have been set and these questions carefully considered, the next step is to devise a plan for implementing and evaluating the goals.  This is best accomplished by focusing on specific rather than on general concerns.  In expressing the scope of the goals in a statement, it's important to concentrate on the particulars.  For example:

GOAL: Develop a training and development program by May 28 after identifying employee needs, interests, staff requirements, and delivery systems.

- 3 -

Had this idea been expressed more generally, say, "Develop a
training and development program," the specific tasks would
not be immediately identified, and time would be lost as the
manager sorted out the specifics of what he or she wanted to
accomplish.  It is not until the tasks or stages are recognized that the manager can assign various components of the
project to staff members.  He or she must then set a tentative completion date for each assignment, and schedule
periodic review meetings.

REVIEWING THE GOALS

    Because goals set early in the year can prove secondary
to others as time passes and needs change, the manager
should carefully and systematically review goals in terms of
relevance and probable achievement.  No goal should be
pursued merely for its own sake or to satisfy the need to
complete a specific project.  Goals that may prove counter-
productive to ongoing individual and corporate needs should
be discarded, especially if they appear outdated or no
longer viable.

CONCLUSION

    Clear goal-setting offers the advantage of preventing
routine activities from taking excessive time from pursuing
key goals.  Clear goal-setting helps managers to accomplish

- 4 -

particular aims and invariably leads to more effective
time management.  The ability to set and achieve selected
goals is crucial to the effective daily performance of all
managers.

# INFORMATION REPORT

## How Much Oil and Gas?

# TABLE OF CONTENTS

# 1. INTRODUCTION

The goal of this booklet is increased public understanding of the petroleum resources that remain in the world after more than a century of exploration and production.

Everyone recognizes that crude oil and natural gas exist in finite amounts, but no one really knows how much of either remains. Since E. L. Drake drilled his first well in 1859, a vast industry has been established and oil has become the world's dominant fuel. But petroleum geologists freely admit that definitive knowledge about the resource base that made this growth possible remains elusive.

Nevertheless, much has been learned and is being learned everyday about the earth and about the oil and gas fields already discovered. With this has come an improved ability to estimate the amount, location, and recoverability of the petroleum that remains to be found. Such information is important because it is widely assumed that oil and gas will together supply more than half the world's energy for the rest of this century, and a substantial portion for many years thereafter. If it were not believed that enough recoverable petroleum is left in the ground to make this feasible, major changes in investment plans, government policies, and the direction of scientific research would be needed.

At any given time, the amount of oil and gas available for consumption depends primarily on two factors: the producibility of already discovered reserves and the production policies of governments in the countries where those reserves exist. Over the long run, however, it is the amount of recoverable oil and gas left in the ground, including those volumes as yet undiscovered, that will be decisive. It is this, along with the economic factors influencing petroleum's supply and demand, that will determine how long the world can rely on crude oil and natural gas and how soon it must develop other sources of energy.

Estimates of the remaining petroleum resource base vary widely. Experts disagree about the size and producibility of individual reservoirs and about the total national and world reserves associated with already discovered fields. They are even further apart when assessing the world's undiscovered potential. This is not surprising when it is remembered that they are making judgments—frequently educated guesses—about hydrocarbons contained in porous rocks many thousands of feet under the earth's surface. Often, they have little more to go on than the data from a few widely dispersed 8-inch diameter holes in existing fields—and still less information in the case of fields expected to be discovered in the future.

The weight of informed opinion is not only that much petroleum remains to be discovered, but also that new reserves will be harder to find and more difficult and expensive to produce. There are limited prospects for finding additional giant fields such as those currently being worked in the Middle East.

Greater awareness of the ultimate limits of the world's petroleum and of the sharply increased costs of finding new supplies has underscored the need to make the most of known resources. For this reason, more attention than ever is now being focused on

1

"improved recovery" from discovered fields. Such methods will add to usable energy supplies—perhaps significantly.

This booklet describes the elements that make up the oil and gas resource base, gives estimates of their magnitude, and explains how these estimates are developed. In the process, it also defines some terms that have given rise to confusion. "Proved," "probable," and potential" reserves are not the same thing, nor are "reserves" the same as "resources," though all have sometimes been used interchangeably.

## 2. TERMS AND DEFINITIONS

Simply stated, the petroleum geologists' challenge is to identify areas where oil and gas are likely to exist in quantities large enough to justify the costs of finding and producing them. The starting point is a *sedimentary basin*, the basic regional geologic unit in which petroleum can exist. A basin is a subsurface area where layers or beds of sedimentary materials—clays or muds (shales), sandstones, or limestones—were deposited over millions of years.

The more promising basins for petroleum are those that originally formed in ancient seas or lakes whose waters contained countless tiny plants and animals. As these died, they were absorbed in the mud on the bottom, subjected over time to heat and pressure, and gradually transformed into petroleum. With the further passage of time, some of this petroleum was squeezed out of the shales and into cracks and pore spaces in adjacent sandstone or limestone beds. When this process took place during or just after vertical or horizontal movements of the earth's crust, a fraction of the oil and gas accumulated in localized traps or reservoirs—the fields which the industry seeks today.

Oil and gas reservoirs are not simply big subterranean caves or caverns. They are sandstone or limestone beds—often only a few feet thick but sometimes extending for miles—in whose pores and cracks oil and gas have been stored for eons. These hydrocarbons must move fairly long distances through those tiny openings in order to reach a few small drainage points (the wells) and be produced. It normally takes 10 to 30 years to fully recover a field's reserves—a tiny fraction of the time it took for its formation.

It would be interesting to know just how much oil and gas was originally in place in each trap. However, use of such figures would be misleading because typically only a portion of the oil in a given trap—often much less than half—is recoverable and, therefore, available to run our cars or heat our homes.

A more practical concept, therefore, is petroleum *resources*, which is defined as all the oil and gas believed to be eventually recoverable, by means of known or expected technologies, out of the total volumes in place. Some of these resources have already been found and are referred to as *discovered resources*. Those expected to be found in the future are *undiscovered potential* resources. The *total resource base* is the sum of the two. The specialist's perception of how much is recoverable is derived from a mixed bag of knowledge, ranging all the way from some relatively firm data to much that is

2

## The Requisites for Recoverable Petroleum to Exist in a Sedimentary Basin

For oil and gas to have accumulated in a reservoir and to be recoverable, all of the following had to be present:

A *source rock*, such as a shale, which was formed millions of years ago when layers of mud containing billions of microscopic animals and plants sank to the bottom of a sea or lake. Over time, as additional layers of sediments built up on top of them, these muds were subjected to heat and pressure, causing them to solidify and form shales. This process also led to the decomposition of the organisms deposited with the mud into compounds of hydrogen and carbon that we now know as petroleum.

A *reservoir rock*, such as a sandstone or limestone layer, which was in contact with source rocks so it could receive petroleum that was squeezed out of the source rocks as they were compressed by overlying sediments. The reservoir rock had to be porous—have cracks and open spaces between its grains—to provide a place to store the petroleum received from the source rocks. It also had to be permeable so that the oil and gas could move through it.

A *trap*, where oil and gas—which are lighter than the water that is also in the reservoir—have accumulated. There are two general types of traps: *structural* traps, formed by the folding or faulting of the reservoir rock layers, and *stratigraphic* traps, created when layers of porous, permeable reservoir rocks are sealed off by superimposed impermeable beds.

A *seal*, which is the dense rock that overlies the trap and prevents the petroleum liquids and gases from escaping.

Not only must all these features have been present; they also must have been properly related in time. The source rock had to be in contact with the reservoir rock after the organic matter was transformed into hydrocarbons so that they could be squeezed out of the shales and into the reservoirs. Similarly, the traps (and the seals) had to exist at the time the hydrocarbons were being forced into the reservoir rocks, in order to limit the movement of the oil and gas and so cause them to accumulate in what we today call oil and gas fields.

highly speculative. Consequently, it changes with time, in response to new geological information, improvements in exploration and recovery technology, and anticipated changes in price trends.

3

**U.S. Companies Required to Report Proved Reserves**

Current Federal securities law regulations require U.S. oil and gas producing companies registered with the Securities and Exchange Commission to include in their annual reports to shareholders estimates of the amount and value of their proved reserves in the ground. The purpose is to give the public—and particularly investors and potential investors—a better understanding of each company's worth and a better means of comparing one company with another.

The goal is worthy. But the fact that such information is published as a supplement to financial statements gives a misleading impression of its accuracy. Estimates of proved reserves are inherently uncertain, no matter how much effort goes into them. Estimates of the value of these reserves are even less accurate because production will occur over a long period during which significant changes may occur: in oil and gas prices, in production costs and production capabilities, and in competitive sources of energy.

Confusion may also arise from the exclusion of other, less certain classes of oil and gas resources (probable reserves, static resources, and undiscovered potential) for which formal reporting is not required.

In some cases, the latter might turn out to be more important than the proved reserves. For example, following discovery of a new field, it normally is necessary to drill several delineation wells to determine the extent of the discovery and to establish commerciality. Particularly in the remote and harsh environments that characterize much current exploration drilling, several years are required to delineate the discovery and to obtain the necessary production data to adequately determine the extent of the reserves. Typically, initial estimates of proved reserves increase with time as more wells are drilled, production experience is obtained, and the prospects for improving recovery are evaluated. Thus, a dilemma is posed: reporting only proved reserves tends to understate a company's petroleum assets in the ground—but including other categories would introduce still further elements of uncertainty.

A more limited but also elusive concept is that of *commercial reserves*, the segment of discovered resources that is thought to be recoverable at current or forecast prices. Of these, *proved* reserves—those whose existence is known with a high degree of confidence and which are commercially producible—are the most widely discussed. This is because petroleum companies regularly report their proved reserves to governments and shareholders. *Probable* reserves are those whose existence is less well known

**4**

and which are expected to be commercial in the future. The non-commercial portion of the discovered resources is called *static* resources. If prices rise, or if a remote area is developed because other fields are found nearby and a pipeline is built, or if drilling indicates a higher reserves volume than originally thought—than a static resource may become commercial and may move into the proved or probable reserves category.

Unfortunately, there is no universally accepted classification system for petroleum resource concepts. The terms used in this booklet are defined in accordance with the system employed by Exxon. Others may use fewer or more categories and may give them somewhat different names. No matter what classification system is used, however, the geologic and economic distinctions are not—and cannot be—precise. What is geologically known and/or commercially feasible changes with time and circumstances.

## 3. METHODS OF ESTIMATION

Geologists and reservoir engineers understandably have a better idea of how much oil and gas remain in fields already discovered than of how much is likely to be contained in fields yet to be discovered. This is because discovered fields always yield some information on which to base reserves estimates whereas projections of undiscovered potential are necessarily much more speculative. Not surprisingly, the methods used to estimate discovered resources and undiscovered potential differ considerably.

### Estimating Discovered Resources

After more than a century of petroleum exploration and production, the industry has developed a fairly substantial data base that can be used to estimate both commercial reserves and static resources for existing fields. Most of the world's major oil and gas fields have been extensively analyzed by the operators, and information on many of them is available publicly in technical journals. Geologic and engineering studies have also been published on many smaller fields in the United States and some other countries.

Depending on the amount and quality of information available, three general approaches are used in estimating the amount of oil and gas recoverable from an existing field:

*Extrapolations,* based on a field's past production. Extrapolation techniques are primarily applicable to the already-drilled and producing portions of a field. Factors taken into account include the production history and decline rates, the existence of undeveloped but potentially productive zones elsewhere in the field, the possibilities for enhanced recovery, and any constraints that may have inhibited past production.

*Theoretical calculations,* based on an existing field's geological and geophysical characteristics. These are especially useful for forecasting production from the

5

yet-to-be-drilled portions of a field. They involve such data as the field's area and the degree to which it is delineated; average thickness of the producing formations; porosity of the reservoir rocks; reservoir pressure and temperature; permeability of the rocks and characteristics of the oil, gas, and water in them; nature of the reservoir energy originally available to move the oil and gas into the well bores; and probable susceptibility of the reservoir to various methods of supplementing the original sources of energy.

*Comparisons* with other, similar fields for which more data are available. This approach is employed when the other two methods are not feasible—for example, in the case of a field which has not yet been developed or for which very little information is available. The assumption is that the new field will yield results like those of other, better-known fields which have comparable geological and/or reservoir characteristics.

Economic considerations determine how much of the discovered resources should be classified as commercial reserves. Questions to be answered about each field are: What capital expenditures will be required to initiate or complete development (a function of average production per well per day, the number of wells required, and anticipated well depths)? What will be the operating conditions (including accessibility, climate, weather conditions and, in the case of an offshore field, the depth of the water)? What quality oil will be produced (gravity and viscosity)? What is the outlook for oil and gas prices?

Usually, the published estimates of remaining reserves for already-discovered fields are in reasonably close agreement. Differences are due mainly to variations in the estimates of how much is likely to be obtained from application of improved recovery methods.

### Estimating Undiscovered Potential

The bases for estimating undiscovered potential—and for identifying locations for exploration—are geologic studies of the world's sedimentary basins. Geologists have identified approximately 600 sedimentary basins scattered throughout the world. About 160 of these are known to be productive or capable of production. Roughly 240 others have been explored to some degree—many only slightly—without the discovery of producible reserves. Another 100 are still essentially unexplored because of hostile physical conditions. The last 100 are judged to have very little chance of yielding petroleum, either because there is enough information on them to indicate that they simply lack the proper geologic characteristics or because they are located in environments beyond the reach of known or imagined technology.

Ultimately, of course, there is no substitute for the knowledge that comes from drilling exploratory wells. These are extremely costly, however, and, if undertaken indiscriminately, would make the discovery of hydrocarbons prohibitively expensive. For this reason, various supplementary techniques have been developed to improve exploration efficiency. These techniques, which utilize knowledge of the geological and

6

geochemical principles that govern hydrocarbon occurrence, help to narrow the range of possible places where oil and gas may be found. They involve gathering and analyzing large quantities of data, including:

Direct geological and geochemical data collected from surface rocks and exploratory wells.

Indirect data from many sources, including seismic surveys (analyses of sonic wave reflections from underground rock layers), gravimetric and magnetic surveys (measurements of the effects of various rocks on the earth's gravity and magnetic fields), and photographs of the earth's surface from satellites and aircraft.

The use of computers to analyze such data has become an important factor in the search for oil. They make it possible to analyze more data in more ways, thus increasing the chances of finding subtle indications of petroleum reservoirs that otherwise might be overlooked.

Even with these sophisticated analytical techniques, the assessment of undiscovered potential requires a great deal of informed judgment. When little information is available, the experts must rely principally on their interpretations of comparisons with better known basins that appear to have similar geologic characteristics. As exploration proceeds and the availability of geologic information increases, the quality of reserve calculations improves. But even in these circumstances, judgment is needed in deciding which data and calculation methods should be employed.

Because of the uncertainties in the assessment process, experts typically assign probabilities of occurrence to each of the various geologic factors which affect the existence and recovery of hydrocarbons. Such probabilities reflect the risk that the necessary geologic elements might not exist, as well as the imperfections in the data used. Putting these various assessments together yields an overall estimate of future undiscovered potential.

## 4. RESOURCE ESTIMATES

Given the ways in which petroleum was formed and stored over time, how much recoverable oil and gas is there in the world, and how is it distributed? What have been the historical trends of discoveries, what is the outlook for finding new oil and gas in the future, and what are the prospects for improving the recovery from existing fields?

### World Oil and Gas Resource Base

Experts, as has been noted, do not agree on the answers. A good example was provided by the 1977 World Energy Conference (WEC), at which twenty-seven petroleum companies, government agencies and individual consultants submitted projections. Estimates of the total oil and gas resource base—including what has been produced, the rest of what has already been discovered, and what is still undiscovered—ranged from about 3,000 to 7,000 billion barrels oil equivalent. (Oil equivalent means crude oil,

7

plus natural gas expressed as its energy equivalent in oil, plus liquids removed from the gas.) Applying statistical analysis to those experts' views indicates the mean—or most likely—result to be around 4,500 billion barrels. It also shows a 95 percent probability that the resource base was at least 3,000 billion barrels but only a 5 percent probability that it could be as high as 6,500 billion barrels.

Table 1 provides a more recent estimate of the world's oil and gas resource base, compiled by Exxon from a variety of industry sources and divided into the categories defined earlier. These figures suggest that the total resource base is between 3,000 and 5,000 billion barrels oil equivalent.

While the more recent total is reasonably consistent with the WEC mean of 4,500 billion barrels, the figures in Table 1 differ significantly from the World Energy Conference data in the estimate of undiscovered potential: the new range is 1,000 to 2,500 billion barrels, compared with 1,000 to 6,500 billion barrels for the WEC. One reason for this is the additional information that has been obtained from the exploration results of the ensuing three or four years; another is the fact that the newer range reflects industry projections only, whereas the WEC survey included a number of non-industry respondents.

## Discovered Reserves

In the more than 120 years since the first oil well was drilled in Pennsylvania in 1859, the world's cumulative production has been about 700 billion barrels oil equivalent. That is around 30 percent of the more than 2,000 billion barrels which have been discovered to date, shown in Table 1.

Table 2 shows that the U.S. is the world leader in cumulative crude oil production, even though it no longer leads in current output. The U.S.S.R., where oil was discovered in 1873, is second in cumulative production; and Saudi Arabia, which had its first

### TABLE 1. World Oil and Gas Resource Base, 1981

|  | Billions of Barrels Oil Equivalent* |
|---|---|
| Remaining Proved Reserves | 1000–1200 |
| Probable Reserves | 300–600 |
| Total Remaining Commercial Reserves | 1300–1800 |
| Cumulative Production to Date | 700 |
| Total Resources Discovered to Date | 2000–2500 |
| Undiscovered Potential | 1000–2500 |
| Total Oil and Resource Base | 3000–5000 |

* Includes crude oil, natural gas expressed as its energy equivalent in oil, and liquids removed from the gas.

8

**TABLE 2.** *Cumulative Crude Oil Production of Leading Countries, as of July 1, 1981*

| Country | Cumulative Production (Billions of Barrels) | Year of 1st Recorded Production |
|---|---|---|
| U.S. | 127 | 1859 |
| U.S.S.R. | 75 | 1863 |
| Saudi Arabia * | 44 | 1936 |
| Venezuela | 36 | 1917 |
| Iran | 30 | 1913 |
| Kuwait * | 22 | 1946 |
| Iraq | 16 | 1927 |
| Libya | 14 | 1961 |
| Canada | 10 | 1862 |
| Indonesia | 9 | 1893 |
| Nigeria | 9 | 1957 |
| Mexico | 8 | 1901 |
| Abu Dhabi | 6 | 1962 |
| Algeria | 6 | 1914 |
| Argentina | 4 | 1907 |
| Qatar | 3 | 1949 |

* Including 50% of neutral zone.
Sources: *Oil & Gas Journal*, U.S. Department of Energy.

discovery in 1938, is third. Reliable data on cumulative natural gas production are not available for many countries. Indeed, historical gas production for the world probably will never be known accurately because an indeterminate, but surely large, amount of gas was flared without being measured in the years before there were markets for it, and before reservoir energy conservation practices were introduced. However, the U.S. is certainly the leader in cumulative gas production, just as it has been for oil, and the U.S.S.R. is undoubtedly second.

Proved oil reserves are the most important part of the resource base, at least for the short term, and are distributed quite unevenly among nations. As illustrated in Table 3, the reported totals for individual countries can rise or fall significantly over the years, depending on production and the timing of additions to reserves. Of the top ten countries, five are in the Middle East, including Saudi Arabia, which is first by a wide margin, and Kuwait, which is second. Saudi Arabia accounts for 25 percent of the total; the top five, 62 percent; and the top fifteen, 92 percent.

Table 4, which aggregates oil reserves by groups of countries, shows that almost two-thirds of the current reserves belong to the thirteen member nations of the Organization of Petroleum Exporting Countries (OPEC). About 13 percent are in the Centrally Planned Economies (CPE) of the U.S.S.R., People's Republic of China, Eastern Europe, and Southeast Asia. Only 10 percent are estimated to be in the principal industrial nations which form the Organization for Economic Co-Operation and Development (OECD) and are the world's major energy consumers. The other 12 percent are in the rest of the world, which means all the developing countries outside OPEC, most

9

**TABLE 3.** *Estimated Proved Crude Oil Reserves of Leading Countries (billions of barrels)*

| Rank | Country | 1/1/82 | 1/1/77 | (Rank) | 1/1/72 | (Rank) |
|---|---|---|---|---|---|---|
| 1 | Saudi Arabia * | 167.9 | 113.2 | (1) | 157.5 | (1) |
| 2 | Kuwait * | 67.7 | 70.6 | (3) | 78.2 | (2) |
| 3 | U.S.S.R. | 63.0 | 78.1 | (2) | 75.0 | (3) |
| 4 | Iran | 57.0 | 63.0 | (4) | 55.5 | (4) |
| 5 | Mexico | 57.0 | 7.0 | (14) | 4.5 | (19) |
| 6 | Abu Dhabi | 30.6 | 29.0 | (7) | 18.9 | (8) |
| 7 | U.S. | 29.8 | 31.3 | (6) | 37.3 | (5) |
| 8 | Iraq | 29.7 | 34.0 | (5) | 36.0 | (6) |
| 9 | Libya | 22.6 | 25.5 | (8) | 25.0 | (6) |
| 10 | Venezuela | 20.3 | 15.3 | (12) | 13.9 | (9) |
| 11 | P.R.C. | 19.9 | 20.0 | (9) | 20.0 | (7) |
| 12 | Nigeria | 16.5 | 19.5 | (10) | 11.7 | (11) |
| 13 | U.K. | 14.8 | 16.8 | (11) | 5.0 | (18) |
| 14 | Indonesia | 9.8 | 10.5 | (13) | 10.4 | (12) |
| 15 | Algeria | 8.1 | 6.8 | (15) | 12.3 | (10) |
| | Top 15 | 614.7 | 540.6 | | 561.2 | |
| | All others | 56.0 | 58.4 | | 70.7 | |
| | World Total | 670.7 | 599.0 | | 631.9 | |

* Including 50% of neutral zone.
Source: *Oil & Gas Journal.*

**TABLE 4.** *Estimated Proved Crude Oil Reserves by Groups of Countries* * *(billions of barrels)*

| | | | | | | |
|---|---|---|---|---|---|---|
| OPEC | 439.0 | 65 | 404.2 | 67 | 438.7 | 69 |
| CPE | 85.9 | 13 | 101.1 | 17 | 98.5 | 16 |
| OECD | 63.9 | 10 | 64.0 | 11 | 63.7 | 10 |
| All others | 81.9 | 12 | 29.7 | 5 | 31.0 | 5 |
| Total | 670.7 | 100 | 599.0 | 100 | 631.9 | 100 |

* Country Groupings:

OPEC— Algeria, Ecuador, Gabon, Indonesia, Iran, Iraq, Kuwait, Libya, Nigeria, Qatar, Saudi Arabia, United Arab Emirates, Venezuela (the Neutral Zone reserves, shared 50/50 by Kuwait and Saudi Arabia, are also included).

CPE—Union of Soviet Socialist Republics, People's Republic of China, Eastern Europe, Cuba, Mongolia, North Korea, Viet Nam, Yugoslavia, Laos, and Kampuchea.

OECD—Australia, Austria, Belgium, Canada, Denmark, Finland, France, Greece, Iceland, Irish Republic, Italy, Japan, Luxembourg, the Netherlands, New Zealand, Norway, Portugal, Spain, Sweden, Switzerland, Turkey, United Kingdom, United States, and West Germany.

Source: *Oil & Gas Journal.*

of which—with the principal exception of Mexico—must import the bulk of their energy supplies.

Proved gas reserves, shown in Tables 5 and 6, also are distributed unevenly, but the list of principal countries shows different rankings and includes four which were not

**10**

**TABLE 5.**  *Estimated Proved Natural Gas Reserves of Leading Countries*
*(trillions of cubic feet)*

| Rank | Country | 1/1/82 | 1/1/77 | (Rank) | 1/1/72 | (Rank) |
|------|---------|--------|--------|--------|--------|--------|
| 1 | U.S.S.R. | 1160 | 918 | (1) | 546 | (1) |
| 2 | Iran | 484 | 330 | (2) | 200 | (3) |
| 3 | U.S. | 198 | 220 | (3) | 270 | (2) |
| 4 | Algeria | 131 | 126 | (4) | 107 | (4) |
| 5 | Saudi Arabia * | 118 | 66 | (5) | 56 | (7) |
| 6 | Canada | 90 | 56 | (7) | 54 | (6) |
| 7 | Mexico | 75 | 12 | (22) | 12 | (17) |
| 8 | Qatar | 60 | 28 | (13) | 8 | (20) |
| 9 | Netherlands | 56 | 62 | (6) | 83 | (5) |
| 10 | Norway | 49 | 19 | (19) | 10 | (18) |
| 11 | Venezuela | 47 | 41 | (9) | 25 | (12) |
| 12 | Nigeria | 41 | 44 | (8) | 40 | (8) |
| 13 | Kuwait * | 35 | 34 | (10) | 35 | (10) |
| 14 | Indonesia | 27 | 24 | (17) | 5 | (33) |
| 15 | Iraq | 27 | 27 | (14) | 22 | (14) |
| | | | | | | |
| Top 15 | | 2598 | 2007 | | 1473 | |
| All others | | 313 | 297 | | 252 | |
| World Total | | 2911 | 2304 | | 1725 | |

* Including 50% of neutral zone.
Source: *Oil & Gas Journal.*

**TABLE 6.**  *Estimated Proved Natural Gas Reserves by Groups of*
*Countries (trillions of cubic feet)*

| | 1/1/82 | % | 1/1/77 | % | 1/1/72 | % |
|------|--------|-----|--------|-----|--------|-----|
| OPEC | 1022 | 35 | 783 | 34 | 554 | 32 |
| CPE | 1195 | 41 | 953 | 41 | 558 | 32 |
| OECD | 466 | 16 | 460 | 20 | 518 | 30 |
| All others | 228 | 8 | 108 | 5 | 95 | 6 |
| | | | | | | |
| Total | 2911 | 100 | 2304 | 100 | 1725 | 100 |

Source: *Oil & Gas Journal.*

among the top fifteen in oil. The U.S.S.R. leads with 40 percent of the world's total, followed by Iran, the U.S., Algeria, and Saudi Arabia. These first five account for 72 percent; and the top fifteen, 89 percent.

OPEC, led by Iran, has 35 percent of the world's proved gas reserves. The Centrally Planned Economies, mainly the U.S.S.R., have 41 percent. The OECD group has about 16 percent, which is considerably more than its share of oil and reflects the significant reserves of the U.S. and the Netherlands. The remaining 8 percent of proved gas reserves are in the rest of the world, again led by Mexico.

11

## *Distribution of Undiscovered Potential*

Projections of undiscovered potential, the most speculative figure of all, vary from 1,000 to 2,500 billion barrels oil equivalent.

The petroleum industry's first century has amply demonstrated how unevenly the known hydrocarbon deposits are distributed around the world. Of the 160 basins so far found to be productive, only 25 have contained more than the equivalent of 10 billion barrels of oil (about the size of the Prudhoe Bay field on the Alaskan North Slope). Nevertheless, those 25 basins contain more than 85 percent of all the hydrocarbons discovered in the world to date. Furthermore, only six of these basins have reserves in excess of 50 billion barrels—and account for 65 percent of the total petroleum discovered so far. And, finally, just one basin, the Arabian/Persian Gulf, contains 40 percent of all the petroleum found to date.

Most experts, therefore, expect that an uneven distribution pattern will apply to the 440 basins which have not yet been demonstrated to contain significant amounts of oil or gas. They estimate that while a fair number of these may eventually turn out to be productive, no more than a dozen or so are likely to contain the equivalent of 10 billion barrels or more of oil. And of those, no more than two or three are expected to have the equivalent of 50 billion barrels of recoverable oil. The consensus, moreover, is that it is unlikely the unexplored basins in the world will rival the richness of the Arabian/Persian Gulf.

Despite all the technical advances made in exploration over the years, the petroleum industry is still unable to determine which of the remaining prospects will contain the major oil and gas fields of the future. The only way to determine this is the time-proven method: by drilling exploration wells. Some geologically promising spots may turn out to be unproductive, while others that appear less promising may yield hydrocarbons in abundance. To illustrate, one need look no farther than the eastern part of the U.S. Gulf of Mexico, which looked promising but turned out to be dry, or the Reforma area of Mexico, which had lain unrecognized and untested for years but which has now turned out to contain a large part of Mexico's currently estimated 57 billion barrel oil reserve. The one sure thing is that until the drill bit chews far into the earth, reserves estimates all are basically guesswork.

## *Outlook for Discovery Rates*

In the quarter century before 1970, substantial oil finds, principally in the Middle East, raised the world's annual rate of discoveries to an average of 20 to 30 billion barrels. As production rates were relatively low, these exploration successes led to a build-up in the inventory of discovered reserves. By the early 1970's, however, the situation had changed. Discoveries had declined to an annual average of about 15 billion barrels. This, coupled with continuously rising production rates, caused the inventory of discovered reserves to begin to decline.

Even assuming continued active exploration efforts, something like the lower overall discovery rates of the last decade is expected to persist in the future. If world oil

12

### Other Hydrocarbon Resources

The crude oil and natural gas resources referred to in this booklet are mostly what are termed "conventional hydrocarbons"—that is, naturally occurring fluids existing in the kinds of reservoirs that the petroleum industry is accustomed to. However, there are other sources of hydrocarbon energy which may be called "unconventional"—either because of their chemical makeup or because of the places where they are found. The unconventional sources most likely to be exploited over the balance of this century are:

Synthetic oil, obtained from the kerogen (an insoluble organic substance which can be converted into a hydrocarbon) found in oil shales.

Synthetic oil and gas, derived from coal.

Crude oil which is extremely viscous to semisolid, deposited in sandstone rocks (oil sands or tar sands, containing bitumen or very heavy oil).

Natural gas trapped in extremely low permeability rocks (tight gas sands).

The unconventional source farthest from current exploitation is natural gas which is trapped subsurface in:

Extremely deep sedimentary rocks (30,000–50,000 ft.).

Geopressured sediments (dissolved in water).

Shallow shale beds (especially Devonian shales).

Coal seams.

Solid hydrates in arctic regions and ocean areas.

Except for limited amounts of very heavy oil and some of the gas in tight sands, none of these other hydrocarbon resources is included in the resource estimates discussed previously. While volume claims for several of them are mind-boggling, there are, unfortunately, few hard data on these resources. Some involve staggering technological, environmental, and economic problems. In fact, it may take more energy to recover some of these resources than can be obtained from them. Others could be even more costly to exploit than future large-scale sources of renewable energy.

consumption holds steady or increases slightly in the years ahead, the decline in the inventory of discovered oil reserves is likely to continue. As a result, oil production eventually will reach a plateau—probably sometime early in the next century—and then begin to drop.

13

Historical information about gas discovery and consumption rates is not as complete and accurate as for oil, and projections for the future are more uncertain. However, present data indicate that, in contrast to oil, the gas discovery rate still exceeds the gas production rate. Moreover, the world is expected to go on building an inventory of discovered gas reserves, even with projected steady increases in gas production, and is not expected to begin liquidating that inventory for some years. Therefore, gas production probably will not reach its peak until well into the 21st century.

Predictions are always risky, but petroleum industry experts are fairly certain about some aspects of the discovery outlook. Finding and developing the world's as yet undiscovered oil and gas resources will be progressively more difficult and costly. The number of unexplored areas where there are chances of finding large fields is steadily diminishing. Furthermore, many of the more promising of these are either in remote, undeveloped locations or involve exceptionally harsh operating environments, such as deep water or the cold of the polar regions. In such places, exploration and production operations are sure to be technologically demanding and the development of new fields will require long lead times.

Experience has shown that the largest discoveries in a basin are usually made first and that the sizes of new fields generally decrease as exploration progresses in that basin. This means that in those areas where production already exists, the fields now remaining to be discovered are likely to be smaller, on average, than past discoveries.

What all of this signifies is that despite anticipated high levels of exploration effort, the world's total remaining discovered resources are expected to decline with time. Eventually—sooner for oil, a little later for gas—there simply won't be enough oil or gas reserves in the world to support further growth and, inevitably, production will begin to decline. When this will happen depends on how rapidly existing resources are produced and the rate at which the industry can find and develop new reserves in the future as well as on the costs of alternatives.

## Improved Recovery Prospects

Improved recovery methods are already employed in many countries, but the potential for broader application and for technology improvement is substantial. In fact, some experts believe that these techniques could double the recovery from many existing fields.

Improved recovery most often comes into play after natural reservoir pressures have pushed out all of the petroleum they can. That usually is from a fifth to a third of the oil in place and half to three quarters of the gas in gas fields. Sometimes, however, natural and improved recovery methods are employed concurrently. In the case of fields containing very heavy oil—that is, crude oil too viscous to be produced in the normal manner—improved recovery techniques may be the *only* feasible way to extract *any* of the oil or gas.

The initial phase of improved recovery—more commonly known as secondary recovery—involves injecting water or gas to displace more oil. These secondary methods already are very widely employed. For example, about half of U.S. production cur-

**14**

rently comes from fields where secondary recovery techniques are utilized. However, these processes still leave behind large quantities of oil and gas.

A more advanced form of improved recovery—tertiary—is used to coax out some more of this remaining petroleum. Tertiary recovery usually takes one of three principal forms: thermal, chemical, or miscible. The approach used in a particular situation depends on the nature of the oil, gas, and water in place and on rock characteristics and reservoir parameters. Among the most important factors are the type of oil—light, medium, or heavy—and the reservoir depth and pressure. Generally:

*Thermal* methods are used in relatively shallow, low pressure reservoirs containing thick, highly viscous oils. The processes, which includes steam injection and in situ combustion, heat the rock and the oil. This reduces oil viscosity and makes it easier for the oil to flow into the producing wells.

*Chemical* methods are applicable to a wide range of oils and a broad variety of reservoir conditions. The processes include flooding with detergent-like surfactants to wash oil from surfaces in a reservoir and injection of polymers which, by "thickening" the water, make it more effective in pushing oil toward producing wells.

*Miscible* methods—best suited to medium and light oils in fairly deep, medium to high pressure reservoirs—include solvent flooding and the injection of carbon dixodie or nitrogen. The objective is to achieve a complete mixture of reservoir fluids and injected fluids, which improves flow characteristics and makes it easier to displace the oil.

The potential attractiveness of these methods has been recognized for a long time. Now, after many years of laboratory experiments and pilot tests, a few commercial-scale tertiary projects are in operation, mostly in the U.S. The slow pace of adoption reflects three things:

First, there have been, and continue to be, significant technical problems. Some of these problems are related to the reservoir fluids and rocks, others to the injected fluids, and still others to surface environmental issues.

Second, the costs—both the initial outlays for facilities and chemicals and the subsequent operating expenses—have been, and still are, very high. Most tertiary projects were not attractive before the increases in oil and gas prices of recent years.

Third, because of the very large initial outlays and significant technical risks, each project must be very carefully studied, planned, and designed. Technical manpower requirements also place limits on the rate at which new projects can be started up.

Some experts think that something like 2,000–4,000 billion barrels oil equivalent would be left in the ground—lost forever—when the existing fields can no longer be produced if it were not for improved recovery efforts (both secondary and tertiary). For the Middle East *alone,* the estimate has ranged from 1,000 to 2,000 billion barrels.

15

Future improved recovery programs, many of them utilizing still-emerging technologies, are expected to further increase the percentages of the in-place hydrocarbons that can eventually be produced. Just how much is uncertain but the range of resource base figures in Table 1 suggests that the industry is anticipating average recoveries of around 50 percent for oil and over 75 percent for gas. This, in turn, means that perhaps as much as a sixth of the current estimate of the world's remaining discovered resources is attributed to tertiary recovery techniques.

## 5. SUMMARY

No one knows for sure the amounts of oil and gas that remain in the earth. Major uncertainties inhere both in resource estimation techniques and in the economic factors governing reserves. The most recent estimates place the world's total resource base between 3,000 and 5,000 billion barrels oil equivalent, of which nearly a third (1,000–1,200 billion barrels) is now considered proved reserves—that is, oil and gas producible in today's circumstances. Since the world's annual oil and gas consumption is expected to average 30–40 billion barrels oil equivalent per year over the next couple of decades, there are sufficient reserves at present. However, by the end of this century there won't be enough reserves to permit production at levels now foreseen, unless substantial quantities of new oil and gas are discovered in the interim.

An understanding of the concepts and terms used in analyzing the petroleum resource base and reasoned estimates of its components are important for public policy. They enable governments and the public to place information about new discoveries in perspective, and they help to insure the timely discovery and development of additional supplies of oil and gas. In addition, they provide a background against which to plan the development of alternative energy sources—both those, such as coal, that can be important in the near term and those, such as synthetic fuels and the renewable forms of energy, on which the world will increasingly depend over the long run.

# PROCESS REPORT

CHASE COMMERCIAL CORPORATION

MARKETING AND SALES MANAGEMENT PROGRAM

May 23-28, 1982

MARKETING & SALES MANAGEMENT

WORKSHOPS

Reprinted by permission of Chase Manhattan Bank.

## INTRODUCTION

The purpose of this series of workshops is to give you
the opportunity to use the concepts and theories that have
been discussed in class to develop marketing and management
strategies for various selected markets in the Chase Commercial Corporation.  While these markets have their own unique
requirements, in general, a clearly articulated marketing
strategy with a high degree of selectivity and focus is
required to serve these markets effectively and profitably.

Marketing is defined as detecting and meeting customer
needs at a profit.  As you go through the process of developing a marketing strategy, it is important to think in terms
of customers and customer needs, not in terms of Chase
products and services.  As Phil Kotler points out, "The
critical difference between selling and marketing is that
selling focuses on the needs of the seller while marketing
focuses on the needs of the buyer."  Marketing strategy must
begin with an assessment of the customer and the customer's
needs.

The market planning and management processes that you
will be using in these workshops is presented in detail in
the Chase document titled A Framework for Strategic Planning
to Support Strategic Management.  You may find it helpful to
refer to this document as you go through the workshops.

For this series of workshops you will be divided into
work groups, each of which will be responsible for developing
a strategy for a different market or product.

- 2 -

   I.  Development of the Regional Asset Based Lending
      Market

  II.  Development of the Regional Equipment Leasing &
      Finance Market

 III.  Development of National Vendor Market

On Thursday afternoon, following the last workshop, each group will present a summary of its strategy to the other groups. Use of flip charts for these presentations is encouraged. In addition, each group will be responsible for preparing a written presentation after the program for the senior managers directly interested in the workshop topic. Senior management will be represented at Thursday's presentation.

INSTRUCTIONS FOR WORKSHOP I

The purpose of Workshop I is to decide upon a method for segmenting the market. Often the pressures of day-to-day job responsibilities create an environment in which attention is focused on individual products rather than customers ("trees") or rather than groups of customers ("the forest"). While this may be appropriate for sales people, a manager with limited marketing and sales resources is faced with a more complex task. The manager must allocate resources in some systematic way in order to generate the maximum total benefit for the CCC.

- 3 -

STEP 1:  Market Definition.  A market is defined as the intersection of a customer class and service/product group.

* Who are the customers?
  - What are the identifying characteristics that enable you to separate customers from non-customers?
* What are their needs?
  - What are the customer needs that CCC could meet through offering its current or potential range of products and services?
  - What are the key steps to relationship enhancement?

STEP 2:  Market Segmentation.

* How should the market be segmented?
  - In addition to the conventional ways of segmenting the market -- i.e., by geography, industry, size -- consider the advantages and disadvantages of these methods of segmentation:
    a.  by service usage (e.g., fee vs. loan)
    b.  by growth potential
    c.  by psychographics (e.g., modern vs. traditional)
    d.  by level of risk
    e.  by type of relationship (e.g., lead bank vs. major bank vs. minor bank)
    f.  other segments
  - Assess each segmentation method in terms of its
    - measurability

- 4 -

- - accessibility
- - substantiality
- Select the segmentation method (or combination of
  them) that most clearly differentiates customer
  groups based on their unique needs and characteristics.
- Identify and describe briefly each of the segments
  derived through the segmentation method you have
  selected.
- Where appropriate, develop a market definition and
  segmentation for each team member.
- Select a team member's market definition and
  segmentation that represents the best quality
  work your team produced.  This will be the model
  you should present on Thursday.

INSTRUCTIONS FOR WORKSHOP II

The purpose of Workshop I was to decide upon a segmentation strategy and to identify the segments derived by using
segmentation analysis.  In Workshop II you are asked to assess
Chase's current position and future objective in each market
segment.  In evaluating Chase's competitive position, you will
probably find it necessary to rely more on managerial judgment than on hard data.

STEP 3:  Market Attractiveness.  A market is considered
         attractive if its potential for providing a

- 5 -

significant contribution to objectives for earnings
growth and ROI is judged to be high.

* How attractive is each of the market segments identified
  in step 1? (High, medium, or low.)
  - In assessing market attractiveness, consider such
    factors as:

    Size

    Expected growth rate

    Profitability to C.C.C. by serving this market
      segment

    Usage of other Chase services/products

    Level of risk in doing business with this market
      segment

    Competitive environment (intensity of competition
      in this market segment)

STEP 4:  Competitive Position.  Competitive position simply
         refers to C.C.C.'s standing relative to major
         competitors.  The key to developing a strong
         competitive position is to identify and build on
         factors that give Chase a competitive advantage
         relative to major competitors in target markets.

  * Who are Chase's major competitors in target markets?

  * What are Chase's weaknesses and strengths (competitive
    advantages) relative to major competitors in each
    market segment?

  * What is Chase's competitive position in each of the
    market segments identified in Step 1?

- 6 -

* Consider these factors:

    Market share (absolute and relative to competitors)

    Profitability

    Perceived quality of services/products

    Breadth of product/service line

* For each market segment, indicate Chase's competitive position (strong, average, or weak).

STEP 5:  Environmental Factors.  Strategic plans are based on certain assumptions about the external environment. It is critical to identify these assumptions if there is a reasonable likelihood that a change in the expected course of events would have a significant impact on the implementation of the strategy.

* What environmental factors are likely to change and thus could significantly affect your competitive position or the attractiveness of the market segments?

    - Consider factors in these areas:

        Government/Regulatory

        Economic

        Technological

        Social (e.g., demographic, attitudinal)

        Other

    - Indicate what the factor is, and what the expected impact is on market attractiveness or competitive position.

STEP 6:  Summary Positioning.  A 3 x 3 matrix can be used effectively to illustrate the current position and

- 7 -

the trends of market segments along the dimensions
of market attractiveness and competitive position.

* Use a matrix to indicate the current position of each
  market segment.
* Use a matrix to postulate any overall trends in the
  market.
* Use a matrix with arrows to indicate current trend and
  future objective.  In deciding the future objective,
  you must assume a constant level of financial and human
  resources.  Therefore, ask both:  where will we put
  more effort and where will we put _less_ effort.


Market Segment A

Investment strategy:  Grow/penetrate

Strategic objective:  Enter market in 1980; achieve
10% market share and $100MM in total revenue by 1984.

Note:  If you do not have enough data to supply hard
numbers by strategic objectives, indicate "increase,"
"level," or "decrease" for each of these three categories:
market share, total revenue, and ROI.


INSTRUCTIONS FOR WORKSHOP III

In Workshops I and II, you segmented the market and
determined the current positioning of each market segment.
In Workshop III you are asked to select an investment
strategy for each segment.

STEP 7:  Investment Strategy.

- 8 -

* Review the alternative investment strategies listed
  in Appendix A.
* For each of the market segments you identified in
  Workshop I, which strategies would you use?  (i.e.,
  grow/penetrate, harvest, withdraw, etc.)

(Note:  Assume a constant level of resources.  This means,
for example, that you cannot use a grow/penetrate strategy
for one segment without making a commensurate reduction in
effort in another segment.)

STEP 8:  Strategic Objective.

* What measurable results to you intend to achieve in
  each market segment?


INSTRUCTIONS FOR WORKSHOP IV

In this workshop you are asked to design specific action
plans for each market segment.  This is the crucial stage
where you must move from concept to ACTION.

STEP 9:  Attack Plans.  "Marketing mix" refers to the set of
         controllable variables that can be used to influence
         the buyer's response.

* Keeping in mind the customer needs unique to each
  market segment and C.C.C.'s competitive strengths and
  weaknesses, determine an effective marketing approach
  for each market segment.

- 9 -

* Consider these elements of the "marketing mix":

Product

- What aspects of the product/service should you
  stress in order to meet customer needs and
  differentiate C.C.C. from your competitors?

Promotion/Communication

- What types of promotion and other means of communication can be used to approach customers in this
  market segment?  (For example, consider:  promotional materials, advertising, use of Chase
  publications, public relations, industry meetings,
  speeches, etc.)

Distribution

- How do you and your Business Development Officers
  approach customers in this market segment?  (For
  example, consider:  call frequency, use of senior
  officers, use of Chase network.)

Price

- How should C.C.C. products/services be priced for
  this market segment?
- Should C.C.C. be a price leader or follower?
- What innovative pricing strategies can be used?


INSTRUCTIONS FOR WORKSHOP V

   In the previous workshops, you focused on your market.
In this workshop, you'll allocate your resources required to

- 10 -

meet your marketing plan.

STEP 10:  Sales Management.

* How would you organize your sales force to face off
  against the markets?  (That is, what system would you
  use to divide customers and customer groups among
  Business Development Officers?)
* Within each market segment:
  - Should efforts be concentrated on a small number
    of accounts or spread over a large number of
    accounts?
  - What percentage of time should be spent servicing
    existing accounts versus new accounts?
* What standards of performance would you establish to
  measure each salesperson's contribution?
* Draft a three to six month work plan for your sales
  force members and/or for your own accounts.

## APPENDIX A

### MARKET SEGMENT INVESTMENT STRATEGIES

| Category | Assessment of Contribution to Earnings | General Objective | Investment Commitment |
|---|---|---|---|
| I Grow/Penetrate | Significant increment to earnings in long run. | Penetrate market to establish strong future position. | Sustained long term investment. Accept high investment risk. |
| II Grow/Balanced | Significant current and long term earnings growth. | Maintain current strong position in growth market with little or no reduction in ROI. | Sustained investment at a rate to maintain growth with market. Accept medium investment risk. |
| III Selectively Invest | Significant current and future earnings but limited growth with stable margins. | Maintain or improve ROI as primary objective. Exploit selective opportunities for volume growth if available. | Limited investments in targets or opportunity. Accept low investment risk. |

APPENDIX A (CONT.)

| Category | Assessment of Contribution to Earnings | General Objective | Investment Commitment |
|---|---|---|---|
| IV Defend | Significant current earnings. Declining margin. Limited volume growth. | Defend earnings base until attractive opportunities can replace. | Invest only in response to competitive inroads. Accept medium investment risk. |
| V Harvest | Significant current earnings from strong position but outlook is for a flat or declining market. | Maximize current earnings. Allow gradual erosion in share if it improves margin. | Disinvest gradually at a rate to avoid collapse of business. |
| VI Restructure/ Rebuild | Opportunity for at least a one time increment in earnings where market share at least average. | Eliminate current deficiencies to restore profitability. | One time investment dictated by nature of deficiencies. Accept medium investment risk. |

APPENDIX A (CONT.)

| Category | Assessment of Contribution to Earnings | General Objective | Investment Commitment |
|---|---|---|---|
| VII Withdraw | Declining market and earnings. Possible one time earnings increment from sale or elimination of loss. | Withdraw from market on most favorable terms. | Disinvest. |
| VIII Hold | Nature of opportunity not established. | Carry out strategy development while maintaining status quo. | No investment until strategy developed. Commit to resources required for strategy development. |

# ECONOMIC FORECAST REPORT

QUARTERLY ECONOMIC REPORT
ECONOMICS GROUP

CONFIDENTIAL
NOVEMBER 1981

## The Business Outlook

In brief:  The economy is moving downward at a good clip and on a broad scale.  The unemployment rate is eight percent, heading toward nine.  Industrial production has dropped by 2.9% in the past three months and is still falling fast.  Auto sales:  terrible; housing starts:  worse; new order:  down all over the place.  In short -- a real, honest to goodness, economic recession.

You want some good news?  We have it:  Everybody now agrees that this is a recession.  And why is that good news?  Because the first and therefore the most essential step in resolving a problem is the recognition that a problem exists.  Recognizing the problem, business has begun to make the necessary adjustments -- in particular, to try to get inventories back under control.  The 1.5% decline of industrial

A quarterly economic forecast report of the Chase Economics Group. The text has been reprinted with permission of Chase Manhattan Bank.

- 2 -

production in October, involving by far the majority of
industries, shows that this objective is being pursued
vigorously.  A fast start on inventory correction does not
by itself assure that a recession will be either brief or
mild.  Nevertheless, "the sooner, the better" is a good
rule of thumb.

It would be nice to think that the public policy
reaction to this recession would be similarly rational.  To
us, "rational" in this circumstance means following monetary
and fiscal policies designed to produce more growth and less
inflation in the long run rather than jeopardizing those
goals with desperate measures to counter a short-term correction in the private economy.  (If you want to know what
that means in detail, just ask.  We never preach in our
regular economic reports.  Well -- hardly ever.)  Can we
expect such sensible behavior out of Washington?  Despite
the increasingly distraught -- and utterly predictable --
utterances from various members of Congress, we have some
hope.  Our operating assumption is that they won't seriously
mess it up.

Add to these ingredients a considerable and continuing
decline in interest rates and further modest improvements in
inflation rates and it is possible to see the outline of the
rest of this misadventure.  Total activity is likely to
decline fairly rapidly for several more months, with the
sharpest drop during the current quarter and a smaller one

- 3 -

in early 1982.  We expect an upturn beginning in the spring,
with a strong recovery in the second half of the year.  The
July 1 tax cut will be a big help.

In spite of the poor beginning, this pattern should
produce reasonably good growth in 1982.  It won't show up in
the year-to-year figures; real GNP on that basis will probably
be down by a small fraction.  Fourth-quarter to fourth-quarter,
however, we expect an increase of about 2½%.  That's not a
really big number, but it should be welcome after the experience of the previous two years.  Real GNP in the current
quarter will be virtually identical (in total if not in
detail) with the figure for the fourth quarter of 1979.  We
also expect the rate of price inflation to improve in 1982,
declining by 1½-2 percentage points.  Sector-by-sector
details of the forecast are discussed in detail later in this
report.  But before we get to those details, we would like to
make a few comments on recent history, which appears to
contain lessons that are relevant for the next several years.

Q.  Isn't the economy behaving rather oddly?

A.  You bet it is.

You don't think you live in unusual times?  In a
period of less than eight years you have experienced the
following:

1)  The longest peacetime economic expansion in
recorded U.S. history.  (Records of such matters date

- 4 -

from 1854.)   That expansion lasted 58 months, ending
with January, 1980.

2)   The <u>shortest</u> (but close to the steepest) <u>economic
contraction</u> in history.   According to the cycle experts,
it lasted six months and ended in July, 1980.

3)   Judging by the information available, <u>one of the
shortest economic expansions</u> in history.

4)   <u>The highest and probably the most variable
interest rates</u> in our history.

You want more?   Even if our forecast of faster growth
in 1982 proves to be correct, total economic growth in the
three years 1980-82 will be less than in any other three
consecutive years since the U.S. reconverted to civilian
production following World War II.   As we can't help noticing
from time to time, that was before a growing number of our
readers were born and before all but a few of you joined this
bank.

No doubt many factors contributed to this remarkable
spree of record-setting.   But why quibble?   The essential
source was inflation.   And the operating mechanisms that produced the new records were changes in the private and public
response to price inflation -- changes that came about as
people finally recognized just how deeply ingrained the
inflationary process had become.

1)   <u>The long expansion</u>.   You may recall that the vast
majority of economic forecasters expected a recession to

- 5 -

begin during 1979.  (Just to show our sincerity, we will
confess that we were among that mistaken majority.)  Why the
widespread error?  In our case, as with many others, the
mistake occurred because the public reacted to its perception of rising price inflation by continuing to spend at
high levels -- not to mention borrowing at record rates to
enhance consumption even further.  We had expected the
opposite.  Always before during the postwar period, consumers had reacted to new bursts of price inflation in quite
a different way; they saved more and bought less.  While we
can't prove this assertion, we suspect that the altered
response reflected a new belief that inflation had become a
permanent phenomenon, and one that was very likely to get
worse rather than better.  Regardless, that consumption spree
may have added as much as a year to the expansion.  It's
worth noting, too, that the personal saving rate has remained
at relatively low levels ever since; people still believe
that inflation is their more or less permanent lot.  (The
saving rate did jump this October -- presumably a transitory
response to the Some Savers Certificate, as we prefer to call
it.)

   2)  <u>The short, sharp, 1980 recession.</u>  The recession
occurred partly because consumers began to run out of borrowing power.  But the principal cause was a change in policy:
The Federal Reserve finally decided that it had to do something effective about inflation and took action in October,

- 6 -

1979.  Over the next three months, short-term rates rose to
extraordinary levels, the bond market collapsed, residential
real estate activity tumbled, and business investment began
to fall.  By February, the economy was in recession.  Then
another anti-inflation policy -- the President's invocation
of the Credit Control Act of 1969 -- accelerated the slide.

The recession ended when credit controls were lifted and
short-term interest rates were permitted to fall sharply.
And the public helped by quickly resuming its free-spending
ways -- with the principal exception, that is, of products
that ordinarily involve the extensive use of credit --
automobiles and major appliances.

3)   One of the shortest economic expansions in history.
That vigorous rebound didn't last long -- about six months,
in fact.  (For various technical reasons, the ensuing out-
right recession probably won't be dated as starting before
August; nevertheless, there has been no real growth since
January.)  The return to hyper-high interest rates did it.
You put the kind of anti-inflation policy that the Fed is
pursuing together with a big Federal deficit, continuing
rapid price inflation and an expanding private economy, and
that's what you get.

An important non-event also was involved in truncating
the recovery.  The reaction of the Congress to the 1980
recession violated a tradition of fifty years standing.
This time, there was no rush to fight recession with new

- 7 -

spending programs (public works, jobs, etc.), or with big new
tax cuts.  (In the euphemistic parlance of the day, we assume
that the latter would now be labeled "negative revenue
enhancement.")  In the past, the full effect of such actions
tended to be felt well after a recovery had started and thus
helped to give it momentum.  It should be noted that this
break with political tradition was also a reaction to
inflation.  The members of Congress had come to recognize
that the public increasingly blamed them for inflation, and
they acted (or more correctly, non-acted) accordingly.

4)  <u>Those amazing interest rates</u>.  The adjustment of
various sections of the economy to the new interest rate
climate is still in its early stages.  One unfortunate form
of adjustment is reflected in the large rise in business
and personal bankruptcies.  On a more positive note, it
could be argued that the new financial climate was a major
reason for passage of the Depository Institutions Deregula-
tion and Monetary Control Act of 1980.

Why this digression from our normal concentration on
the specifics of the outlook?  (Aside, that is, from self-
pity over the uncommon difficulty of forecasting these days.)
Two points:

First, the path of economic growth is likely to remain
choppy, and total growth unsatisfactory, until something
gives.  That is, until there is a fundamental change in Fed
policy, or the Federal deficit, or the public's spending

- 8 -

habits, or the inflation rate itself.  But who knows which, or when?  Our forecast for the next year or so in effect assumes no basic shifts in any of these, although we have allowed for some decline in the inflation rate and a modest rise in the rate of saving.

Second, Reagonomics has now been added to the picture. At the moment, his program is being treated in the press as if it were a guaranteed recipe for economic disaster in 1983 or 1984.  That is a premature judgment, for at least a couple of reasons.  For one, this program, like all programs, will be significantly modified as time passes.  For the other -- and this is one of the reasons for the past few pages of observations -- the program is being imposed on an economy that is already behaving in ways for which there is only very recent and limited precedent.  To predict the outcome with any degree of conviction requires more gall than we feel is justified by the current state of economic knowledge.  We can probably hope, at best, to minimize surprise at the results if we are exceptionally observant.

### Elements in the Outlook

Consumer spending was a sustaining force in the economy through the third quarter of this year, but now appears to be weakening.  Detroit's attempts at self-levitation through repeated temporary price cuts and special sales inducements have finally run out of steam.  Total car sales will run at

- 9 -

an annual rate under 8 million units in the current quarter,
with domestic models only a shade over 5.5 million. The
comparable figures for all of last year -- bad as it was --
were 9 million and 6.6 million. Sales of soft goods have
held up better, but no longer show much strength. The
recent tax cut could provide a little help in this sector.
Nevertheless, the outlook for the rest of the Christmas
selling season is somewhat less than prepossessing.

The first quarter next year doesn't look much better
for consumer spending. Incomes will be adversely affected
by the recession, and also by lower interest rates;
personal interest income rose by close to $50 billion
(about 19%) in 1981, but won't be doing nearly so much for
the next few months. (Interest available for spending will
weaken even further, now that substantial earnings have been
tied up in tax-free savings certificates. The new IRAs will
have much the same effect throughout 1982 and beyond.) And
the dismal state of residential real estate markets will
continue to limit the availability of housing-related
capital gains, which provided major support for consumer
spending during the late 1970s.

Spring should bring the beginning of a revival, and we
expect strong consumer spending later in the year when the
next individual income tax cut becomes effective. All
major classes of products should benefit. We do remain
cautious on auto sales, however. Our 1981 estimate is 9.2

- 10 -

million units, up from 8.7 million this year.  We understand
that forecasts by the domestic automobile companies are in
the same neighborhood, with one big qualification:  If
interest rates come way down, and stay down, at least one of
them thinks sales could go as high as 10.5 million units.
We wouldn't go quite that far.

    Once a cyclical downturn gets under way, the path
followed by business inventories always becomes a key deter-
minant of the depth and duration of recession.  As noted at
the beginning of this report, business has made an early and
determined start on the necessary inventory correction.
Because the current inventory excess is almost entirely due
to declining sales -- rather than, as in 1974, a combination
of falling sales and speculatively over-built inventories --
the correction need not be a major one.  It is likely to be
concentrated in the first quarter of next year, and to end
around mid-spring.  This factor, more than anything else,
will determine the length of the recession.

    Business capital investment has been declining in real
terms since early 1981 and will go down some more.  With the
operating rate in manufacturing down to 76.9% in October and
clearly heading lower, there is little incentive to add
capacity.  The fall McGraw-Hill preliminary survey of 1982
investment plans indicated no change in real terms in 1982.
When taken near cyclical turning points, this survey tends to
underestimate gains.  So we think that investment will show

- 11 -

a marginal decline -- 1% or so in real terms -- in 1982.  The
drop would be a good deal sharper but for petroleum refining
(reacting to a change in both input and output mix) and
communications.

This outlook could be considered disappointing in view
of the significant investment incentives contained in the new
tax law.  Until final demand improves, however, the enhanced
cash flow from liberalized depreciation is likely to be used
in good measure to improve corporate balance sheets rather
than be pumped right back into additional new investment.
Given the state of some of those balance sheets, that may not
be such a bad idea in the short run.  As final markets
improve later in 1982, investment should begin to pick up;
1983 could be quite a good year.

And then there is housing.  The faint of heart among
you may wish to skip this section.  Come to think of it, we
feel vaguely squeemish ourselves when dealing with the
subject.  So let's be uncharacteristically succinct.

Residential real estate activity, in all its aspects,
is in truly tattered shape.  This sector is, of course, the
prototypical victim of super-high interest rates.  The sole
comprehensive cure consists of lower rates.  Mortgage rates
have begun to slip just a little but and should come down
some more over coming months.  Housing starts should hit
bottom within the next couple of months and begin to improve
early next year.  But the recovery will be only partial in

- 12 -

1982; this really is a seriously damaged industry. We
estimate new housing starts at about 1.1 million units in
1982 -- just a shade over the 1981 figure, which will be the
worst in more than three decades.

Federal government purchases of goods and services will
rise about in line with overall economic activity during
1982, with defense purchases more than responsible for the
gain. State and local purchases are another matter. We
expect them to be close to flat, and they could decline
significantly; currently, they are about 2% lower, in real
terms, than they were a year ago. State revenues are under
a multi-pronged assault: the recession hurts them; Federal
assistance, which provided close to one quarter of S&L
revenues in recent years, is being cut back; because many
state and local taxes are computed on a base established by
Federal tax statutes, the ongoing program of Federal tax
cust also erodes S&L revenues; and the proliferation of tax-
limiting laws is a further constraint. It is not so long
since state and local employment was growing by 400,000 a
year; it fell by that amount in the past year, and the
fiscal squeeze is still on.

# STATUS REPORT

CENTER FOR PUBLIC RESOURCES

December 14, 1982

The Honorable Alan J. Dixon
456 Russell Office Building
United States Senate
Washington, DC  20510

Dear Senator Dixon:

It is my pleasure to convey to you <u>Basic Skills in the U.S.</u>
<u>Work Force</u>, a report from the Human Resources Executive
Program of the Center of Public Resources (CPR) detailing
the results of a national survey of business, school systems, and organized labor regarding the basic academic
skills deficiencies of high school youth entering the work
force.  We felt that these survey findings might be of
assistance to you in your work on the Committee on Labor and
Human Resources.

The problem facing secondary education in the U.S. today
are ones in which companies, as the employers of youth, and
school systems, as the educators of youth, have a significant stake.  Each possesses clear incentives for pursuing
active cooperation towards resolution of the problems.  Yet,
as the CPR report makes clear, business, labor and school

The Honorable Alan J. Dixon
December 14, 1982
Page Two

systems differ significantly regarding the nature and level
of basic academic skills required for initial employment,
and regarding the present state of basic skill competencies
of high school youth.  The various sectors are largely
talking past one another on what is a prime issue for the
economic strength of our country.  The survey, nevertheless,
disclosed a strong desire on the part of all involved to
seek closer collaboration to resolve the problem.

CPR and its Human Resources Executive Program offer this
report in keeping with CPR's goal to mobilize business
resources to address public problems in ways that are
consistent with business needs and objectives.  We hope
the report will not represent just another collector of
dust on bookshelves, but rather will provide a stimulus to
greater understanding and cooperation among business, labor
and secondary school officials in the interests of increased
national economic productivity.  Indeed, CPR is now moving
forward with a series of follow-up activities to assist in
the creation of those cooperative partnerships.

Your comments on the report or those of your staff would be
most welcome.

                                    Sincerely,

                                    *J. F. Henry*

                                    James F. Henry
                                    President

JFH:jf
Enclosures

# Basic Skills in the U.S. Work Force
## *The Contrasting Perceptions of Business, Labor, and Public Education*

**James F. Henry**
*President*

**Susan Ueber Raymond, Ph.D.**
*Vice President, Program Operations*

**Project Assistants**
*Anne Glauber*
*Victorina Nichols*
*Valerie Mann Watts*

# TABLE OF CONTENTS

## EXECUTIVE SUMMARY

*A youngster has to be drawn by schools and community into an educational life that ensures the acquisition of basic skills. Those skills, as this report indicates, are sorely lacking for too many young people and severely limits their own employment futures as well as the potential for economic growth of our communities.*

*Established enforced standards with back-up assistance that helps individual children when and as they need help in learning these basic skills is the right that both business and schools must insist upon from their local, state and national government. The greater linkages urged by this report between business and education can and should be there—after all, that is a link that* should *be a national one.*—Frank J. Macchiarola, Chancellor, New York City Public Schools

### Statement of the Problem

A strong national economy in the 1980's will require expanded industrial productivity which, in important part, is dependent on an adequately skilled work force. Yet, 13% of white, 43% of black, and 56% of hispanic seventeen-year-olds are functionally illiterate. Between 40 and 50 percent of all students in urban areas have serious reading problems.

Considerable attention has been given by educators and public policy makers to identifying the nature of the problem and to determining methods for its resolution. Studies focusing on questions of educational methodology and curriculum development have been developed by school teachers and administrators.

Seldom, however, have policy makers attempted to understand the business perspective in analyzing basic education problems of the secondary schools and to match that perspective to the views of public educators. The independent initiatives of business to overcome basic skills deficiencies, whether in the existing work force, or among newly hired employees, have been largely ignored.

Yet as a potential and actual employer of secondary school graduates and non-graduates, it is perhaps American business which best understands the need to improve basic skills deficiencies.

Since business is grappling daily with the economic implications of the basic skills crisis, it possesses immediate incentives and experience to join in a partnership with the public school system to overcome skill deficiencies. While there has been increased recognition over the past two years regarding the need for cooperative efforts between public and private sectors on these issues, the theory and philosophy of cooperation have seldom been accompanied by a broad base of hard facts describing the

1

problem, the perceptions and initiatives of business, and the perceptions and initiatives of the school systems.

### Survey, Basic Skills in the U.S. Work Force

Recognizing the importance of the basic skills crisis, members of CPR's Human Resources Executive Program, described later in this summary, selected the problems of secondary school education as the first issues to be addressed by the Program.

With support from the Ford and Charles Stewart Mott Foundations, and corporate grants from AT&T, the Prudential Insurance Co., and the Gannett Company, CPR organized a Task Force of leading corporate executives and public educators. The agenda of the Task Force was to define the problem of basic skills deficiencies from the business, union and school perspectives, and to devise new methods for generating cooperation between companies and school systems at the community level.

To define the problem, and to begin to generate the data needed to construct cooperative initiatives and locally-appropriate pilot projects, CPR recently completed a national survey of corporations, school systems and trade unions. Survey findings underscore the breadth of the problem, and the need for cooperation in its resolution. Among the findings were the following:

- *A significant gap exists between business and school system perceptions of basic skills "adequacy".*

  The majority of companies surveyed identified basic skill deficiency problems in the majority of job categories listed. Over 75% of the school systems, however, assessed the majority of graduates entering the work force as "adequately prepared" for employment.
- *School systems appear to have underestimated the importance of basic (academic vs. vocational) skills for successful employment of students entering the work force.*

  For their part, however, businesses have a hard time translating their general perceptions of basic skills deficiencies among employees into specific assessment of the nature and level of those deficiencies compared to job requirements.
- *Businesses and unions identified speaking/listening, mathematics, and science skills as most frequently deficient, vs. "reading" skills more usually cited by educators.*
- *Even in less advanced job categories, both businesses and unions identified widespread deficiencies in mathematics and science,* a trend with serious implications for youth in the future, particularly with regard to increasingly technological job markets.

  It appears that the basics of the physical sciences are increasing in importance for job success as technology begins to affect virtually every factory and office job. A quarter of the responding school officials listed science as "of little importance." Few listed such skills as "of great importance."
- *Two-thirds of the companies and most unions noted that basic skills deficien-*

2

*cies limit the job advancement of employees,* with the result being employee frustration and high turnover rates.

In hiring a new employee, business has a "human resources concept," thinking perhaps of a 35-year investment in the individual. School systems seem to educate only for the "first job," rather than for long-term viability of the individual in the working world.

- *While the survey identified a variety of cooperative business-school system activities focused on vocational or career education, there were only a few cooperative models aimed specifically at basic skills.*
- *The overwhelming majority of companies have not estimated the cost of basic skills deficiencies, either in terms of direct or indirect costs.*

There is a general perception that the costs are high, but the perception is subjective. It is not based on objective analysis and hard data.

- *On a subjective, rank-order basis, businesses overall rank "general productivity" costs as first in importance, "management/supervision time" costs as second, and "product quality" costs as third.*
- *The overwhelming majority (90%) of respondees from all sectors expressed a desire to examine first-hand the viability of cooperation to resolve the problem.*

Particularly surprising was the recognition by both school system and business respondees that the latter would have to articulate its needs more precisely, and be willing to assist with curriculum development and classroom instruction, if business' expertise is to have an impact on preventing (rather than just coping with) basic skills deficiencies.

· · ·

## I. INTRODUCTION

> *The quality of education available in America's junior and senior public high schools is by no means as poor as the most vocal critics of public education have announced, but it is nowhere as good as it must be to prepare our young people for entry into the labor force or for entry into universities and colleges. Although there are some very bright spots in secondary education, almost none of them are in the areas of science, mathematics, computer technology, or languages. When we 'won' the space race with Russia, the Nation's priorities shifted, and the resources that once were poured into education were diverted to other interests. The documented results are not only sad, they are generally alarming.*—Shirley M. Hufstedler, Former Secretary, Department of Education

3

## Nature of the Problem

A crisis is smoldering beneath the surface of our troubled economy that threatens to erupt and impede the nation's potential for real economic recovery and growth. This crisis—over which considerable national concern has been expressed—involves the lack of basic academic capabilities (in reading, writing, math, science, speaking/listening, and reasoning) among high school youth and its detrimental impact upon the country. That recently, President Reagan called attention to this crisis, by noting, "the education of American schoolchildren in science and math had reached such a deplorable state that it threatened the nation's military and economic security".[1]

Indeed the parameters of the problem are striking. Our educational system costs the nation more than $120 billion annually. Yet, 13% of white, and 56% of Hispanic seventeen-year-olds are functionally illiterate.[2] Experts estimate that 44% of black youth leaving high school at age 18 are unable to read at or above the 4th grade level.[3] A leading authority in the education field reported that at least one in ten students cannot accomplish basic reading tasks by the end of high school.[4] Over the past fourteen years, Scholastic Aptitude Tests measuring basic reading and math comprehension have continued to decline nationwide with a 49 point drop in verbal tests and a 32 point drop in math (on a scale of 800). Hopefully, recent upward trends in those test scores, especially regarding reading skills, mark a reversal of this downward movement for the majority of high school students.

Unfortunately these alarming data understate the problem as they do not include high school dropouts who number over 700,000 a year and who have a high illiteracy rate. According to a Ford Foundation report on adult illiteracy in the United States, more than one half of the adult population in nine states (Kentucky, South Carolina, North Carolina, Arkansas, Georgia, Mississippi, Alabama, Tennessee, West Virginia) have not completed high school.[5]

Urban schools confront an even more intense situation. In Chicago an average of 54,000 students are absent every day and more than 15,000 students drop out each year.[6] The Office of Education estimates that 40 to 50 percent of all students in urban cities have serious reading problems.[7] Chicago School Superintendent Ruth B. Love reported that the average reading level for eighth grade students is 7.3 (seven years and three months), considerably lower than the national norm.[8] Twenty personnel managers from major Chicago corporations were surveyed regarding the capabilities of high school graduates. Only three managers felt that more than 40% of the graduates were ready for employment, six said less than 20%, and nine said between 20% and 40% were ready for employment.[9]

The impact of these trends on various aspects of American life is profound.

Business is the major consumer of public high school graduates. Eighty percent of the jobs in the United States are in the private sector, and private enterprise will contribute nearly 100% of the projected net growth in numbers of jobs in the 1980s. Yet, perceived concern with the economic aspects of basic skills deficiencies in the work force rises and falls in direct proportion to the general state of the national economy. In periods of high unemployment, the number of unemployed high school graduates

**4**

increases, and the soft labor market eliminates problems for many companies in finding adequately skilled employees. On the other hand, in periods of peak employment, when business finds greater difficulty in identifying sufficient numbers of well-prepared youth, the perceived importance of basic skills deficiencies grows.

Yet, the reality of the impact of basic skills deficiencies on the labor force is a fundamental, albeit uniquely different problem at both high and low periods of economic performance. The linkages among economic growth, work force employability, and work productivity are tightly forged, and basic skills competency is a common factor in the linkage.

.  .  .

## II. WHAT ARE "BASIC SKILLS" AND WHAT IS "COMPETENCY"?

Early in the design of the survey mechanism it became clear that perceptions and interpretations of "basic skills" varied across sectors and were usually highly generalized concepts. Yet, it was also clear that in order to undertake a valid comparison of the perceptions of business, union, and school executives, one (preferably specific) definition of "skills" and "competency" in skills was necessary.

Prior to 1978, the basic competencies used to determine literacy in the U.S. were reading, writing, and arithmetic. In 1978, the Primary-Secondary Education Act was amended to add speaking and listening to this list. However, the functional definitions of these "skills" was not specific. Perceiving the need to attach a certain depth of functional specificity to academic expectations regarding these (and other) basic skills competencies of high school graduates, a group of school and college teachers and administrators, under the auspices of the College Board's "Project Equality", developed during 1980–81 definitions of "Basic Academic Competencies . . . ; the Outcomes of Learning and Intellectual Discourse."[1]

While the College Board had developed the definitions for application to college-bound high school graduates, CPR felt that the definitions provided a starting point for specifying "basic skills" and "competency" to survey recipients. Alterations were made in the College Board definitions to remove the college-bound assumption. In addition, a category, "Scientific Competencies", was added, with definitions determined at CPR. While there can be considerable debate as to improvements in the College Board definitions—indeed the Board is in the process of gaining such opinions as of this writing—the CPR survey relied for the most part on the best state-of-the-art available at the time.

The resultant skill categories and competencies used in the survey were as follows:

**READING COMPETENCIES**
- The ability to identify and comprehend the main and subordinate ideas in a written work and to summarize the ideas in one's own words.

5

- The ability to recognize different purposes and methods of writing, to identify a writer's point of view and tone, and to interpret a writer's meaning inferentially as well as literally.
- The ability to vary one's reading speed and method according to the type of material and one's purpose for reading.
- The ability to use the features of printed materials, such as table of contents, preface, introduction, titles and subtitles, index, glossary, appendix, bibliography.
- The ability to define unfamiliar words by decoding, using contextual clues, or by using a dictionary.

WRITING COMPETENCIES
- The ability to organize, select, and relate ideas and to outline and develop them in coherent paragraphs.
- The ability to write Standard English sentences with correct:

> Sentence structure.
> Verb forms.
> Punctuation, capitalization, possessives, plural forms, and other matters of mechanics.
> Word choice and spelling.

- The ability to improve one's own writing by restructuring, correcting errors, and rewriting.
- The ability to gather information from primary and secondary sources; to write a report using this research; to quote, paraphrase, and summarize accurately; and to cite sources properly.

SPEAKING AND LISTENING COMPETENCIES
- The ability to engage critically and constructively in the exchange of ideas.
- The ability to answer and ask questions coherently and concisely, and to follow spoken instructions.
- The ability to identify and comprehend the main and subordinate ideas in discussions, and to report accurately what others have said.
- The ability to conceive and develop ideas about a topic for the purpose of speaking to a group; to choose and organize related ideas; to present them clearly in Standard English.

MATHEMATICAL COMPETENCIES
- The ability to perform the computations of addition, subtraction, multiplication, and division using natural numbers, fractions, decimals, and integers.
- The ability to make and use measurements in both traditional and metric units.
- The ability to use effectively the mathematics of

> Integers, fractions, and decimals.
> Ratios, proportions, and percentages.
> Roots and powers.
> Algebra.
> Geometry.

6

- The ability to make estimates and approximations, and to judge the reasonableness of a result.
- The ability to use elementary concepts of probability and statistics.

SCIENTIFIC COMPETENCIES
- The ability to understand the basic principles of mechanics, physics, and chemistry.
- The ability to distinguish problems whose genesis is in basic mechanics, physics, or chemistry.
- The ability to apply basic scientific/technical solutions to the appropriate problems.

REASONING COMPETENCIES
- The ability to identify and formulate problems, as well as the ability to propose and evaluate ways to solve them.
- The ability to recognize and use inductive and deductive reasoning, and to recognize fallacies in reasoning.
- The ability to draw reasonable conclusions from information found in various sources, whether written, spoken, tabular, or graphic, and to defend one's conclusions rationally.
- The ability to comprehend, develop, and use concepts and generalizations.
- The ability to distinguish between fact and opinion.

In addition, the survey form was structured so as to allow respondees freedom to suggest additional skill categories. As will be noted later in this report, both business and school respondees often did so.

## III. NATURE OF THE SKILLS COMPETENCY NEED

> *Not being able to read is to lack one of the most important skills needed for full and proper participation in our society. In addition to the skill deficiency, the person's very personality and spirit are affected, as non-readers always have low or no self esteem. In most cases, the non-reader is unemployable, or working in a very menial position. Productivity is affected because a non-reader cannot totally comprehend job responsibilities. This puts a drain and strain on the overall economy, and touches us all.*—Wally Amos, Founder/Chairman, The Famous Amos Chocolate Chip Cookie Corporation

### Introduction

For many years, the means for ensuring adequate basic academic skills among secondary school students have been widely discussed in educational circles. Only re-

7

cently, however, has the question of basic skills competency become a priority issue for businesses. This new awareness has stemmed not only from declining academic competencies of high school youth as described in Section I, but also from U.S. business' growing concern about its international competitiveness. Business leaders have begun to examine a variety of factors affecting productivity, including the relative academic preparedness of U.S. versus the competitive work forces of other nations.

Changes in the nature of the jobs available for out-of-high-school youth have also been a factor in expanded business concerns. To use one example, many high school graduates were hired in the past for essentially rote clerical jobs—typing forms all day. Changing technology (e.g., the word processor), however, has eliminated such jobs and introduced a need for the new hiree to be able to handle more comprehensive tasks, based more on such basic skills as reading, writing, and listening than on such "vocational" skills as typing. Analogies abound from the assembly line to the warehouse to the construction job site. What one executive has called "the lift, place, take, put jobs", purposely engineered to be viable regardless of worker education levels, are rapidly being replaced by technology.

Thus, to examine the basic skills areas needing emphasis in corporate-school system cooperative programs, one first must have an understanding of the type and level of basic skills competency required for employment.

## A Note on the Corporate Responses

In order to specify from the corporate perspective the impact of skill competency on employability and job performance, the survey requested corporate respondees to self-select relevant job categories and to rank the skill competencies necessary for those jobs according to whether they were high, medium, or low competencies, or not applicable. "Medium" is defined as the requirement to fulfill those skill functions set out in Section II of this report; "high", the requirement for a greater number of functions; and "low", the requirement for fewer competency functions.

## Corporate-School System Comparisons

### The Four "R's"

Generally, *school and business executives had relatively consistent views regarding the importance of reading, writing, and reasoning as basic skills for entry level employment.* Generally, medium-competency levels were viewed by business as important for most job categories in all industries. Eighty-eight percent of school systems ranked reading and 66% ranked reasoning as of great importance as a job requirement.

Business executives saw high competency in writing skills as of importance only in secretarial/clerical and managerial positions. Though not asked to specify job categories, school system executives similarly viewed writing skills as important but not critical to job entry and retention.

Greater contrast was seen in the comparative view of mathematics. *Medium-to-high levels of mathematics skills are required across job categories, according to re-*

8

*sponding business executives, with consistently high levels required in the manufacturing, utilities, and finance industries.* However, *fully half of the responding school systems viewed mathematics as of important but not critical relevance* to out-of-high-school employment.

Stronger opinions are, of course, available. As Shirley Hufstedler, former Secretary of the Department of Education, has noted, U.S. secondary school science and mathematics training has failed to keep pace with that of our international competitors: "Every year more than 3 million students graduate from Soviet high schools with two full years of calculus . . . By contrast, barely 100,000 American high school graduates have even taken one year of calculus."[1] The two educators brought in to salvage the educational program at South Boston High School emphasize that "the crucial curriculum focus in urban schools is math, not reading," if urban students are to be able to compete successfully in today's urban job market. The need at South Boston was clear: 91% of the incoming 9th grade class in 1979 tested below grade level on standardized math tests; of this, 52% tested below 6th grade level and 15% below third grade level.[2]

It should be noted that, in the CPR survey, school systems in the West and in suburban areas differed the most from the overall averages, with mathematics viewed as "of great importance" in 60% of these responses.

*Speaking/Listening*

On the CPR survey responses, *business executives nearly always noted speaking/listening skills as required at high-to-medium levels. This was true for all job categories in all industries. Moreover, the limited labor union data available indicates that these verbal communication skills are also of the most importance across job categories from the union point of view.* This ranking is consistent with a 1979 survey carried out by the University of Wisconsin among 45 corporate executives in which listening was overwhelmingly ranked as the most important basic communication skill, although only 9 provided any internal training to employees to improve their listening capabilities.[3]

*School system leaders appear to be in full agreement.* Eighty-five percent of school system respondees listed speaking/listening skills as crucial to job entry.

*Science*

Job requirements, even at entry level positions, for a basic grounding in science appear to be surprisingly high. As the applications of computers and electronic technology become more widespread, a basic knowledge of technological sciences becomes important. Yesterday's tool-clad telephone repairman today must be as well versed in dealing with computer-controlled machinery as in soldering wire.

*Many of the companies responding to the CPR survey saw medium levels of basic science capability as necessary for jobs not only in the skilled labor and technical areas, but also in secretarial positions (30% of respondees) and supervisory positions (85%).* This trend was also seen in early 1982 at a meeting in Denver of business executives and school system leaders convened by the College Board to review the "basic skills" definitions described in Section II of this report. At that meeting, the ex-

9

ecutives recommended that the College Board add "technology" skills to its list of basic competencies required of secondary school graduates for job entry and promotion.[4]

It appears that the basics of the physical sciences are viewed as increasingly important, as technology begins to affect virtually every factory and office job. As one business observer noted, "The net outcome will be more jobs, probably better jobs at better pay; but getting there is going to be painful for many Americans"[5] because of the current lack of science/technology education in secondary school education.

*Twenty-six percent of school system officials responding to the CPR survey, on the other hand, listed "sicnece" as of little importance for job-seeking high school students. Fewer than a dozen respondees listed such skills as of great importance.*

*Other Skills*
It should also be noted that *corporate, school, and union responses frequently added the requirements of "human relations" and "work behavior" as essential skills,* including punctuality, appropriate attire, and ability to work within group settings. *High levels of these skills were usually required.*

.  .  .

## IV.  NATURE OF BASIC SKILLS DEFICIENCIES

*The data cited in the* Basic Skills in the U.S. Work Force *report are cause for serious concern. Over the next decade we expect advances in technology and the corresponding impact on work force skill requirements to accelerate. The next generation must be adequately prepared if they are to achieve productive and satisfying careers in industry. AT&T has worked with educators at all levels and will continue to do so. The cooperative programs described in this report, particularly Curriculum Development and Work Study Programs, deserve serious consideration.—H. Weston Clarke Jr., Vice President, The Bell System*

### *General Findings*

.  .  .

*Overall, the majority of companies responding to the survey identified basic skill deficiency problems of at least one degree in the majority of job categories listed.* For example, a manufacturing company listing four job categories (e.g., secretarial/ clerical, skilled labor, unskilled labor, and supervisors) would identify deficiencies (re-

**10**

quirement versus capability) in, for example, reading, speaking/listening and mathematics for at least half of the above categories.

It should be noted that the CPR business survey focused on corporate employees, those who were hired from a pool of applicants, rather than those who were not hired. In general, companies have a great deal of difficulty retrieving detailed information on the latter set of applicants. Interviews have elicited some information on the skill level of this group. Given the survey's focus, however, the reader should note that *the level of deficiencies found by the surveys is an underestimate of the overall problem.*

In terms of those who are not hired, the general information available to CPR is episodic, but no less disturbing. One utilities company executive in the Northeast noted that, although their out-of-high-school personnel were in general adequately skilled, the company has had an increasingly difficult time finding such personnel from among job applicants. Only 10% of those interviewed for a typical job are thought sufficiently promising to be tested. Of those given the set of standardized mathematics and reading comprehension tests, half fail at least one test and fully a third fail both. Echoing this situation, a utilities executive in the West noted that in 1981, 39% of out-of-high-school job applicants scored below standard on the company's entry-level mathematics and verbal tests and were not hired for this reason.

In contrast to this business perception of the basic academic capabilities of the out-of-high school work force, *over three quarters of the school systems responding to the CPR survey assessed the majority of their graduates entering the work force as adequately prepared in the basic academic skills for employment in that work force.* As might be expected, school system officials in large urban areas more frequently evaluated students as inadequately prepared than did their counterparts in medium-sized urban or suburban areas.

. . .

## V. THE COSTS OF DEFICIENCIES

> *Economic productivity is impossible without educational productivity. We educate for more than vocational skill, yet there is no skill of the sort our economy requires that is possible without a good basic education.*—David Mathews, President, Charles F. Kettering Foundation

The skill deficiency problems analyzed in Section IV obviously involve financial and other costs to business and society in general. Direct costs include the amounts of money diverted within corporations to cover the costs of training. Just as important are costs incurred by companies—and the consumer—in terms of lost productivity and poor product quality. In one company, for example, a worker who did not understand how to read a ruler mismeasured sheet steel and lost the company $700 worth of ma-

11

terial one morning.[1] In another, 70% of outgoing correspondence must be corrected and retyped at least once because typists working from recorders do not know how to spell or punctuate sentences.[2]

Despite the prevalence of such illustrative examples of costs incurred by companies due to basic skill deficiencies and the provision of remedial training to correct those deficiencies, only five corporate respondees to the survey had attempted to estimate the costs to their companies of basic skills deficiencies in their work force. One of the five indicated that the results of the company study were not reliable. Two of the remaining four—both manufacturing companies—provided estimates of the costs of the necessary remedial skill development activities in their companies. Another company, a medium-sized manufacturing company in the Northeast, estimated annual costs of $250,000 in rework and materials waste.

The two companies providing training figures both estimated corporate cost at a quarter of a million dollars each for remedial training that should have been accomplished in the 9th and 10th grades. And that figure is growing, as illustrated by one company that ten years ago hired one training director at $15,000 and today has six full-time, twenty part-time, and several consultant remedial education trainers with an estimated budget in salaries and material of $250,000.

Anticipating that few companies would have data available estimating the financial impact of skill deficiencies, the CPR survey asked company respondees to rank order the cost factors which, in their professional judgment, had the most significant corporate impact. The results are summarized in Table V.1.

As Table V.1 indicates, *overall "general productivity" costs were ranked first in importance, the additional "management/supervision time" necessary second, "product quality" third, "time and effort spent to increase skills" fourth, and dangers to "worker safety" fifth.*

This rank order showed no significant variations except by company size, with medium-sized companies ranking "management/supervision time" equally frequently

**TABLE V.1.  *Corporate Cost Category Ranking***

| Rank | General Productivity | Product Quality | Worker Safety | Management/ Supervision Time | Time and Effort to Increase Skills | Other* |
|------|--------|--------|--------|--------|--------|--------|
| 1 | 41%** | 21% | 3% | 24% | 6% | 4% |
| 2 | 29% | 26% | 4% | 28% | 11% | 2% |
| 3 | 23% | 21% | 9% | 32% | 12% | 1% |
| 4 | 2% | 19% | 22% | 12% | 39% | 1% |
| 5 | 2% | 7% | 50% | 5% | 34% | 2% |
| 6 | — | 9% | 82% | — | — | 9% |

* Includes "lost sales", "turnover", and "customer dissatisfaction."
** Percentages refer to the percent of responding companies listing the cost category as the rank specified (e.g., 41% of companies ranking a first priority ranked "general productivity" as No. 1, 21% ranked "product quality" as No. 1).

Number 1 as "general productivity". The priority of the supervision cost to a medium-sized firm can perhaps be attributed to more constrained and thinly spread management/supervisory resources. Time diverted to increased supervision due to worker skill deficiencies is thus relatively more costly than in a larger company, with correspondingly greater supervisory resources.

Unions responding to the CPR survey or interviewed for the Project distinguished internal (union management) from external (company relations) costs. The internal costs associated with improving the basic skills of union representatives to better serve union membership was viewed as the most important cost category. Ranked second in importance was the increased number of grievances needing to be addressed which are traceable to basic skill deficiencies. Third in importance was the failure of union members to adhere to union policies or negotiated agreements (e.g., safety procedures) because of such problems as reading deficiencies. Fourth in importance was insufficient membership use of negotiated benefits due to reading and/or listening deficiencies.

Improving the level and quality of information regarding the costs to the corporation of remedial training for employees with poor basic academic skills is an important undertaking. It is exactly that type of "bottom line" information that human resources executives find most useful in convincing corporate management to become involved in cooperative efforts directed at public education. To the extent that such information could be quantified, a greater level of corporate involvement, measured in terms of the number of companies involved and the depth of commitment of individual companies, could ensue.

It is equally important to recognize, however, the difficulties of the undertaking. Data regarding the payouts, direct and indirect, of corporations for remedial training are available within corporations, especially within the larger and more sophisticated companies. These data would be useful indicators to corporate executives, school officials and public policy makers in appreciating the additional investment made by the *private* sector in individuals for whom the *public* education investment has been ineffective.

However, quantitative estimates of the total economic costs of the basic skills deficiencies will be extremely difficult to derive. Few methodological tools are available for relating quantitative productivity loss and other opportunity costs to the educational level or capability of a given work force. The relevant causal factors are so varied and interrelated that quantitative attribution of, for example, productivity decreases to basic skills deficiencies would be extremely difficult.


## VI.  RESOLVING THE PROBLEM

> *Sometimes I feel discouraged that so many of us in public education still see corporate involvement as a matter of volunteerism or philanthropy. Productive working relationships seldom endure without* quid pro quo, *as there is no accountability*

*on either side. It's time for the managers of public resources to stop trying to pick corporate pockets, and to start helping our private sector companies find cost-justified approaches to coupling the business interests of their shareholders with spending huge amounts for many of the same purposes. Why not pool resources and jointly design programs for equal or better returns for each partner at less cost? This, not volunteerism and not philanthropy, is the classical notion of partnership. We should be asking corporations to invest, not give—to invest in developing the human capital that is required by corporate America for productivity, profitability and growth.*—Floretta Dukes McKenzie, Superintendent of Schools, District of Columbia Public Schools

## Introduction

In addition to defining the various perceptions of the nature and level of basic skills deficiencies, the CPR survey attempted to add to the current understanding of what exists in terms of models of practice addressing basic skills competencies both within business and school systems and cooperatively between the two sectors.

*While the survey identified a wide variety of cooperative business/school system activities focused on vocational or career education, most addressed academic skills only peripherally.*

Few examples were identified of innovative, cooperative models of practice aimed specifically at basic skills. The relative paucity of specific basic skills models appears to be due to three factors. First, many companies conduct a wide variety of remedial education programs within their own organizations and thus have dealt with the problem with an *internal* "curative" rather than an external or cooperative "preventive" strategy targeted at school system improvement. While most do not necessarily prefer this strategy compared to a stronger educational system, development of such programs has, in the past, been perceived as more easily accomplished than improving fundamental aspects of public education. Second, as described in Section I of this report, corporate concern with the extensiveness of basic skills deficiencies is fairly recent, paralleling changes in job parameters and employment needs. Third, cooperative involvement in improving the basic academic skills obtained by secondary school students implies business-school system communication and collaboration on the *fundamental* responsibilities of educational institutions. Such cooperative involvement goes to the heart of secondary school responsibilities in ways that, for example, career or vocational education cooperation do not. Consequently, the disincentives to cooperation have often outweighed the incentives.

*Those models that are available, nevertheless, represent potentially replicable activities for communication to those companies and school systems who recognize their basic skills problem but carry out no activities aimed at its resolution.*

.   .   .

14

Activities pursued by corporations and/or school systems fall into three basic categories:

1. Intra- or inter-business activities focused on basic skills improvements, some of which may provide useful training models or methods for use in school systems.
2. School system efforts to improve systematic knowledge of the basic skills needs of the private sector.
3. Business-school system cooperative efforts aimed in whole or in large part at basic skills improvements, and representing models of practice with replication potential.

### Internal Corporate Programs

Seventy-five percent of all companies replying to the CPR survey carry out some type of basic skills competency program *within* the company for existing employees. Forty-three percent of the responding companies having such programs provide remedial training in the basic skills discussed in this report, with an overwhelming emphasis on mathematics and speaking/listening skills. The second largest area of activity mentioned was the provision of financing for outside skill enhancement via tuition assistance (35% of companies with basic skills activities). Medium-sized companies more frequently had instituted remedial training programs than had large companies (50% versus 35%). Insurance and manufacturing companies were more likely to have instituted internal training programs rather than tuition aid (50% of companies in each category had internal remedial training programs and 30% had tuition aid programs) and utilities more likely to choose tuition reimbursement (55% tuition aid versus 20% internal training).

Finally, 20% of the companies responding to the CPR survey noted that, to some extent, the remedial training provided employees was itself carried out jointly with other corporations in the community.

Few companies responding to the survey were involved in government-sponsored youth training programs or, if so involved, considered their experience with those programs to be positive. Business respondees generally viewed the costs of participation in such programs, in terms of bureaucracy and regulations, as greater than the benefits received by either the company or participating youth.[1]

In addition to the sheer number of companies actively involved in internal remedial training, it is equally important to emphasize the degree to which internal corporate activity is directed at the development of training tools and techniques, targeted on basic skills, which might be applicable to the secondary school but have not yet found their way into the classroom to their full potential. McGraw Hill's "Numbers Skills Program," for example, is widely used in industry to teach accuracy in computation and numerical transcription. The Program uses a tachistoscope (a speed-reading pacer adapted to work with numbers), filmstrips, and individual trainee workbooks as training aids.

Control Data has developed a computerized "Basic Skills Learning System" called

15

PLATO, designed to individualize instruction in reading, mathematics, and the language arts thus giving students the opportunity to learn at their own pace. The computers determine the students' level of learning and prescribe appropriate lessons and activities. PLATO provides instant feedback to student responses, in the event of error, providing advice and clues as to how to seek the correct answer.

Bankers Life Company of Des Moines, Iowa has also developed and adapted a series of audio-tutorial, modular material for writing and speaking skills that approximates one-to-one tutoring. Similarly, the training material targeted at listening skills, developed by Lyman Steil with the assistance of the Sperry Corporation and used throughout industry, is easily adaptable to school settings. Few school systems in the country either make use of it or have the formal speaking/listening curricula emphasis which would encourage its use.

. . .

## VII.  WHAT FURTHER CAN BE DONE?

> *Strong evidence reveals the willingness and readiness of business/industry to work with the schools. The schools, once reluctant to share responsibilities thought to be theirs alone, seem now, in desperation, to be ready to accept partnership. The schools, however, must take the initiative in inviting the partnership and sharing actively in its design and function.*—Sidney P. Marland, Jr., Former U.S. Commissioner of Education

There is general agreement among corporate and school system respondees to the CPR basic skills survey that there is an appropriate and perhaps expanded role for business to play in resolving the basic skills deficiencies of out-of-high-school youth. Yet, perceptions of how that role can best be played out are varied. Moreover, where dissent is present, it is strongly held.

### *The Corporate Perspective*

*1. The Business Role*
Overall, 76% of corporate respondees to the survey responded positively when asked if an expanded corporate role in basic skills improvement—especially as regards school partnerships—was advisable. Specific responses as to what more business could do fell into three categories: communication, expanding current activities, and moving "upstream" in the educational process by becoming involved in school planning and curriculum development. As the National Institute for Work and Learning has pointed out, "the quality and effectiveness of a community's total teaching/learning and human resources delivery system is dependent upon the extent of accurate communica-

16

tion among the various providers in all the formal sectors: education, business, labor, government, (and) community service."[1]

Respondees were generally self-critical regarding the effectiveness of past efforts to communicate their needs and problems to school systems, teachers and students. The common theme throughout the responses was that business must communicate its basic skills problems more fully and effectively to school systems if it is to be justified in expecting improved competency on the part of job applicants. Moreover, it was also acknowledged that business must attempt to convey that same message to students via increased speaking engagements and expanded work-study programs. As one executive noted "A factor in job failure is the demoralization/disillusionment of students who are unused to what can be the tedium and discipline of entry level positions." Over half of the 76% agreeing to the appropriateness of expanded corporate activity cited these communication elements as important actions to be undertaken by business.

Another 15% of the suggested actions involved expanded efforts in areas already cited as successful from the business viewpoint, especially in-house remedial training, tuition reimbursement, and improved screening programs. It should be noted, however, that, while willing to expand on-the-job remedial programs, corporate respondees overall saw attempts at prevention of the problem via school cooperation as more appropriate.

Twenty percent of the corporate respondees advocated active business roles in core aspects of the school system's operation, from curriculum development to the provision of personnel for teaching appropriate basic skills classes. Such roles, it was felt, were necessary if the stream of basic skills problems encountered in the corporation were to be prevented in the school rather than cured on the job.

Also emphasized by survey respondees was the increasing need for corporations to become political advocates for the public education system. As other observers have noted,[2] with demographic changes the constituency for public education is dropping. Yet, business continues to rely on that education system for its basic personnel needs. A block-grant approach to federal involvement in education will place much decision making in the hands of states and communities. Thus, business has a stake in filling the role of "educational advocate" and the very real opportunity to see the budgetary fruits of its advocacy determined at the local level.

The fundamental nature of the educational system questions raised by widespread basic skills deficiencies implies a need for movement toward deeper "collaboration" between business and school systems, i.e., "joint review of the three basic functions educating institutions provide—advisement, instruction and certification—and discussions of what schools and employers would do to ensure that youths have the learning opportunities in and out of school that will teach and reinforce skills and habits required of competent and responsible young adults."[3]

Those corporate respondees dissenting from these views did so largely on three counts, noting first that it is the schools' responsibility to ensure basic skills and that business can only react to the problem, not initiate solutions; second, that schools need to expect more from students if they expect to get more in terms of competency;

17

and third, that school system administrators simply are not willing to accept that practicality is essential in a high school education. These three dissenting points, although generally expressed, are succinctly summarized in the comments of one responding executive.

> I do not see many opportunities for business initiatives that would have meaningful impact on basic skill levels of students coming out of secondary schools. Certainly learning occurs once they are on the job, but how to have them come to us with better basic skills seems to me a difficult thing for business to achieve, other than to convey to students that the skill levels coming out of the school system are not good enough and where there is an alternative, individuals with low skill levels won't be hired. The change really has to occur back in the school years.
>
> As to what happens there, I attach great importance to the home environment, the part the parents can play in the education process.
>
> As to the school system itself, . . . my observation has been that educators have proceeded down a course which in effect says that education is desirable in the abstract, almost as though business—where most students will spend most of their later lives—did not exist. It could well be that students would be well served if education was imbued from the very beginning with the proposition that business or similar careers are where the students are headed and they are going to need basic skills when they get there. Writing business into the curriculum, so to speak, from day one could provide a better or additional reason to learn, be it reading, writing, speaking/listening, math, science or whatever.

### 2. *The School Role*

Whatever actions undertaken by business, corporate survey recipients were asked for their views as to what further actions were needed on the parts of schools and government to improve basic skill levels of secondary school graduates and non-graduates.

The nearly unanimous corporate view was that government could play no appropriate role, and indeed was functionally not responsive enough to individual school needs to establish meaningful policies or programs in this area.

The majority of responding companies felt that the most important action for schools to take was to develop and enforce stringent basic skills competency standards. Responding companies overwhelmingly stated that unless such programs and standards were enforced, any "partnership" between the sectors was not likely to affect the basic skills competency of the high school graduate entering the work force.

The average hourly amount spent per public school per school day in 1980 was $2.39,[4] hardly enough to support both a firm grounding in the basic skills and a wide array of elective courses. It is, in the business view, that firm basic academic grounding which is essential to employment as the demand for essentially unskilled labor to fill rote jobs declines (e.g., currently General Motors employs one skilled worker per 5–6 assembly line workers; by the year 2000 that ratio is projected to be one-to-one[5]). Thus, schools, in business' view, should reinstitute more advanced basic skills requirements and ensure that those requirements result in competency. It should be noted that 18 states require such competency testing for high school graduates. Five states explicitly prohibit such testing for either graduation or grade promotion. In a few states, competency testing is currently being challenged in the courts.[6]

It should be emphasized that this business viewpoint of necessary school actions was usually not expressed in a critical or negative manner, but rather as a necessary albeit not sufficient action for improving the skills problem in the *context* of expanded business activity.

.   .   .

## VIII.  CONCLUSIONS

> *The public high school is the most seriously troubled institution in American education. High dropout rates, marginal performance for far too many students, and declining teacher morale have all contributed to widespread loss of confidence in schools. Also, there is a growing gap between the world of education and the world of work. Many students in their upper teens feel unwanted and unneeded. They leave school without having tested either their aptitude or their interests. They even leave without having mastered the central objective of all formal learning—the achievement of literacy. The failure to master language is absolutely calculated to lead to educational and social failure.*—Ernest L. Boyer, President, Carnegie Foundation for The Advancement of Teaching

The data and discussion in this report can be summarized in six points:

- There is a serious problem of basic skills deficiencies among secondary school graduates and non-graduates entering the work force, from the perspective of business.
- Those deficiencies are pervasive across job categories, types of skills, and types of companies.
- The deficiencies affect not only the performance of entry-level positions, but also the possibilities for job advancement.
- A considerable mis-communication exists between business and school systems regarding the quality of academic skills required on the job, and the seriousness of the deficiencies which exist.
- Corporations do a considerable amount of "curative" remedial training, BUT
- There are relatively few specific precedents for preventive cooperation to address the basic academic skills problem directly. Solutions and efforts are normally tangential aspects of vocational, career, or counseling programs.

The question remaining, of course, is how best to bring private sector concern with and independent activity to remedy basic skills deficiencies together with public secondary school systems. The good news is that the vast majority of companies, unions, and school systems responding to the survey saw increased mutual cooperation tar-

19

geted specifically at basic skills problems as appropriate and potentially beneficial. The willingness to explore new methods of cooperation on the fundamental academic skill questions raised in this report is clearly present on all sides.

The bad news is that developing successful cooperation on such fundamental aspects of education, even with a broad consensus on the merits of such cooperation, is extremely difficult. The barriers to effective cooperation are rooted on the one hand in what Diane Ravitch, associate professor of history and education at Columbia University's Teachers College, calls "the dilemma of American education," i.e., providing education for all while taking account of individual differences in ability.[1] Public education's main problem, at the community, state, or national level, is that the public itself lacks consensus as to the specific, common objectives public education is to achieve.

If that lack of consensus stymies the substantive agenda for cooperation, equally problematic is the "service delivery" barrier in the educational structure that impedes the process of cooperation. As Seeley has noted at length, the educational system has come to view itself—and be viewed by others—as the producer of a commodity, education, and the community as the consumer. As an increasingly bureaucratized and professionalized producer, the public education system has become removed from the community, parents, businessmen, and students engaged with it in the educational process, the definition of its needs and the development of solutions. It is this producer-client relationship that must be broken if effective cooperation is to be developed. As Seeley has summarized, "The chief characteristic of a partnership is common effort toward common goals. Partners may help one another in general or specific ways, but none is ever a client because the relationship is mutual. Providers and clients can deal with one another at arm's length; partners share an enterprise, though their mutuality does not imply or require equality or similarity. Participants in effective partnerships may be strikingly different, each contributing to the common enterprise particular talents, experiences, and perspectives and sometimes having different status within the relationship and control over aspects of the work to be done."[2]

One of CPR's main goals in developing the Corporate Roles in Public Education Project, conducting its national basic skills survey, and issuing this report has been to contribute information and leadership to overcome both of these barriers: *information* targeted at assisting local communities in defining and developing their individual educational consensus, and *leadership* from business, organized labor and education to encourage partnership alternatives to current producer-client structures in secondary education. It is hoped that CPR's efforts to date have represented a useful point of departure for further efforts to bring the various sectors closer together in coordinating their activities in the interests of better educated, more productive youth.

A note is thus appropriate as to the areas of activity to be undertaken by the CPR Corporate Roles in Public Education Project to follow up on this initial survey work and assist in building these partnerships.

From the outset, CPR and the Project Task Force have known that while a generalized view of the basic skills problem and the precedents for its resolution was essential, the initiatives needed for sustained cooperation targeted at youth employability

**20**

must be developed at the local level. It is there that the incentives for, and barriers to, cooperation must be examined. Available "models of practice" must be evaluated locally for their viability.

As is clear from this report, some local partnerships have been formed to address the basic skills problem. The CPR survey identified many more school systems and companies wishing to address cooperatively the issue but lacking the structures and information necessary to catalyze a partnership. An important task, then, is on the one hand, to provide assistance (information, expertise, etc.) to bolster those partnerships currently underway and, on the other hand, to aggregate the leadership of these experienced groups to provide the information, insight, and program design details necessary to assist those school systems and businesses still searching for locally appropriate partnership vehicles.

Over the next year, therefore, CPR will seek to expand the available information in areas identified by the survey as poorly understood, e.g., the private sector costs of remedial basic skills training, and the basic skills needs of the high-demand jobs of the future. The results of this research will be made available to a broad audience of school, business, and community leaders via occasional published research monographs.

Moreover, CPR and the Project Task Force will seek to assist in the actual development of new local partnerships, and the support of existing efforts, by making broadly available, via workshops and printed communications, knowledge of what partnership methods have worked and why, and by assisting local groups in identifying the models of experience most applicable to their needs.

It is those partnerships which must lead the way in the pragmatic re-establishment of the pre-eminence of basic academic skills at the high school level and thus, in part, in restoring the strength of the U.S. work force. As Ernest Boyer, President of the Carnegie Foundation for the Advancement of Teaching, has noted, "The downward spiral in public education threatens the economic, social and political fabric of the nation. The nation's future is inextricably linked to the future of the public schools where 90% of our students are taught. It is an inescapable conclusion that those who wish to strengthen this great country must place public education as the top priority on their agenda."

## END NOTES

**Chapter I**

1. "Reagan Warns Schools are Failing to Meet Science, Math Needs," *New York Times*, May 13, 1982, page B18.

2. George McGovern, "Illiteracy in America—A Time for Examination," *USA Today*, May 1980.

3. Data from the Adult Illiteracy Program, New York, N.Y., 1981.

4. McGovern, *op cit.*

5. James Henter and David Harmen, *Adult Illiteracy in US*, New York: Ford Foundation, 1979.

6. "Who Will Save Our Schools," *Chicago*, October 1981, page 191.

21

7. Dr. Mary Hoover, "Literacy and the Inner City Child," Teacher Center, 1978.

8. "Who Will Save Our Schools," *op cit.*

9. David Robison, "Training and Job Programs in Action: Case Studies in Private Sector Initiatives for the Hard-to-Employ," Washington, D.C.: Committee for Economic Development, Work in America Institute, Inc., 1978, page 14.

**Chapter II**
1. "Preparation for College in the 1980's: The Basic Academic Competencies and the Basic Academic Curriculum," New York: The College Board, 1981.

**Chapter III**
1. Personal communication, October 1982.

2. Geraldine Kozberg and Jerome Winegan, "The South Boston Story: Implications for Secondary Schools," *Phi Delta Kappa*, vol. 62, no. 8, April 1981, pages 565–69.

3. Susan Mundale, "Why More CEO's are Mandating Listening and Writing Training," *Training and Human Resources Development*, October 1980, page 37.

4. "Summary: Seminar on High School Preparation for the World of Work," College Board, mimeo.

5. "Work Won't Be the Same Again," *Fortune*, June 28, 1982, page 58.

**Chapter V**
1. "Employers Take Over Where Schools Fail to Teach Basics," *Wall Street Journal*, January 22, 1981.

2. *Ibid.*

**Chapter VI**
1. For similar findings, see *Review of the Literature: Expanded Private Sector Involvement.* Washington, D.C.: Youthwork, Inc., April 1980.

**Chapter VII**
1. *Industry-Education-Labor Collaborative*, National Institute for Work and Learning, Washington, D.C.,1982, page 19.

2. Gene I. Maeroff, "Enrollment Drop Growing Threat to Public Schools," *New York Times*, September 7, 1982.

3. Robert I. Wise, "Schools, Business and Education Needs: From Cooperation to Collaboration," *Education and Urban Society*, vol. 14, no. 1, November 1981, page 79.

4. "Employers Take Over Where Schools Fail to Teach Basics," *Wall Street Journal*, January 22, 1981.

5. *Ibid.*

6. *The Condition of Education, 1980.* Washington, D.C.: National Center for Education Statistics, U.S. Department of Education, 1981.

**Chapter VIII**
1. Diane Ravitch, "The Schools We Deserve," *The New Republic*, April 18, 1981, pages 23–27.

2. David S. Seeley, *Education Through Partnership: Mediating Structures and Education*, Cambridge, Massachusetts: Ballinger Publishing Company, 1981.

# AUDIT REPORT

153 EAST 53RD STREET
NEW YORK, NEW YORK 10022
212-371-2000

To the Shareholders and Board of Directors of W. R. Grace & Co.

In our opinion, the accompanying consolidated balance sheets and the related consolidated statements of income, shareholders' equity and changes in financial position present fairly the financial position of W. R. Grace & Co. and subsidiary companies at December 31, 1979 and 1978, and the results of their operations and the changes in their financial position for the years then ended, in conformity with generally accepted accounting principles consistently applied. Our examinations of these statements were made in accordance with generally accepted auditing standards and accordingly included such tests of the accounting records and such other auditing procedures as we considered necessary in the circumstances.

*Price Waterhouse & Co.*

February 11, 1980

### Management's Responsibility for Financial Reporting

Management is responsible for the preparation as well as the integrity and objectivity of Grace's financial statements. The financial statements have been prepared in conformity with generally accepted accounting principles and necessarily include amounts which represent the best estimates and judgments of management.

For many years, management has maintained internal systems which include careful selection of personnel, segregation of duties, formal business, accounting and reporting policies and procedures and an extensive internal audit function to assist them in fulfilling their responsibilities for financial reporting. While no system can ensure elimination of errors and irregularities, the systems have been designed to provide reasonable assurance that assets are safeguarded, policies and procedures are followed and transactions are properly executed and reported. These systems are constantly reviewed and modified in response to changing conditions.

The Audit Committee of the Board of Directors, which is comprised of directors who are not officers or employees of W. R. Grace & Co. or its subsidiaries, meets with senior financial officers, the internal auditors and independent accountants and reviews audit plans and results as well as management's actions taken in discharging their responsibilities for accounting, financial reporting and internal control systems. The Committee reports its findings to the Board of Directors and also recommends the selection and engagement of independent accountants. Management, the internal auditors and independent accountants have direct and confidential access to the Committee.

Independent accountants are engaged to conduct an examination of and render an opinion on the financial statements in accordance with generally accepted auditing standards. These standards include a review of the systems of internal controls and tests of transactions to the extent considered necessary by them to support their opinion.

**Management Discussion and Analysis of Earnings**

**1979 vs. 1978**    Record sales of $5.3 billion were achieved in 1979, an increase of 18 percent over 1978 sales of $4.4 billion which have been restated for the effects of poolings of interests transactions. Excluding sales of units which were divested or planned to be divested, the rate of growth was 28 percent. While all lines of business contributed to the sales increase, a particularly strong showing was made in Specialty Retailing where sales advanced 90 percent primarily due to the acquisition of Daylin, Inc. in 1979 which brought to Grace the Handy Dan home improvement chain and the Diana women's apparel shops. Additionally, in the Natural Resources area, 1979 sales grew to $456 million, an increase of 44 percent which is greatly attributable to escalating prices for oil and gas as well as continued strength in the service related businesses of Grace's natural resource operations. Cost of goods sold and operating expenses increased 16 percent, two percent lower than the rate of sales growth, reflecting the effects of improved margins in the Natural Resources line of business and disposal of lower margin businesses. Rapid expansion and resultant preopening expenses in the Restaurant and Specialty Retailing areas, coupled with continued inflation in all lines of business, contributed to the 27 percent increment in selling, general and administrative expenses.

Dividends, interest and other income amounted to $41.8 million in 1979, an increase of 89 percent. The primary factors causing this increase were higher interest rates, increase in interest bearing deposits and gains on sales of securities and properties. Equity in earnings of partnerships and less than majority owned companies decreased by $8.0 million in 1979. Contributing to this decrease was the divestment in 1979 of Grace's interest in Voyager Petroleums Ltd. and nonrecurring disproportionate capital contributions in 1978 by Grace's partner in mining ventures.

Interest expense of $106.3 million was 27 percent greater than the 1978 amount of $83.4 million and is primarily attributable to both higher interest rates and larger average borrowings in 1979. The increase in research and development expenses of $5.1 million or 13 percent is analyzed by functional expenditure category in the Financial and Statistical Review on page 31.

Net foreign exchange losses in 1979 amounted to $5.3 million compared to $13.8 million in 1978. This favorable decrease was caused, in part, by the lower decline in the value of the U.S. dollar versus other currencies than that experienced in 1978. Net foreign exchange losses in 1979 and 1978 were partly offset by favorable translation effects relating to FAS No. 8 of $3.1 and $11.7 million, respectively, included in cost of goods sold and operating expenses.

Net gains on disposal of businesses were $12.8 million in 1979 versus $8.0 million in 1978. An analysis of these gains by line of business is contained in Note 10 of the Notes to Financial Statements.

**1978 vs. 1977**    Sales amounted to $4.4 billion, an increase of seven percent over 1977 sales of $4.2 billion which have been restated for the effects of poolings of interests transactions. Excluding sales of units which were divested or planned to be divested, the rate of growth was 15 percent. All lines of business reported higher 1978 sales. Cost of goods sold and operating expenses increased five percent, two percent lower than the sales growth, reflecting positive effects of the disposal of lower margin businesses. Selling, general and administrative expenses, however, increased 12 percent primarily as a result of continued inflationary pressures and expanded operations.

Dividends, interest and other income increased in 1978 by $3.5 million, or 19 percent primarily due to interest income generated from the investment of proceeds received upon disposals of businesses and higher interest rates. Equity in earnings of partnerships and less than majority owned companies increased by $8.3 million to $9.4 million in 1978, primarily caused by the full year operations of businesses which in 1977 were in the development stage.

Research and development expenses rose $6.3 million or 19 percent in 1978. An analysis of the specific areas in which these expenses were incurred appears in the Financial and Statistical Review on page 31.

Net foreign exchange losses in 1978 amounted to $13.8 million compared to $5.8 million in 1977, an increase of $8.0 million reflecting the decline of the U.S. dollar against most major foreign currencies. The 1978 loss is partially offset, however, by the favorable translation effect relating to FAS No. 8 of $11.7 million in cost of goods sold and operating expenses.

Net gains on disposal of businesses amounted to $8.0 million in 1978 versus a loss of $17.2 million in 1977. An analysis of the 1978 gain is in Note 10 of the Notes to Financial Statements.

2

## Sales ($ millions)

$3,722  $3,779  $4,168  $4,448  $5,267

1975  1976  1977  1978  1979

## Net Income ($ millions)

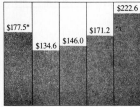

$177.5*  $134.6  $146.0  $171.2  $222.6

1975  1976  1977  1978  1979

*Includes gain on sale of a portion of the Company's interest in Jacques Borel International S.A. of $35.6

## Shareholders' Equity Per Common Share

$26.04  $27.79  $29.45  $31.72  $34.74

1975  1976  1977  1978  1979

## Total Capital Including Long Term Debt ($ millions)

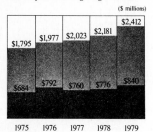

$1,795  $1,977  $2,023  $2,181  $2,412
$684  $792  $760  $776  $840

1975  1976  1977  1978  1979

▬ Total Capital Including Long Term Debt
▬ Long Term Debt

## Financial Summary — 1969 to 1979* *($ thousands except per share)*

| | 1979 |
|---|---|
| **Earnings Statistics** | |
| Sales | $ 5,266,629 |
| Other income | 43,221 |
| Cost of goods sold and operating expenses | 3,475,458 |
| Interest expense | 106,256 |
| Net gains (losses) on disposal of businesses | 12,764 |
| Depreciation, depletion and lease amortization | 168,591 |
| Income before taxes and extraordinary items | 411,883 |
| Income taxes | 189,303 |
| Income before extraordinary items | 222,580 |
| Extraordinary items | — |
| Net income | 222,580 |
| **Financial Position** | |
| Cash and marketable securities | $ 154,157 |
| Notes and accounts receivable—less allowances | 729,401 |
| Inventories | 767,440 |
| Total current liabilities | 1,065,134 |
| Working capital | 635,272 |
| Properties and equipment—net | 1,629,361 |
| Long term debt | 839,802 |
| Shareholders' equity—common stock | 1,563,402 |
| **Data per Common Share** | |
| Earnings per common share: | |
| Income before extraordinary items | $ 5.02 |
| Extraordinary items | — |
| Net income | 5.02 |
| Earnings per share assuming full dilution: | |
| Income before extraordinary items | 4.79 |
| Net income | 4.79 |
| Weighted average number of shares (thousands) used in computing: | |
| Earnings per share | 44,249 |
| Earnings per share assuming full dilution | 46,954 |
| Cash dividends per common share paid by the Company | 1.975 |
| Shareholders' equity per common share | 34.74 |
| **Other Statistics** | |
| Working capital provided by operations | $ 417,726 |
| Cash dividends on common stock paid by the Company | 85,386 |
| Capital expenditures | 477,688 |
| Current ratio | 1.6:1 |
| Debt ratio (including capitalized leases) | 34.8 % |
| Debt ratio (excluding capitalized leases) | 30.5 % |
| Common shareholders | 47,598 |
| Employees | 82,100 |

*Data for the years 1975 through 1978 have been restated to include businesses combined in poolings of interests transactions and for the effects of FAS No. 19 in accordance with a policy of restatement of data for the four immediately preceding years. Amounts previously reported in 1978 are shown in the table to the right.

3

| | 1978 | 1977 | 1976 | 1975 | 1974 | 1973 | 1972 | 1971 | 1970 | 1969 |
|---|---|---|---|---|---|---|---|---|---|---|
| | $4,448,184 | $4,167,961 | $3,779,251 | $3,721,614 | $3,601,464 | $2,889,817 | $2,397,623 | $2,105,043 | $1,973,745 | $2,047,743 |
| | 31,447 | 19,627 | 17,954 | 21,291 | 25,916 | 25,667 | 19,579 | 19,728 | 20,784 | 22,214 |
| | 2,989,889 | 2,851,481 | 2,613,019 | 2,538,304 | 2,511,683 | 2,045,962 | 1,694,856 | 1,506,740 | 1,399,636 | 1,460,232 |
| | 83,381 | 79,382 | 73,183 | 83,038 | 78,813 | 58,422 | 42,663 | 42,829 | 41,890 | 46,530 |
| | 7,982 | (17,158) | 810 | 26,370 | (17,339) | (4,426) | — | — | — | — |
| | 160,824 | 143,833 | 126,222 | 105,622 | 88,617 | 72,989 | 64,185 | 60,251 | 58,271 | 66,700 |
| | 322,740 | 273,015 | 257,520 | 324,587 | 255,646 | 161,895 | 112,937 | 85,465 | 85,785 | 83,733 |
| | 151,543 | 127,063 | 122,871 | 147,056 | 130,988 | 77,272 | 49,867 | 43,405 | 36,294 | 36,725 |
| | 171,197 | 145,952 | 134,649 | 177,531 | 124,658 | 84,623 | 63,070 | 42,060 | 49,491 | 47,008 |
| | — | — | — | — | — | (6,266) | 3,232 | (6,195) | (30,851) | 14,356 |
| | 171,197 | 145,952 | 134,649 | 177,531 | 124,658 | 78,357 | 66,302 | 35,865 | 18,640 | 61,364 |
| | $ 263,160 | $ 190,989 | $ 245,012 | $ 111,283 | $ 168,211 | $ 138,982 | $ 143,993 | $ 105,855 | $ 83,824 | $ 107,264 |
| | 629,861 | 564,505 | 515,380 | 497,544 | 521,790 | 438,050 | 384,129 | 341,526 | 329,742 | 341,850 |
| | 712,005 | 635,998 | 610,836 | 576,424 | 667,092 | 493,185 | 419,400 | 382,823 | 356,654 | 390,762 |
| | 891,496 | 804,984 | 764,888 | 737,900 | 860,648 | 628,284 | 522,054 | 432,007 | 442,339 | 443,155 |
| | 747,715 | 627,250 | 638,543 | 584,946 | 532,028 | 467,119 | 446,808 | 417,971 | 348,479 | 416,094 |
| | 1,293,231 | 1,220,726 | 1,137,695 | 1,069,741 | 959,895 | 770,650 | 664,755 | 608,878 | 576,376 | 648,519 |
| | 775,825 | 760,041 | 791,791 | 683,856 | 721,505 | 633,604 | 520,069 | 526,654 | 407,616 | 436,383 |
| | 1,396,356 | 1,254,190 | 1,176,189 | 1,101,651 | 858,662 | 765,973 | 729,971 | 671,279 | 661,935 | 673,819 |
| | $ 3.98 | $ 3.43 | $ 3.17 | $ 4.63 | $ 3.51 | $ 2.56 | $ 1.92 | $ 1.40 | $ 1.72 | $ 1.67 |
| | — | — | — | — | — | (.19) | .10 | (.21) | (1.08) | .52 |
| | 3.98 | 3.43 | 3.17 | 4.63 | 3.51 | 2.37 | 2.02 | 1.19 | .64 | 2.19 |
| | 3.72 | 3.20 | 2.96 | 4.25 | 3.23 | 2.38 | 1.82 | 1.39 | 1.70 | 1.66 |
| | 3.72 | 3.20 | 2.96 | 4.25 | 3.23 | 2.21 | 1.90 | 1.19 | .69 | 2.15 |
| | 42,795 | 42,407 | 42,307 | 38,182 | 35,364 | 32,788 | 32,450 | 29,819 | 28,537 | 27,671 |
| | 46,991 | 46,885 | 46,874 | 42,811 | 40,029 | 37,455 | 37,130 | 31,466 | 30,489 | 29,117 |
| | 1.85 | 1.775 | 1.70 | 1.625 | 1.525 | 1.50 | 1.50 | 1.50 | 1.50 | 1.50 |
| | 31.72 | 29.45 | 27.79 | 26.04 | 24.13 | 23.16 | 22.69 | 22.49 | 22.92 | 24.03 |
| | $ 349,831 | $ 333,850 | $ 280,957 | $ 295,836 | $ 259,784 | $ 186,585 | $ 139,751 | $ 121,839 | $ 117,419 | $ 122,630 |
| | 71,393 | 65,913 | 60,932 | 50,654 | 45,390 | 41,886 | 38,295 | 34,949 | 32,214 | 29,948 |
| | 284,879 | 275,100 | 233,271 | 308,712 | 302,737 | 174,304 | 135,272 | 98,129 | 104,731 | 130,800 |
| | 1.8:1 | 1.8:1 | 1.8:1 | 1.8:1 | 1.6:1 | 1.8:1 | 1.9:1 | 2.0:1 | 1.8:1 | 1.9:1 |
| | 35.6% | 37.6% | 40.0% | 38.1% | 45.4% | 45.0% | — | — | — | — |
| | 32.5% | 34.5% | 37.4% | 35.1% | 42.6% | 42.5% | 41.3% | 43.6% | 37.7% | 38.9% |
| | 48,458 | 57,528 | 58,986 | 59,143 | 56,357 | 52,071 | 49,423 | 47,644 | 49,646 | 49,835 |
| | 68,500 | 68,700 | 63,800 | 65,300 | 79,100 | 75,700 | 73,900 | 66,900 | 63,900 | 70,000 |

| ($ thousands except per share) | 1978 | 1977 | 1976 | 1975 |
|---|---|---|---|---|
| Sales | $4,309,588 | $4,063,646 | $3,699,454 | $3,659,308 |
| Net Income | 170,403 | 145,739 | 137,947 | 174,442 |
| Earnings per share | 4.23 | 3.63 | 3.44 | 4.86 |

4

# FINANCIAL REPORT

## THE CBS ORGANIZATION

# *Management's Financial Commentary*

A financial report prepared by the CBS Organization. Portions of
the text have been reprinted with permission from CBS, Inc.

## MANAGEMENT'S FINANCIAL COMMENTARY

The complex developments in our businesses in recent years are difficult to understand solely by use of standard financial statements. The following presentation is offered to clarify not only the operating trends and results, but also the investments, divestments and other cash flows that have occurred while we have repositioned some of these businesses. Financing transactions and capital structure of the Company are also shown.

Revisions to previously published figures have been made for a new accounting rule related to the method of accounting for broadcast license agreements. Details of this adjustment can be found in the footnotes to the financial statements.

### Revenues

Total revenues rose 10 percent in 1983, after increasing modestly in 1981 and 1982, with all groups showing improvement. Broadcast Group revenues increased 10 percent in 1983 as all divisions, led by the Television Network, advanced. Records Group revenues improved 9 percent in 1983 following two years of decline. Domestic revenues increased significantly in 1983 with all labels showing improvement. This strong performance more than offset a modest decline in international revenues primarily caused by unfavorable foreign exchange rates. Columbia House and CBS Songs also contributed to the Group's improved performance. Publishing Group posted a 9 percent increase in 1983 due principally to improvement in the Magazines Division. Columbia Group revenues rose 11 percent in 1983 primarily due to increases in the Toys Division. The 1982 increase was related to the acquisition of the Ideal Toy Corporation.

### Operating Profits

Operating profits increased 32 percent in 1983 reflecting a strong turnaround from the decline recorded in 1982. Broadcast Group profits rose 8 percent in 1983 despite higher network programming costs in sports and evening entertainment, partially offset by successful cost management programs in all divisions. Profit increases were posted by all divisions.

Records Group profits, led by the resurgence of the domestic records division, rebounded strongly in 1983 following a series of difficult years. Strong product and improved market trends, combined with cost reductions derived from the 1982 realignment of the Division's operations, contributed significantly to these results. Included in 1982's results was a pretax loss of $13.1 million due to the shutdown of manufacturing operations in Terre Haute, Indiana. International operations improved profits in 1983 primarily due to successful cost management. This followed a decline in 1982 due to difficult economic conditions abroad. The declining value of foreign currencies affected both years negatively but was partially offset, especially in 1983, by increased interest income, particularly in Brazil. Columbia House continued a three-year period of growth with a significant increase in 1983. CBS Songs' profits improved principally because of the inclusion of a $4.5 million pretax gain on the sale of certain music publishing print rights and materials.

Publishing Group operating profits rose 45 percent in 1983 due to a turnaround in the Magazines Division related primarily to women's magazines. Educational and Professional Publishing recorded a slight increase in 1983.

Columbia Group recorded a loss in 1983 with both divisions reporting losses. In Toys, the loss was principally attributable to the very troubled marketplace for video games which caused the Division to close down its domestic video development and distribution operations. Musical Instruments, however, substantially reduced its losses, from the level recorded in 1982, due largely to the Steinway and Fender product lines.

Other reflected losses in 1981 through 1983 primarily due to development spending for Venture One, CBS Theatrical Films and CBS Video Enterprises, partially offset by income from tax benefit lease transactions. Gains from the sales of Canadian cable television investments and a Company aircraft were recorded in 1980. Included in 1979 was profit on the sale of the television syndication rights to the Cinema Center Films library.

1

| | 1983 | 1982 | 1981 | 1980 | 1979 |
|---|---|---|---|---|---|
| | (Dollars in millions) | | | | |
| CBS/Broadcast Group . . . . . . . . . . . . | $ 2,389.4 | $ 2,165.2 | $ 1,921.1 | $ 1,701.4 | $ 1,525.5 |
| CBS/Records Group . . . . . . . . . . . . | 1,158.8 | 1,066.7 | 1,218.3 | 1,338.0 | 1,287.1 |
| CBS/Publishing Group . . . . . . . . . . | 587.0 | 538.7 | 507.7 | 486.6 | 399.8 |
| CBS/Columbia Group . . . . . . . . . . . | 342.7 | 308.5 | 253.0 | 271.5 | 257.0 |
| Other . . . . . . . . . . . . . . . . . . . . . . . | 67.6 | 51.0 | 61.5 | 59.1 | 37.9 |
| Elimination of Intergroup Revenues . . . . . . . . . . . . | (5.3) | (7.3) | (5.7) | (4.6) | (6.4) |
| **Total Revenues** . . . . . . . . . . . . . . . . | **$ 4,540.2** | **$ 4,122.8** | **$ 3,955.9** | **$ 3,852.0** | **$ 3,500.9** |
| Foreign . . . . . . . . . . . . . . . . . . . . . . | $ 642.1 | $ 664.5 | $ 721.2 | $ 753.8 | $ 653.3 |
| Domestic . . . . . . . . . . . . . . . . . . . . . | 3,898.1 | 3,458.3 | 3,234.7 | 3,098.2 | 2,847.6 |

| | 1983 | 1982 | 1981 | 1980 | 1979 |
|---|---|---|---|---|---|
| | (Dollars in millions) | | | | |
| CBS/Broadcast Group . . . . . . . . . . . . | $291.5 | $270.8 | $316.9 | $247.1 | $269.3 |
| CBS/Records Group . . . . . . . . . . . . . | 109.4 | 22.2 | 58.9 | 72.3 | 68.4 |
| CBS/Publishing Group . . . . . . . . . . . | 55.2 | 38.0 | 43.1 | 45.0 | 42.7 |
| CBS/Columbia Group . . . . . . . . . . . . | (15.7) | 3.2 | 11.1 | 24.5 | 24.3 |
| Other . . . . . . . . . . . . . . . . . . . . . . . | (29.8) | (24.0) | (22.8) | 17.0 | 19.3 |
| **Operating Profits** . . . . . . . . . . . . . . | **$410.6** | **$310.2** | **$407.2** | **$405.9** | **$424.0** |
| Foreign . . . . . . . . . . . . . . . . . . . . . . | $ 69.8 | $ 64.9 | $ 71.7 | $ 72.2 | $ 68.0 |
| Domestic . . . . . . . . . . . . . . . . . . . . . | 340.8 | 245.3 | 335.5 | 333.7 | 356.0 |

### Income From Continuing Operations

General Corporate Expenses rose in 1983 primarily due to lower unallocated employee benefit expenses in 1982. Corporate interest expense net of interest income decreased in 1983 due primarily to lower commercial paper borrowings and more favorable rates. This followed a sharp rise in 1982 caused by increased borrowing levels. Foreign Exchange Losses rose dramatically in 1983, primarily due to losses in Brazil, which has a highly inflationary economy. In the prior three-year period these losses had remained level although varying on a country-by-country basis. Joint Ventures represents the CBS share of the operations of The CBS/FOX Company and Tri-Star Pictures, which began operations in 1982 and 1983, respectively. Amounts related to Tri-Star, however, are not significant.

The effective income tax rate for the Company returned to a more typical level in 1983 after declines in 1981 and 1982. The drop in the 1981 rate was due primarily to a $6.5 million settlement of the Company's 1962-1971 investment tax credit on film refund claims. The 1982 decrease was largely related to a federal tax audit settlement for the years 1977 through 1979 and higher than normal investment tax credits due to the purchase of three satellite transponders.

### Net Income

In 1981 and 1982, the Company discontinued certain businesses. There were no discontinued operations in 1983. In 1982, CBS Cable, an advertiser-supported cable programming service, was discontinued and the Specialty Stores Division, which retailed home entertainment products, was discontinued and subsequently sold. The mass market paperback book business was discontinued in 1981 and subsequently sold.

Operating results and losses on disposal from these businesses have been classified as Discontinued Operations. Net Income is arrived at by combining the after-tax results of these Discontinued Operations with Income From Continuing Operations.

### Internal Cash Generation

Funds provided from operations after dividends rose substantially to $201 million in 1983 due to the increased operating profits previously described and the absence of any discontinued operations. This followed a sharp decline in 1982 primarily related to the drop in operating profits. Discontinued Operations in 1981 and 1982 include the net losses from those operations (excluding items not affecting funds, such as depreciation and amortization of intangibles) and the net losses on disposal.

### Cash From External Sources

Since 1979 commercial paper and short-term debt have supplemented internally generated funds. In 1982 the Company issued $150 million of ten-year notes, which reduced commercial paper borrowings, and sold 1,650,000 shares of common stock to the public.

3

| | 1983 | 1982 | 1981 | 1980 | 1979 |
|---|---|---|---|---|---|
| | (Dollars in millions, except per share amounts) | | | | |
| **Operating Profits** | $410.6 | $310.2 | $407.2 | $405.9 | $424.0 |
| General Corporate Expenses | (49.9) | (44.9) | (44.4) | (42.2) | (43.5) |
| Corporate Interest, net | (25.4) | (32.1) | (8.1) | (15.9) | (11.1) |
| Foreign Exchange Losses | (15.9) | (5.1) | (5.4) | (5.2) | (2.9) |
| Joint Ventures | 7.0 | 1.9 | | | |
| **Income From Continuing Operations Before Taxes** | 326.4 | 230.0 | 349.3 | 342.6 | 366.5 |
| Income Taxes | (139.2) | (81.6) | (146.4) | (152.9) | (168.2) |
| **Income From Continuing Operations** | $187.2 | $148.4 | $202.9 | $189.7 | $198.3 |
| **Earnings Per Share From Continuing Operations** | $ 6.31 | $ 5.29 | $ 7.27 | $ 6.80 | $ 7.13 |

| | 1983 | 1982 | 1981 | 1980 | 1979 |
|---|---|---|---|---|---|
| | (Dollars in millions, except per share amounts) | | | | |
| **Net Income** | $187.2 | $110.8 | $165.5 | $183.8 | $198.7 |
| **Earnings Per Share** | $ 6.31 | $ 3.95 | $ 5.93 | $ 6.59 | $ 7.14 |
| **Dividends Per Common Share** | $ 2.80 | $ 2.80 | $ 2.80 | $ 2.80 | $ 2.65 |

| | 1983 | 1982 | 1981 | 1980 | 1979 |
|---|---|---|---|---|---|
| | (Dollars in millions) | | | | |
| **Income From Continuing Operations** | $187.2 | $148.4 | $202.9 | $189.7 | $198.3 |
| Depreciation and Amortization | 97.0 | 80.8 | 70.6 | 66.0 | 55.6 |
| Deferred Income Taxes | 3.1 | 21.0 | 22.2 | 5.6 | 23.9 |
| Undistributed Share of Equity Income | (3.2) | (4.6) | (7.4) | (8.7) | (6.4) |
| Discontinued Operations | | (35.3) | (33.8) | (2.0) | 4.4 |
| | 284.1 | 210.3 | 254.5 | 250.6 | 275.8 |
| Dividends | (83.1) | (78.4) | (78.3) | (78.2) | (73.9) |
| **Internally Generated Funds** | $201.0 | $131.9 | $176.2 | $172.4 | $201.9 |

| | 1983 | 1982 | 1981 | 1980 | 1979 |
|---|---|---|---|---|---|
| | (Dollars in millions) | | | | |
| Commercial Paper and Other Debt | $ (53.0) | $ (37.4) | $ 8.4 | $ (64.2) | $186.6 |
| Ten Year 14½% Notes | | 150.0 | | | |
| Common Stock Offering | | 92.9 | | | |
| **Total Cash From External Sources** | $ (53.0) | $205.5 | $ 8.4 | $ (64.2) | $186.6 |
| **Average Corporate Interest Rate** | 10.8% | 12.0% | 14.3% | 11.6% | 10.0% |

4

---

### Investment Program

"Total Funds Available" for investment in the Company's businesses includes cash from both internal and external sources. This table details how those funds were utilized.

Capital expenditures, acquisitions and investments in internally developed businesses accounted for 75 percent of the investment program over the last five years. These are detailed further in the following sections. In addition, the Company made major investments in broadcast program rights. Tax benefit leases were purchased in 1981 and 1982 and resulted in a 1982 federal income tax refund receivable of $35.8 million due to carry-back investment tax credits. This was included in other current assets in 1982 and was collected in 1983. Further discussion of the Investment Program is contained in the Working Capital Section.

---

### Capital Expenditures

The level of capital expenditures has been in the range of $100-135 million over the last five years. The majority of these expenditures were related to updating Broadcast Group facilities and to the construction of recorded music manufacturing plants.

The Broadcast Group implemented an equipment and facilities modernization program starting in 1981 which included the updating of the Broadcast Center in New York, which is expected to be completed in 1985. In addition, three satellite transponders were purchased in 1982.

The Records Group made major expenditures both internationally and domestically over the period. Recorded music plants were erected in England and Brazil in 1979 and 1980. In 1983, major modernization expenditures were made in Brazil, Holland and Mexico. Domestically, construction in Carrollton, Georgia began in 1979 and spending for this plant continued through 1983 in line with the consolidation of domestic manufacturing facilities.

---

### Depreciation

Depreciation of Property, Plant and Equipment increased gradually over the last five years, reflecting the capital expenditures previously described.

---

### Expenditures for Major Acquisitions and Internally Developed Businesses

The major expenditures over the period related to the Publishing Group's acquisition of *Family Weekly* in 1980, the Columbia Group's acquisition of the Ideal Toy Corporation in 1982, the Company's investments and advances related to the CBS/FOX and Tri-Star Pictures joint ventures in 1982 and 1983 and the Company's investments in various internally developed businesses from 1980 through 1983. These businesses, primarily CBS Theatrical Films, CBS Video Enterprises, CBS Software and CBS Cable (discontinued in 1982) are included in Other. Some of the assets of CBS Video Enterprises were contributed to the CBS/FOX joint venture in 1982.

Also included in the table are the Broadcast Group's acquisition of a small cable television system in Texas in 1982, the Records Group's investment in the CBS Catalogue Partnership in 1983, and the Publishing Group's acquisitions of several magazines in 1979, 1980 and 1982 and a small English publishing company in 1982.

5

| | 1983 | 1982 | 1981 | 1980 | 1979 |
|---|---|---|---|---|---|
| | | (Dollars in millions) | | | |
| Capital Expenditures | $ 101.5 | $ 131.3 | $ 122.4 | $ 107.9 | $ 121.6 |
| Acquisitions and Internally Developed Businesses | 71.8 | 139.1 | 19.3 | 62.4 | 7.6 |
| Broadcast Program Rights, net | 8.4 | 28.9 | 46.7 | (12.0) | 62.9 |
| Tax Benefit Leases | (39.8) | .9 | 33.1 | | |
| Other Net Assets excluding Cash | (8.8) | 37.3 | 37.8 | (13.1) | 108.1 |
| **Total Investments** | **133.1** | **337.5** | **259.3** | **145.2** | **300.2** |
| Total Funds Available | 148.0 | 337.4 | 184.6 | 108.2 | 388.5 |
| **Increase (Decrease) in Cash** | **$ 14.9** | **$ (.1)** | **$ (74.7)** | **$ (37.0)** | **$ 88.3** |

| | 1983 | 1982 | 1981 | 1980 | 1979 |
|---|---|---|---|---|---|
| | | (Dollars in millions) | | | |
| CBS/Broadcast Group | $ 58.4 | $ 79.0 | $ 49.9 | $ 27.2 | $ 30.2 |
| CBS/Records Group | 21.5 | 20.9 | 36.3 | 54.2 | 66.0 |
| CBS/Publishing Group | 4.3 | 4.5 | 4.5 | 4.4 | 4.2 |
| CBS/Columbia Group | 9.2 | 7.2 | 6.0 | 9.3 | 6.4 |
| Corporate and Other | 8.1 | 19.7 | 25.7 | 12.8 | 14.8 |
| **Total** | **$ 101.5** | **$ 131.3** | **$ 122.4** | **$ 107.9** | **$ 121.6** |

| | 1983 | 1982 | 1981 | 1980 | 1979 |
|---|---|---|---|---|---|
| | | (Dollars in millions) | | | |
| CBS/Broadcast Group | $ 25.2 | $ 20.5 | $ 16.2 | $ 15.0 | $ 13.7 |
| CBS/Records Group | 18.3 | 17.6 | 17.3 | 17.8 | 14.8 |
| CBS/Publishing Group | 3.7 | 3.3 | 3.3 | 2.9 | 2.6 |
| CBS/Columbia Group | 7.9 | 6.2 | 4.8 | 4.1 | 3.5 |
| Corporate and Other | 10.6 | 10.0 | 9.0 | 7.5 | 6.4 |
| **Total** | **$ 65.7** | **$ 57.6** | **$ 50.6** | **$ 47.3** | **$ 41.0** |

| | 1983 | 1982 | 1981 | 1980 | 1979 |
|---|---|---|---|---|---|
| | | (Dollars in millions) | | | |
| CBS/Broadcast Group | | $ 15.0 | | | |
| CBS/Records Group | $ 13.9 | | | | |
| CBS/Publishing Group | | 8.6 | | $ 52.2 | $ 7.6 |
| CBS/Columbia Group | | 57.5 | | | |
| Other* | 24.4 | 41.2 | $ 19.3 | 10.2 | |
| Joint Ventures | 33.5 | 16.8 | | | |
| **Total** | **$ 71.8** | **$ 139.1** | **$ 19.3** | **$ 62.4** | **$ 7.6** |

*Includes net asset buildup of developing businesses. Income or loss from these operations is included in "Internal Cash Generation."

6

### Identifiable Assets

Broadcast Group identifiable assets have grown over the five-year period because of higher receivable levels related to increased revenues and due to the previously described capital expenditures program and investments in network programming. In the Records Group, the closing of the Santa Maria and Terre Haute facilities in 1981 and 1982 partly offset the investments in Carrollton and the foreign record plants. The 1983 increase is due primarily to the investment in the CBS Catalogue Partnership and increased receivables related to higher revenues. In addition, in recent years, the book value of foreign assets was affected negatively by declining exchange rates on the translation of those assets into dollars. Publishing Group assets remained level over the period since the *Family Weekly* acquisition in 1980. Columbia Group had a substantial increase in 1982 due to the acquisition of the Ideal Toy Corporation and rose again in 1983 due to increases in accounts receivable and inventory levels. Corporate and Other declined in 1983 primarily due to the sale of the Specialty Stores Division.

### Working Capital

The current ratio remained relatively stable over the five-year period 1979-1983. Notes and accounts receivable, net, remained at approximately the same level between 1979 and 1982 while increasing 13 percent in 1983 on a fourth quarter sales increase of 17 percent. Despite revenue increases over the period, inventories remained constant, decreasing slightly at year-end 1983.

The Company's investments in program rights and feature films increased significantly over the period. The impact of these increases on profit performance is discussed in the Operating Profits section. $35.8 million of the increase in prepaid expenses and other in 1982 relates to a federal income tax receivable discussed in the Investment Program section.

On the liability side, in addition to increases in liabilities for talent and program rights, income taxes payable increased from $13.8 million at the end of 1982 to $88.4 million at the end of 1983 primarily due to increased profits in 1983 and the effect of tax benefit lease transactions on the 1982 year-end balance. The 1981 tax liability was also lower due to the first tax benefit lease transaction.

### Capital Structure

In 1982 the Company strengthened its balance sheet. The maturity of total debt was significantly lengthened through the issuance of $150 million of AA rated ten-year 14½% notes in June 1982. The public sale of 1,650,000 shares of common stock in December 1982 added to the Company's capital base and enhanced debt capacity, providing greater flexibility for financial planning. In 1983, commercial paper and other current debt were substantially reduced. With the Company's ability to generate cash internally and a low level of total debt to capital, the Company believes its ample liquidity and capital resources position it well for the competitive environment of the 1980's.

7

| | 1983 | 1982 | 1981 | 1980 | 1979 |
|---|---|---|---|---|---|
| | | | (Dollars in millions) | | |
| CBS/Broadcast Group . . . . . . . . . . . . . | $1,152.9 | $1,101.8 | $ 954.9 | $ 806.1 | $ 748.1 |
| CBS/Records Group . . . . . . . . . . . . . | 836.2 | 733.7 | 746.9 | 818.2 | 829.2 |
| CBS/Publishing Group . . . . . . . . . . | 309.8 | 307.4 | 313.2 | 326.7 | 238.3 |
| CBS/Columbia Group . . . . . . . . . . . . | 394.2 | 335.8 | 217.2 | 211.7 | 190.8 |
| Corporate and Other. . . . . . . . . . . . . | 296.7 | 350.8 | 359.5 | 301.4 | 299.8 |
| **Total** . . . . . . . . . . . . . . . . . . . . . . . | **$2,989.8** | **$2,829.5** | **$2,591.7** | **$2,464.1** | **$2,306.2** |
| Foreign . . . . . . . . . . . . . . . . . . . . . . | $ 494.4 | $ 437.6 | $ 447.8 | $ 445.6 | $ 452.4 |
| Domestic . . . . . . . . . . . . . . . . . . . . . | 2,495.4 | 2,391.9 | 2,143.9 | 2,018.5 | 1,853.8 |

*December 31*

| | 1983 | 1982 | 1981 | 1980 | 1979 |
|---|---|---|---|---|---|
| | | | (Dollars in millions) | | |
| Notes and accounts receivable, net . . . . | $ 829.6 | $ 733.5 | $ 713.3 | $ 720.2 | $ 726.2 |
| Inventories . . . . . . . . . . . . . . . . . . . . | 295.3 | 307.0 | 306.9 | 315.7 | 309.9 |
| Program rights and feature film productions . . . . . . . . . . . . . . . | 490.9 | 439.0 | 391.6 | 321.6 | 332.2 |
| Prepaid expenses and other . . . . . . . . | 150.9 | 172.1 | 111.4 | 99.5 | 76.8 |
| Total current assets excluding cash . . . . . . . . . . . . . . . . | 1,766.7 | 1,651.6 | 1,523.2 | 1,457.0 | 1,445.1 |
| Liabilities for talent and program rights . . . . . . . . . . . . . . . . | 247.4 | 199.0 | 196.7 | 173.7 | 144.6 |
| Commercial paper . . . . . . . . . . . . . . | 64.8 | 80.8 | 5.6 | | 182.2 |
| Income taxes . . . . . . . . . . . . . . . . . . | 88.4 | 13.8 | 29.4 | 52.6 | 79.2 |
| Other current liabilities . . . . . . . . . . . | 735.6 | 742.7 | 658.5 | 629.0 | 562.2 |
| Total current liabilities . . . . . . . . . . . . | 1,136.2 | 1,036.3 | 890.2 | 855.3 | 968.2 |
| **Working capital excluding cash** . . . . | **630.5** | **615.3** | **633.0** | **601.7** | **476.9** |
| Cash and cash equivalents . . . . . . . . . | 42.8 | 27.9 | 28.0 | 102.7 | 139.7 |
| **Working capital** . . . . . . . . . . . . . . . . | **$ 673.3** | **$ 643.2** | **$ 661.0** | **$ 704.4** | **$ 616.6** |
| **Ratio of current assets to current liabilities** . . . . . . . . . . . . . . | **1.59:1** | **1.62:1** | **1.74:1** | **1.82:1** | **1.64:1** |

*December 31*

| | 1983 | 1982 | 1981 | 1980 | 1979 |
|---|---|---|---|---|---|
| | | | (Dollars in millions) | | |
| Current Debt . . . . . . . . . . . . . . . . . | $ 75.5 | $ 123.1 | $ 25.8 | $ 22.8 | $ 199.9 |
| Long-Term Debt . . . . . . . . . . . . . . . | 232.5 | 238.0 | 222.6 | 217.2 | 104.3 |
| Total Debt . . . . . . . . . . . . . . . . . . . | 308.0 | 361.1 | 248.4 | 240.0 | 304.2 |
| Shareholders' Equity . . . . . . . . . . . . | 1,440.5 | 1,336.3 | 1,245.2 | 1,183.6 | 1,071.1 |
| **Total Capital** . . . . . . . . . . . . . . . . . | **$1,748.5** | **$1,697.4** | **$1,493.6** | **$1,423.6** | **$1,375.3** |
| **Debt as a Percentage of Capital** . . . . | **17.6%** | **21.3%** | **16.6%** | **16.9%** | **22.1%** |

8

# DESCRIPTIVE REPORT

TRAINING DEPARTMENT GOALS & COURSES


Prepared for

Mr. Leonard Schwartz

Treasurer


Prepared by

Mr. Aldo Vannucci


Schwartz-Snidermann, Inc.

330 Fifth Avenue

New York, New York 10001

May 27, 1982

CONTENTS

INTRODUCTION

The purpose of the Training Department is to provide
newly hired or about-to-be-promoted employees with the
product knowledge and vocational skills needed to perform
their jobs successfully.  This report describes the training
courses that have been devised to effect this goal.

I.  DESCRIPTION OF COURSES

The following courses will be offered to members of our
sales staff on a regular basis each business quarter.

A.  Customer Contact Course

The course is designed for existing sales personnel
trained before 1979.  Selection of participants is determined
by the district manager.

The length of the course is 23 hours in three consecutive days.  The course's objective is to train sales personnel
to recognize and communicate with various types of customers,
to deal with difficult customers using a business-like
attitude, and to sell customers the best rate and service.

The course consists of formal classroom training using
lecture, programmed instruction, and sound recordings with
heavy emphasis on role playing.  This course is modeled on
the highly successful Customer Contact Course used in our
West Coast division.

All participants are required to complete a written
evaluation of the course after they return to their sales
districts.

- 2 -

B. <u>Sales Training Course</u>

The course is designed for new sales representatives
and those with one to three months field experience.  The
length of the course is approximately 72 hours.  The
objective is (1) to increase product knowledge and (2) to
increase client contact effectiveness when calling on
accounts.  The course will focus on the ability to initiate
customer contact, to sell our products successfully, and to
maintain long-term customer satisfaction.

The course employs a substantial variety of training
techniques.  In addition to lecture and demonstration by
instructors, major objectives are met through competitive
teamwork, hypothetical sales projects, role playing, group
discussion, programmed notes, and films.

All participants are required to complete a written
evaluation of the course upon completion.

C. <u>District Sales Manager</u>

The course is designed for existing and about-to-be
promoted district sales managers.  The course length is
undetermined at this time, but will probably run three days.
Its objective is to deal with problems of transition encountered by those assuming new and diverse responsibilities.
Also, the course stresses methods for implementing company
sales policy and procedures, as well as ways of handling
field representatives' problems and needs.  The course will

- 3 -

consist of instruction and discussion, as well as role-
playing exercises.

All participants are required to complete a written
evaluation of the course upon conclusion.

D.  Management Training

The course will instruct about-to-be promoted line
managers in operational functions and management techniques.
Its goals are to develop individual management skills and
expand existing management capabilities.

Duration of the course is two weeks, and instruction
focuses on developing management-related skills and techniques.
Through programmed instruction, general discussion, and on-
the-job training, management trainees will learn all facets
of corporate operations.

In addition to a written evaluation at the end of the
course, participants will review the course content through
correspondence with the Training Department.

II. CONCLUSION

The implementation of these training courses will fulfill
these corporate objectives:

1.  Standardize wherever possible all divisional sales
    training to achieve maximum employee motivation
    performance at the least possible cost.

- 4 -

2. Decrease employee turnover.

3. Effect better communication between corporate management and sales representatives.

III.  RECOMMENDATIONS

In view of the importance of these training courses to our corporate goals, I recommend the following:

1. The Training Department should initiate these courses as soon as possible.

2. The training program should be expanded to include post-class instruction.

3. All courses should be evaluated on a regular basis to ensure quality instruction and up-to-date content.

4. The Training Department should publish and distribute to all employees notification of new courses and programs.

# ORAL REPORT

From:   J.P. Morgan & Co. Incorporated
        23 Wall Street
        New York, N.Y. 10015
        (212) 208-3690


Remarks of Robert V. Lindsay, President, J.P. Morgan & Co.
Incorporated, at the annual meeting of the company's stockholders, April 11, 1984

Those of you who've read our 1983 annual report will
remember that the first section of the report mentioned three
principles that guide Morgan's efforts to maintain a leading
position in today's highly competitive market for financial
services.  They are:

  First, we must maintain a very strong capital base;
  Second, to generate earnings we must concentrate on the
      sophisticated financial services that our clients value
      most; and
  Third, we must strive to improve profitability.

The first and last points are fairly straightforward,
but what we mean by concentrating on the "services our
clients value most" is perhaps less obvious.  So I'd like to
take a few minutes this morning to outline three recent
transactions that show how Morgan draws on a variety of
specialized skills to meet the financial needs of our
customers.

A report prepared by J. P. Morgan & Co., Incorporated. The text
has been reprinted by permission of Morgan Guaranty Trust
Company of New York.

- 2 -

The first transaction I'll describe was quite complex.  Our objective was to provide financing in French
francs to the French subsidiaries of several U.S. multinational corporate clients.  But there were a number of
problems to overcome before we could supply these subsidiaries with the funds they needed to finance their business activities in France.  Our Paris office couldn't simply
lend to these companies because of limits on direct French
franc lending imposed by French regulations.  Neither could
we use a French franc currency swap -- in other words, lend
the companies dollars and then swap the dollars for francs
-- because swaps involving francs are not permitted by
French foreign exchange controls.  So we came up with another
approach that met with the French Treasury's approval.
Morgan took dollars from the U.S. parent companies and lent
them to a French bank, which in turn provided francs for the
subsidiaries of the U.S. corporations.  The attraction of
this arrangement for the French bank was a new source of
dollar financing.

But there was another complication in the deal.  To
complete it, we had to use a technique called an interest
rate swap, which is simply an agreement between two parties
to assume the interest payments on each other's obligations.
This technique made it possible to provide funds at either
fixed or floating rates of interest, according to the needs
of each participant in the transaction.  We ended up making
several interest rate swaps, all arranged by Morgan Guaranty
Ltd, our Euromarket subsidiary.

Once these mechanics were worked out, our Paris
office set the wheels in motion and coordinated each step of
the transaction.  By the time it was complete -- and believe
it or not I've left out the details -- no fewer than eight
Morgan offices and eight multinational clients were involved.
The bankers responsible for our relationships with the U.S.
corporations, the treasury desks at several of our European
offices, corporate finance specialists in London and New
York, and of course officers in Paris worked as a team to

- 3 -

achieve the original objective:  finding a source of French franc financing for the subsidiaries of our multinational clients.

The second transaction I'd like to highlight is important because it involves one of Morgan's newer activities.  In this transaction we served as dealer in the issuance of commercial paper for a major American corporation, which required substantial short-term financing to meet a special need.  After analyzing this need, we advised our client that a commercial paper program would be the least expensive way to raise money.  Morgan's commercial paper advisory group helped the company design a suitable $300 million program.  The bankers responsible for the client relationship established a backstop line of credit for the commercial paper and provided a temporary $300 million loan to bridge the gap between when the client needed the funds -- that is, immediately -- and the issue date.  Money market specialists priced the issue and placed it with investors.  To satisfy the client's requirements, they also invested the proceeds of the issue in Eurodollar time deposits for a positive return.  Finally, Morgan served as issuing and paying agent, which meant that commercial paper operations specialists played an important role, too.

In the last transaction on my list, Morgan served as financial advisor in the friendly merger of two midwest banks.  Here we drew on the talents of merger and acquisition specialists and financial analysts, as well as bankers. First we won the appointment as advisor to the acquiring bank.  Working with our merger and acquisition experts, Morgan financial analysts studied the institution being acquired and provided a valuation of its assets -- a key step in developing a suitable structure for the acquisition agreement.  The transaction ultimately recommended by Morgan, which was agreed on by the banks and approved by their shareholders, involved two steps:  a cash tender offer and an exchange of shares.

- 4 -

Morgan served as dealer-manager for the tender offer, which means that we both advised our client on strategic questions concerning the offer and handled the mechanics involved in making it.  When the need for bank financing became apparent, as the structure of this deal evolved, we also extended credit to finance the purchase of shares.  Just recently, we began a dialogue with our client about how the holding company for the new merged bank might be structured.  Counsel on this issue would be provided by Morgan's corporate finance specialists.

The three transactions I've summarized have something very important in common:  they integrate capital market activities with more traditional banking and operations services.  The old distinctions between these areas have all but completely faded.  We're convinced that the ability to combine financial skills and resources in imaginative ways will be critical to Morgan's success in the markets of the future.  Regrettably, outdated laws restricting the ability of bank affiliates to underwrite and deal in corporate securities in the U.S. keep us from competing as aggressively as we'd like in the converging financial markets.  We think this restriction of competition carries serious long-term costs for both commercial banks and U.S. business.  Morgan intends to take an active role in the public debate on this issue, and you'll hear more about it from us in due course.

Let me just say a word about allegations made from time to time that, as banks expand their financial advisory activities, they will be tempted to condition a customer's access to credit on his use of those services.  This is nonsense.  The tying of services is not only forbidden by law, but as a practical matter would be pointless.  Corporate lending today is a buyers' market, in which bankers can't afford not to compete vigorously for business.

- 5 -

We at Morgan are striving to integrate credit, corporate finance, and operations services in new ways to address
our clients' worldwide needs.  Our ability to design sophisticated solutions to complex problems is a great competitive
strength -- one that commands a premium in the market and
contributes substantially to our profitability.  People from
every area of the company work hard on transactions like
those I've highlighted today, where responsibility and teamwork count most.  I salute them for the important part they
play in making Morgan a leader.

Mr. Preston, let me return the meeting to you.

# APPENDIX C

# Sample Questionnaires

The questionnaires that follow illustrate two of the many formats used to gather information.

## READER SURVEY: COLOR-PRINT FILM PROCESSING

If you have had color-print film processed within the last year, please complete the following questions. Your experiences will contribute useful information to an upcoming report on color-print film processing. Please return your completed questionnaire by February 1.

1. What size color-print film do you normally shoot?
   110 ....... ☐    126 ....... ☐    135(35mm) ....... ☐

2. In the last year, about how many rolls of color-print film have you had processed?
   Less than 5 .......... ☐    10-19 ..................... ☐
   5-9 ..................... ☐    20 or more ............. ☐

3. Listed below are four factors that might be considered in selecting a film processor. Rank the factors in terms of how important each is to you, giving a 1 to the *most* important, a 2 to the second most important, a 3 to the third most important and a 4 to the least important factor.

   Cost of processing ............................................ ____
   Location of processor ...................................... ____
   Quality of prints ............................................ ____
   Speed of processing ........................................ ____

4a. Check below the one *primary* place you've used to process color-print film in the last year.

4b. Check any *other* places you've used in the last year (check all that apply).

|  | Primary Place | Other Places |
|---|---|---|
| Camera store ......................................... | ☐ | ☐ |
| Department store ................................ | ☐ | ☐ |
| Drug store .......................................... | ☐ | ☐ |
| Film and film-processing-only store (e.g. Fotomat) ..................... | ☐ | ☐ |
| Mail order, submitting payment with order .................. | ☐ | ☐ |
| Mail order, using pre-paid mailers ........... | ☐ | ☐ |
| Supermarket ........................................ | ☐ | ☐ |
| Other _____ | ☐ | ☐ |

5. What is the name of the primary place, checked above, to which you take or send your color-print film?

   _____

PLEASE ANSWER QUESTIONS 6 THROUGH 13 ABOUT YOUR *PRIMARY* COLOR-PRINT FILM PROCESSOR.

6a. Do you specify or select a particular brand of processing when you use this processor?
   Yes ................ ☐    No ................ ☐

6b. If yes, what brand do you specify? _____

7. How long do you generally have to wait to get your processed film returned by this processor?
   One-hour service .. ☐    3 days to 1 week ............ ☐
   Same-day service .. ☐    Between 1 and 2 weeks .. ☐
   Within 2 days ....... ☐    More than 2 weeks ........ ☐

8a. Do you get a free or discount replacement roll of film when you have a roll of film processed?
   Yes, a free roll of film ......................... ☐
   Yes, a discount roll of film ................. ☐
   No ...................................................... ☐

8b. If you get a free or discount roll of film from this processor, which brand do you get?
   Kodak ................................................................ ☐
   Company's own brand of film .............................. ☐
   Other _____

9a. What kind of guarantee is given by this processor?
   Money-back guarantee if not completely satisfied.. ☐
   Credit for unprinted frames ............................... ☐
   I am charged only for processed prints ................ ☐
   I am charged only for prints I keep .................... ☐
   I don't know ...................................................... ☐
   Other _____

9b. Have you used the guarantee in the last year?
   Yes, and I was satisfied with the results ............... ☐
   Yes, but I was not completely satisfied
       with the results ............................................ ☐
   No .................................................................... ☐

10. If you get credit slips for unprintable negatives, how often do you use them?
   Always ............... ☐    Rarely ................... ☐
   Sometimes .......... ☐    Never ................... ☐

11a. Has any of your film been lost either in the mail or by this processor in the last year?
   Yes ............... ☐    No ................. ☐

11b. If yes, how were you compensated?
   Not compensated ................................................ ☐
   Free roll of film only .......................................... ☐
   Free roll of film and free processing .................... ☐
   Other _____

12a. Have you ever sent negatives back to this processor for additional prints?
   Yes .................... ☐    No ............. ☐

12b. If yes, how satisfied were you with the reprints?
   Very satisfied ..... ☐    Dissatisfied ................ ☐
   Satisfied ............ ☐    Very dissatisfied ........ ☐

13. Please use the following scale to rate your primary processor on each of the factors listed below.
   1 = Excellent  2 = Very Good  3 = Good  4 = Fair  5 = Poor

| Factor | Rating |
|---|---|
| Cost of processing ............................................. | ____ |
| Location of processor ...................................... | ____ |
| Quality of prints:  color rendition .................. | ____ |
|                     sharpness ........................... | ____ |
| Service ............................................................ | ____ |
| Speed of processing ........................................ | ____ |

14a. In the last year have you received prints *from any* processor that were unacceptable because of poor picture quality?
   Yes ................... ☐    No ............ ☐

14b. If yes, did you try to get the prints reprinted? (if more than one incident, answer for the most recent time.)
   Yes ...................... ☐    No ............ ☐

14c. If yes, were they reprinted to your satisfaction?
   Yes ..................... ☐    No ................. ☐

15a. Have you used any processors in the last two years that you will not use again?
   Yes ..................... ☐    No .............. ☐

15b. If yes, which one? (If more than one, answer about most recent incident.) _____

15c. Why did you stop using this processor? _____
   _____

15d. If you stopped using this processor because of a particular problem, did the problem occur .....
   During original processing ................................... ☐
   When having reprints made ................................ ☐

16. What is your zip code? _____

   If you have any additional comments, feel free to write them on a separate piece of paper. Thank you for your help!

## BASIC SKILLS AND THE U.S. WORK FORCE
## SURVEY INSTRUCTIONS

The attached survey is divided into four sections. Please note that the definition for "competency" in each of the skills covered is attached to the end of the survey.

Section  I:   Requests brief background information on your union and the nature of its membership.

Section II:   Elicits your perception of the nature and level of basic skills required for jobs typical of those held by secondary school graduates and non-graduates who are members of your union, compared to the competency possessed by the average secondary school graduate and/or non-graduate hired into those entry-level job categories.

Section III:  Elicits your evaluation of the areas of union operation most affected by basic skill deficiencies.

Section IV:   Requests a description of efforts your union has undertaken—on its own as well as with others—to resolve basic skill deficiency problems in its membership and/or among secondary school students.

Throughout the questionnaire, the terms "secondary school graduates and non-graduates" refers to that portion of the workforce which has not graduated from a college-level institution. For purposes of this questionnaire, vocational schools are *not* considered to be college-level institutions.

Instructions for completion of individual questions are self-explanatory within each section. If you have additional comments on these or related issues, please do not hesitate to include them, using additional pages as necessary.

Please return the completed questionnaire as soon as possible to:

Center for Public Resources
680 Fifth Avenue
New York, New York 10019

A return-addressed envelope is attached.

## CENTER FOR PUBLIC RESOURCES
## BASIC SKILLS AND THE U.S. WORK FORCE

### BASIC SKILLS SURVEY

#### Section I: Background
(a) Name of union _____

(b) Name and title of person(s) responding to survey

_____

_____

(c) Total number of union members _____

(d) Number of Locals in the union _____

(e) Approximate number (if unavailable, percentage) of members who are

       secondary school/vocational school graduates    _____

       not secondary school graduates    _____

       college graduates    _____

#### Section II: Perception of the Problem
In this section we seek your best professional judgment as to the nature and scope of basic skills problems among secondary school graduates and/or non-graduates entering the workforce and membership in your union.

Note that full definitions of "competencies" for basic skills listed here are derived from the College Board's "Project Equality" and are appended to this survey.

(a) To assist us in comparing your perspective to that of other unions responding to the survey, please indicate three or four examples from your union membership of the job categories into which secondary school graduates and non-graduates are initially hired.

      Graduates  1. _____    Non-graduates 1. _____
                      2. _____               2. _____
                      3. _____               3. _____
                      4. _____               4. _____

1

(b) Please assess the level of basic skills competency required of secondary school graduates and non-graduates entering the types of jobs listed above. "Medium" level of competency is defined as the required skill functions listed in the skill definitions appended to this survey; "Low" indicates that fewer functions are required; "High" indicates that a greater number of functions are required. (Indicate level with an "X" in the appropriate column.)

| | *Level of Competency Required* | | | |
|---|---|---|---|---|
| | *High* | *Medium* | *Low* | *Not applicable* |
| *Graduates* | | | | |
| Reading | | | | |
| Writing | | | | |
| Speaking/Listening | | | | |
| Mathematics | | | | |
| Science | | | | |
| Reasoning | | | | |
| Other (specify) | | | | |
| _____ | | | | |
| _____ | | | | |
| *Non-graduates* | | | | |
| Reading | | | | |
| Writing | | | | |
| Speaking/Listening | | | | |
| Mathematics | | | | |
| Science | | | | |
| Reasoning | | | | |
| Other (specify) | | | | |
| _____ | | | | |
| _____ | | | | |

2

(c) Please assess the level of basic skills competency generally possessed by the average secondary school graduate and non-graduate entering the above listed job categories and union memberships. "Medium" indicates an ability to perform the functions of the skill, as detailed in the appended definitions; "Low" indicates an inability to perform even those functions; "High" indicates an ability to perform skill functions in excess of those listed in the appended definitions. (Indicate level with an "X" in the appropriate column.)

| | *Level of Competency Possessed* | | |
|---|---|---|---|
| | *High* | *Medium* | *Low* |
| *Graduate* | | | |
| Reading | | | |
| Writing | | | |
| Speaking/Listening | | | |
| Mathematics | | | |
| Science | | | |
| Reasoning | | | |
| Other (specify) | | | |
| _____ | | | |
| _____ | | | |
| *Non-graduate* | | | |
| Reading | | | |
| Writing | | | |
| Speaking/Listening | | | |
| Mathematics | | | |
| Science | | | |
| Reasoning | | | |
| Other (specify) | | | |
| _____ | | | |
| _____ | | | |

3

## Section III: Impact of Skill Deficiencies

We recognize that it is extremely difficult to quantify the costs to unions or to companies of basic skill deficiencies among youth entering the workforce. This section is an attempt to understand your subjective assessment of the areas of union operation which are most significantly affected by basic skills deficiencies of secondary school graduates and non-graduates entering the workforce.

Please rank order the following areas of cost of basic skills deficiencies, with "1" being the most significant/costly impact:

Ranking

- Increased numbers of grievances traceable to basic skill deficiencies

- Worker inability to understand union policies

- Inability to follow instructions

- Insufficient use of negotiated benefits

- Violation of company/union agreed safety standards

- Other _____

_____

_____

## Section IV: Resolving the Problem

We are interested in identifying and communicating to other organizations any initiatives you may have undertaken to address the problem of basic skills deficiencies set out in this survey. This section asks you to briefly describe your union efforts in this area and to evaluate their impact. If you have printed materials describing these efforts, simply attach them with your returned survey; you need not repeat the information here.

Please describe activities your union has undertaken within its own membership or organization to improve the basic skill levels of its members (e.g., union-sponsored remedial training, English as a second language):

_____

_____

_____

_____

4

# Selected Bibliography

Barzun, Jacques. *Simple and Direct*. New York: Harper & Row, 1975.

———— and Henry F. Graff. *The Modern Researcher*, 3d ed. New York: Harcourt Brace & World, 1977.

Berdie, Douglas R. and John F. Anderson. *Questionnaires: Design and Use*. Metuchen, N.J.: Scarecrow Press, 1974.

Berenson, Conrad and Raymond Colton. *Research and Report Writing for Business and Economics*. New York: Random House, 1971.

Bernstein, Theodore M. *The Careful Writer: A Modern Guide to English Usage*. New York: Atheneum, 1965.

Brown, Harry. *Business Report Writing*. New York: Van Nostrand, 1980.

Brusaw, Charles T., Gerald J. Alfred, and Walter E. Oliu. *The Business Writer's Handbook*, 2d ed. New York: St. Martin's Press, 1982.

Carr-Ruffino, Norma. *Writing Short Business Reports*. New York: McGraw-Hill, 1980.

Ewing, David. *Writing for Results*, 2d. ed. New York: Wiley, 1979.

Flesch, Rudolf. *The Art of Readable Writing*, Rev. ed. New York: Harper & Row, 1974.

Flower, Linda. *Problem-Solving Strategies*. New York: Harcourt Brace Jovanovich, 1981.

Gunning, Robert. *The Technique of Clear Writing*. New York: McGraw-Hill, 1968.

Harty, Kevin. *Strategies for Business and Technical Writing*. New York: Harcourt Brace Jovanovich, 1980.

Keenan, John. *Feel Free to Write.* New York: Wiley, 1982.

Janis, Harold J. *Writing and Communicating in Business,* 3d ed. New York: Macmillan, 1978.

Lesikar, Raymond V. *Basic Business Communication.* Homewood, Ill.: Irwin, 1979.

———. *Report Writing for Business,* 6th ed. Homewood, Ill.: Irwin, 1981.

Londo, Richard. *Common Sense in Business Writing.* New York: Macmillan, 1982.

*New York Times Manual of Style and Usage,* 2nd ed. New York: Quadrangle/McGraw-Hill, 1976.

Payne, Stanley. *The Art of Asking Questions.* Princeton, N.J.: Princeton University Press, 1951.

Rivers, William E. *Business Reports: Samples From the "Real World."* Englewood Cliffs, N.J.: Prentice-Hall, 1981.

Strunk, William Jr. and E. B. White. *The Elements of Style,* 3d ed. New York: Macmillan, 1978.

Timm, Paul R. and Christopher G. Jones. *Business Communication: Getting Results.* Englewood Cliffs, N.J.: Prentice-Hall, 1983.

Treece, Malra. *Successful Business Writing.* Boston: Allyn and Bacon, 1980.

———. *Effective Reports.* Boston: Allyn and Bacon, 1982.

Walter, Otis M. and Robert L. Scott. *Thinking and Speaking: A Guide to Intelligent Oral Communication,* 4th ed. New York: Macmillan, 1979.

Whalen, Doris. *Handbook for Business Writers.* New York: Harcourt Brace Jovanovich, 1978.

Wilkenson, C. W., Peter B. Clarke, and Dorothy C. M. Wilkenson. *Communicating Through Letters and Reports,* 7th ed. Homewood, Ill.: Irwin, 1980.

Zinsser, William. *On Writing Well.* New York: Harper & Row, 1979.

# Index